Shattered Images

Victoria Lane

This is a work of fiction. Any
resemblance to persons living or
dead is purely coincidental.

Manufactured in the United States of America
ISBN: 1-4392-4236-4

Library of Congress Catalog Card No.: 92-90811

0 9 8 7 6 5 4 3 2 1

This book is dedicated to the two most important people in my life: my father, Joseph, and my husband, Richard. They provided me with support, kindness, and never-ending love. Without them, I would never have survived to write this book. Special thanks to David Bradley, whose kindness will always be remembered.

I give thanks to God for showing me that nothing meaningful in this life comes easy or without pain.

Shattered Images

CHAPTER ONE

The year was 1984. The place, La Guardia Airport, New York City. It was 10:00 A.M., October 17. I was waiting for a taxi by the curb. I was dressed very casually, with my luggage beside me. I began to search through my purse for a cigarette. This waiting was aggravating. For me, Jennifer Vicci, this was a dream come true.

I had just received an advance on my book, and for the first time, I was going to get the chance that I'd prayed for. At last, I would be a published author.

Just as I lit my cigarette, a cab pulled up beside me. The driver jumped from the cab and held the door open for me. I got into the cab as the driver loaded the luggage in the trunk. I gave the driver instructions and put my head back on the seat and allowed myself the luxury of dreaming.

I began to think about my husband, Tom. He was still back in Boston. He wanted me to take this trip by myself. "Just like a big girl" was how he put it. To know me would be to unveil many truths about my disappointments and trials. Only Tom, my husband, knew me, comforted me, and stood beside me.

I was still deep in thought when the driver, trying to be friendly, broke the silence. "Would you like me to give you a tour of the city as we ride or have you been to New York before, miss?"

"This is not my first time in New York, but I never really saw the city before. I was in the city once before on business. I never really took in the sights or even noticed my surroundings. I would appreciate it if you could show me any points of interest. That is, if it's not putting you out."

"Oh, no, miss. You see, we're right on the scenic route, and with all this traffic, you have nothing better to do than to wait and look around." I chuckled as the driver smiled and started to point out several items of interest to me, as I looked out of the window.

I did not listen to what he was saying. My mind was a million miles away. I was thinking about the future.

The driver was still chatting away when I snapped out of it. All of a sudden, I was brought back to reality, somewhat embarrassed, for I

1

had not heard even one word of what he had been saying. I gazed out the window at the overwhelming view of New York City.

The driver said that we were not far from our destination. I began to get nervous as the tension began to build up. I had a nervous habit of brushing back my hair from my face even when my hair was in place. I noticed the grin on the driver's face as I glanced through the rearview mirror. "Well, did you enjoy your tour of the city, miss?"

"Oh, yes, I did," I replied, not wanting him to notice that I had not been listening.

Tension began to mount as we neared my destination. I was thinking about my hometown of Boston, Massachusetts. I thought about my husband and my friends. This was a new venture. It should be a pleasant experience. I had had few pleasant experiences in my life; Boston had many painful memories.

My family had been cruel to me. They would not miss me if I never came back. My husband, Tom, had been my only support for many years, and I loved him very much.

I was about to meet my publisher for the first time. I was hoping that it would mean a new life for me. We had only talked on the telephone, and I was apprehensive about our first meeting.

As the taxi pulled up to the publisher's office building, I thanked and paid the driver. When I got out of the cab, I looked up at the huge building that housed the publisher. Tears stung my eyes, as the sun blazed strong upon me. I ran my fingers through my hair to make sure that I was neat. After all, this would be my first meeting with Jason Ross, my publisher, and I wanted to make a good impression.

I picked up my valise and walked through the rotating glass door of the building. I went up to the security guard, who was sitting in the middle of a circular desk in the lobby. I cleared my throat and asked, "Excuse me, could you please tell me how to get to Jason Ross's office?"

The guard politely pointed toward the elevator and told me to take it to the thirteenth floor. I thanked him and walked toward the elevator.

When I reached my floor, the elevator door slid open to expose very plush, royal blue carpeting, with beautiful Mediterranean accessories and long, flowing, white, custom-made drapes. They were drawn to let the sunlight illuminate the office and soften the colors.

I trembled as I approached the reception desk. I walked over to the young woman behind the desk. "Excuse me, could you tell me where Mr. Ross's office is?"

The young woman asked, "Do you have an appointment?"

"Yes, I do," I replied. "Tell Mr. Ross that Jennifer Vicci is here to see him."

"Oh, yes, Miss Vicci, Mr. Ross is expecting you. Please follow me."

I followed her to Mr. Ross's office at the end of a very long corridor. Along the corridor were framed dust jackets of books that they had published. Stacy, the receptionist, escorted me to Mr. Ross's office and told me to make myself comfortable. I sat in a very sturdy and plush wing chair.

Moments later, Mr. Ross walked into the office. He was a tall, stately man in his late fifties. He walked over to me with a wide smile on his face and held out his hand. "Well, Miss Vicci, how was your trip? You must be tired."

"Yes," I replied, "but excited over the entire trip."

"You're not at all what I pictured you to be."

"Oh," I replied, "should I take that as a compliment?"

"Well, of course," said Mr. Ross.

When he smiled, his whole face lit up. He was not what I had envisioned either. Just then he said, "How about a drink, Miss Vicci?"

"No thank you, Mr. Ross."

"Oh, come on, Miss Vicci. This is a special occasion. It's not every day that you become an author."

"Call me Jenny, Mr. Ross."

"In that case, call me Jason."

We felt at ease with each other. I felt as though I belonged. It was as if my pain, loss, and suffering had paid off.

Jason was busy mixing a pitcher of martinis. He walked over with two glasses, handed me one, and said, "All right, young lady. This is to our business arrangement." He raised his glass and toasted, "To us."

Jason sat down next to me and said, "Jenny, your book is overwhelming, to say the least. How old are you?"

I started to laugh. "Now isn't that a bit of a personal question to ask a lady?"

Jason also laughed. "No, no, Jenny. What I meant is that you appear too young to have experienced everything in your book."

"I'm not so young, Jason. I'm forty-seven years old."

"Well tell me, Jenny. How does your husband, Tom, feel about your new-found fame?"

"Well, Jason, Tom has been through so much with me; I often wonder why he stays. I guess at this point nothing would faze him. He told me to stay in New York for a while and sort things out. After all, now we can afford what we want."

"Whoa!" Jason replied. "Let's focus on the book. You could not get your whole life in one book. You should consider a sequel."

My thoughts turned to my family, and I thought, *I wonder what Ma would think now.* Criticism and rejection could no longer affect me. When I was very young, my mother planted and nurtured a deadly seed, a seed that almost destroyed me. I managed to survive and finally prosper. "I want to make the right decision," I said out loud. "I've made so many wrong ones. This book presents opportunities that I have never had before. I want to chose the right ones."

Jason looked at me sympathetically. "You must be very tired, Jenny. Would you prefer to go to lunch or your hotel room to freshen up?"

"Well," I replied, "I am rather tired; this has been quite an ordeal. I think I'll go to the hotel. I want to take something for a headache."

"Well," replied Jason, "why don't I have my chauffeur drive you to your hotel? Get some rest, because tonight you're in for a real surprise."

"Jason, you're spoiling me."

Jason then turned around and pushed the intercom button. He told Stacy to get Hans, the chauffeur, to take me to my hotel. He then said that his penthouse would be available should my stay be extended. He said, "I want to accommodate your every need. This book will be a best-seller. This is just the beginning."

Just then, the buzzer rang to inform Jason that Hans was here to pick me up. "Well, your ride is here. I'll pick you up around 8:00 P.M. Wear something comfortable. We'll make it an early evening."

"See you then," I replied.

I followed Hans down the corridor and into the elevator. As the doors closed, I thought, *I did it; I did it. Somebody pinch me. I'm somebody today, and I earned it all by myself.*

Hans led me to a black stretch limousine. He opened the door, and I climbed in. Hans told me that reservations had been made for me at the Americana. "Mr. Ross wanted to make you as comfortable as possible. He said that you were to be treated like royalty."

I thought how different this trip to New York was from my last. I asked Hans how long he had been working for Mr. Ross. "Approximately three years," he replied. He then continued to tell me about Mr. Ross. His wife had passed away from cancer about a year ago. He had since become something of a recluse; he did not socialize except for business affairs. Mr. and Mrs. Ross were very close, and he was devastated when she died.

"I appreciate your filling me in. I like to know about the person with whom I am dealing. I had a very bad experience with another publisher, an experience that I want to avoid."

Hans pulled up to the hotel. The doorman walked over to the limousine and opened the door, picked up my luggage, and escorted me to the front desk. The desk clerk asked, "Your name, please?"

"Yes. Vicci, Jennifer Vicci."

"Your room is on the eighth floor, number 8024."

He then rang for the bellboy, who escorted me to my room. "If you need anything, ma'am, just check the book by the telephone. It's a room service directory."

"Thank you," I replied, as I opened my purse to tip him.

"No, ma'am, everything's been taken care of. Have a nice stay," he replied, as he left the room and closed the door.

I walked over to the bed and collapsed on it. As I lay there, my thoughts floated back to my childhood, which had been traumatic. At a young age I developed psychosomatic asthma. My childhood was a web of tangled emotions and confusion. At a young age, I was sent away to a convent. I never understood why my parents sent me away, since they kept my younger brother at home. That was the beginning. I was always an outsider to my own family.

CHAPTER TWO

I was born in Boston, Massachusetts, in the Italian north end, on April 1, 1937, to Angelina and Dominic Vicci. I only had one sibling, my brother Salvatore, but since my mother was one of thirteen children, I had more cousins than I could count. We lived in an old brownstone townhouse on Prince Street, near the outdoor market. My first vivid recollection was leaving that house and starting school.

It was not long after my fifth birthday that I started school. Unlike my friends, who were sent to the neighborhood school, I was sent to a school that seemed millions of miles from home but in reality was closer to twenty miles away in Salem, Massachusetts. This was not like the public school that my friends attended; it was a convent.

One of my earliest memories was of that first day of school. I was a frail and frightened child, and this new experience was especially terrifying because I would be leaving home for the first time. My first day at the Catholic Academy for Girls is vivid in my memory. I was driven there by my mother. She was dressed to perfection. Every article of her clothing matched. Her hair was perfectly coiffed in a bouffant style, and her makeup was applied to hide any traces of wrinkles or bags. Her facial expression and attitude appeared cold and apathetic, and she gave no indication of sympathy for my plight.

There was a long driveway that led up to big black wrought-iron gates. The driveway was framed with large oak trees, and the school was covered with ivy, only the windows peeking through. To the left of the building was a very large tomato patch where sisters were working the harvest in full black habits. I had never seen farm work before, and I was fascinated watching the nuns working in the field.

My concentration was broken when my mother grabbed me by the arm and yanked me out of the car. My blue chiffon dress caught on the car door and caused me to stumble. My mother picked me up, brushed the dirt off of my knees, and combed my blonde curly hair. After I was made presentable, she dragged me up the steep front steps of the school and rang the bell. I remember the fear and anxiety that I felt at that moment. My stomach felt as though it were filled with butterflies. I was desperately in need of reassurance, someone to tell me that everything would be all right. I was looking up at my mother, with my little, blue, soft-looking eyes seeking comfort. Unfortunately, she did not provide this comfort; instead her expression was cold and stern.

The nun who opened the door was a large woman with a round, friendly face. As I looked at this woman, my fear escalated and I began to cry, as I had a strong premonition that I would never see my family again. At this point my mother said, "Listen to me, Jennifer. I don't want you to cause a scene. If you're a real good girl, Daddy and I will come and visit you." She said that within earshot of the nun. She then pulled me aside, close to her, and whispered in my ear, "If you don't behave, you'll never see us again."

My crying, which had been subdued at this point, developed into a loud, wet scream. I threw my arms around my mother's waist and pleaded, "Please, please, don't leave me, Mommy. I don't want to live here without you and Daddy."

My mother responded in a cold, unemotional tone. "That is why Daddy didn't come with us; he could not bear to see you cry. I am more in control of situations."

My mother was so right! She was more in control of situations than my father, who was emotional and empathic with me. She then tore my arms from around her waist, grabbed me by the wrist, and led me into the darkened hallway of the school.

As the nun greeted my mother, I remember how big and imposing she was in that rigid black uniform. At the time the nun was so frightening to me that as soon as I saw her I tried to hide behind my mother. This did not work, because the nun then looked down at me and gave me a warm smile that did not seem appropriate, given her large size and formal attire. She tried to console me by introducing herself. "There, there, my dear. I am Sister Maryanne. We are going to be great friends."

She reached for my hand and pulled me close to her. She told my mother that everything was okay and that I was a big girl that could be left at the school. Of course, I was not consulted for my opinion. I was still scared to death of having to live in this strange place with these strange people. My mother gave me a kiss that seemed ice-cold. She then turned and left without even a good-bye!

At this point I was very scared and lonely. Sister Maryanne kept trying to reassure me with comforting words, but it was not working. She even took me close to her and hugged me, but having to stare at the black habit at close range just added to my fright. My terror must have been apparent, as other nuns joined us and tried to help Sister Maryanne make me comfortable. Sister Maryanne then said in a soft voice, "Jennifer, I'm taking you up to the dormitory, where you will be living."

I had never seen such a cold place. The floor was marble, and the walls were a dark gray. I saw the nuns on their hands and knees scrubbing the floor as Sister Maryanne led me down the hall and up a long flight of stairs. I was tightly grasping her hand, as my initial fear did not abate. When we reached the top of the stairs, she started to stroke my head in a comforting and endearing manner. "It will be all right, dear. You're one of us now." Her comforting words and gesture were in vain, as I began to sob again.

She took me into the dormitory, which had twenty beds, ten on a side. Since this was a rest period, all the beds except one were filled. My future roommates were aged from five to fifteen, and my being among the youngest only added to my insecurity. As we entered the room, all the girls sat up and stared at us. Sister Maryanne then loudly clapped her hands and, in an authoritative voice, declared. "All right, girls. This is our new boarder, Jennifer Vicci." All nineteen girls responded with a respectful but unenthusiastic "Hello."

Sister led me to a bed at the far end of the room. It was unmade, but the bedding was neatly piled at the foot of the bed. Sister Maryanne then called to Lisa, who was one of the fifteen-year-olds, to show me around and explain my duties to me.

Being passed to another stranger did nothing to ameliorate my terror. As Sister Maryanne left the room, the girls circled around me and started to bombard me with questions. "Jennifer, are you an orphan?" "Are your parents divorced?" "Are you here because you are just not wanted?" I answered these questions by shaking my head and sobbing. They told me that the nuns did not like crybabies and that the sooner I adjusted to my new life the better it would be for me.

I still could not accept this as my new life. I was convinced that my mother would change her mind at any moment and take me home. Unfortunately, I was wrong and was destined to spend the next ten years here.

Lisa told the other girls to get back in bed, and she began her assignment as my guide and instructor. She stayed by my side the next few days teaching me my responsibilities, such as how to properly make a bed and clean my living area. The orientation included the issuance of my uniform. I had always been dressed in frilly, brightly colored outfits and felt alienated when I saw my new wardrobe. I was issued a long black dress, black tights, and black oxfords with a navy blue pea coat and a black beret. I was not only the youngest of the group, I was also small for my age, so considerable alteration was required on my new wardrobe.

My schedule at the school was very rigid. I awoke at five in the morning and attended mass. I returned to my dormitory, made my bed, then went to breakfast. This was followed by one hour of religious training, one hour of music, a study period, and then lunch. The afternoon consisted primarily of meditation and prayer, along with two other classes.

This was a hectic and rigid schedule compared to what I had been used to at home. I was still very homesick, even after I had spent several months at the school. When the lights were out and the other girls were sleeping, I would lie in bed and cry, wishing I were back home. I frequently got out of bed and stared out of the window, searching for my parents. When it was apparent that they were not coming that evening, I would start to cry again and not stop until my aggravated roommates would throw a pillow or some article of clothing my way.

Within moments the dormitory would be filled with screams and flying objects. This would attract the attention of Sister Maryanne, who slept in the next room. She would open the dormitory door, dressed in a long black habit with white bonnet and carrying a flashlight. She would move the light slowly around the room, targeting each girl. As the beam hit each girl, she would settle down.

My special friendship with Sister Maryanne began during one of these melees. When the beam found me, I was still crying. She walked over to where I was standing, wrapped her arms around me, and carried me out of the dormitory and into her private cell. She put me into her bed and began to lovingly stroke my hair and whisper reassuring words into my ear. It affected me deeply when she said, "My dear little girl, you touched my heart; there is nothing to fear." I put my head on her breast and fell asleep.

This ritual lasted several weeks, because I would not be able to fall asleep unless I was comforted by Sister Maryanne, who by this time had become my surrogate mother.

One of the most memorable aspects of the convent was the music. I would go to the music room, curl up in a bentwood rocker, and listen to the nuns play their instruments. My favorite piece was the Warsaw Concerto. By rocking along with the music I felt as though I were part of their orchestra. The nuns would pretend that I was not there and continue their playing. I would frequently fall asleep listening to the soothing sounds and be carried back to the dormitory by one of the nuns.

After one of these performances, I was wakened by Sister Maryanne, who told me in her soft voice, "Jennifer dear, your mother and father will be here tonight. I sent for them. You are too young to be away from them." I just gazed into her big brown eyes as she pulled me close. "Maybe, Jennifer, they will take you home after I tell them that you are too young to be here."

I threw my arms around her and kissed her neck. She put me back on the floor, patted my behind, and told me to get washed so that I would look presentable when my parents came.

After I'd washed I went to the music room and waited for my parents in my favorite rocker. After what seemed like hours, Lisa came into the room and led me to Sister Maryanne's office. When we reached the office, Lisa had me wait outside while she informed Sister Maryanne that I was here.

As I waited outside, I could hear Sister Maryanne talking to my parents. Both Sister Maryanne and my father had soft voices. My mother has an extremely loud and cackling voice, which makes it almost impossible for her to say anything in hushed tones. It surprises many people that a woman who is only four feet, seven inches tall can have a voice louder than most men.

The first voice that I heard was Sister Maryanne talking to my mother. "Mrs. Vicci, calm down. Jennifer belongs home with both of you. She is still a baby and too immature to be here. She is a wonderful, expressive child. These are the most precious years in a little girl's life. If you had problems, I could understand your sending her here, but it appears that you and Mr. Vicci have the means to care for her."

My mother responded, "Look, Sister, I know you mean well, but, to put it simply, she has been a difficult child and her father spoils her. She is out of control. All she wants to do is sit on her father's knee and be cuddled. I think this is abnormal behavior."

Sister Maryanne then broke in. "Just a minute, Mrs. Vicci. I have not heard a word from Mr. Vicci. Don't you have anything to say about Jennifer's future?"

I barely heard my father's soft response. "Well, Sister, Jennifer is a problem. My wife is having to make huge sacrifices to care for her."

Sister Maryanne pleaded, "Your daughter is just a baby. The other young children are here because they do not have a family to go home to. Jennifer needs her parents. Can you take her home, because she is not adapting here?"

"I am sorry, Sister, that we have to do this, but I love my daughter and her mother is just not able to deal with her. What can I do? I have to work and I want to give Jennifer the best childhood possible."

"All right, Mr. Vicci, we'll keep her here on certain conditions. She is to be taken home every weekend, and she is to be home every summer

10

when school is out. Now, is that agreeable to you?" He nodded. "Good, let's get Jennifer."

The door opened and Sister Maryanne motioned me into the room. I immediately ran to my father, threw my arms around him, and hugged him, as he lifted me with one arm and brushed my hair. "Hey, Jennifer, we're forgetting Mother. Come on, honey, give her a kiss."

I walked over to my mother and extended my arms to her. Instead of accepting my affectionate gesture, she took my arms and placed them by my side and gave me an emotionless kiss on the cheek. I then walked over to my father and clutched his hand as tightly as I could.

My mother looked at us with a pained expression. "Sister, I think that this unexpected visit has left my daughter exhausted. I think, for her sake as well as my husband's, that we should leave now. We will be back on Friday to take her home for the weekend."

My father walked over to Sister Maryanne, shook her hand, and thanked her for taking such good care of me. He then picked me up, held me close, and whispered, "Don't worry, honey; we will be taking you home for the weekend." He gave me a big kiss on the cheek, then held me out in his outstretched arms for Sister Maryanne to take me. I began to kick and scream as Sister took me from my father, but I settled down as my parents left the office and went home.

Sister was still holding me in her arms as she left her office, mumbling, "Some women should never be mothers." She carried me into the music room. "Here, Jennifer, we are in your favorite place. Sit in the rocker and I will play the piano for you." She played "Ave Maria" and did it beautifully. I slowly began to rock to the music, as several of the sisters entered and began to sing along. I felt that I was in the company of angels. I drifted off into a peaceful sleep.

On Friday morning, I was awakened by Lisa, who was assigned by Sister Maryanne to help me get my uniforms ready for my weekend furlough. Lisa told me what to pack for the weekend and helped me organize my personal belongings. She then helped me carry my things to Sister Maryanne's office, where I waited for my parents.

As I sat in her outer office, I heard her speaking to my father. He was telling her that my mother was ill and could not make the trip. When Sister Maryanne called me into the office, I ran into my father's outstretched arms. He picked me up and carried me to his car and placed me in the front seat. He went back into the building, got my bags, and threw them into the trunk.

Although I did not know it at the time, my experiences at the school, pleasant as they were, did not adequately prepare me for the challenge that I would face later in life. The curriculum was intense but limited

11

to three subjects: music, French, and religion. I entered the school in the early days of World War II, well before the feminist revolution. My parents believed that a genteel education was all that a girl required, and there were plenty of schools such as the Catholic Academy for Girls to provide it. I was essentially schooled in the art of femininity as it was conceptualized at that time. I was trained to be a sweet, mild-mannered woman, get married, have children, and live happily ever after. Unfortunately, years later when I left the school, that scenario became skewed.

My first weekend home came after about three months at school! As I rode in the car alongside my father, I felt eager to get home to more familiar surroundings. The ride home lasted about an hour, and I passed the time singing some of the songs that I had learned at school. Both Salem and Boston are along the Massachusetts coastline, and during much of the ride home I enjoyed watching the seascapes.

The trip home proved to be more enjoyable than my life at home. My parents were complete opposites. My father was a warm, compassionate, and kind man. My mother was cold and callous. On my weekends at home, my parents frequently fought over me. My father gave me lots of attention. We would listen to the radio, play board games, and spend lots of time talking. He would hug and kiss me and tell me all the reassuring things that a little girl likes to hear.

Mother was the disciplinarian, even when no discipline was required. My mother would go crazy with no justification. If I were to spill my milk, soil my clothes, or do something else equally innocuous, my mother would go into a rage, telling me that I was clumsy and stupid. This would precipitate shouting matches between my parents. She would tell my father to stop worrying about his "baby harlot." At the time I did not understand what this phrase meant, but it became a permanent part of my mother's lexicon.

These shouting matches frequently became bloody physical battles. My mother was short and very well built, with a huge bosom that looked almost freakish on a woman well under five feet tall. My father was about a foot taller, with a medium build. He had a full head of thick, black, wavy hair and kindly soft hazel eyes.

Though my father was somewhat larger than my mother, the battles were won by her, due to my father's reluctance to hit a woman. My mother's main weapon was her nails. When Father tried to protect me from my mother's assaults she would claw at him and frequently scratch him badly. Rather than strike back, he would retreat and nurse his wounds. I would then be left to face my mother's wrath.

By this time I would be sobbing wildly. Mother would scream, "Stop it! Stop it! Don't cry in this house!" She would then shake me so much that I thought my head would fall off.

Unfortunately, her cruelty did not end there.

I would usually be able to break away, but she would catch me and drag me by my hair into the kitchen, which became her favorite torture chamber. She would turn on the electric stove. As I would be kicking and screaming she would put her arm around my waist and pick me up and position me next to the hot electric stove. She would then grab my wrist and force my fingers to touch the hot burner. I let out a bloodcurdling scream and went into a spasm that forced my mother to drop me.

As I lay crumpled on the floor, holding my injured hand, she just stared at me with a glazed, almost dreamy look. I then cried out, "Please, Mommy, don't hurt me anymore! I'll be good! Please get away!"

She then put her hand under my chin, stared into my eyes, and screamed, "If you tell anyone, it will be worse the next time! Do you understand?" She then grabbed me by the shoulders and shook me. When she was through, I was like a little rag doll lying in a heap in the middle of the kitchen floor.

Once after this happened and I was lying in a corner of the kitchen floor, I looked up and saw my father staring at me with tears streaming down his face. He knelt down, put his arms around me, and lifted me up. He grabbed a kitchen towel, wet it, and washed the tears off my face. He then looked down and saw my burned hand. "What happened, my God, what happened!" He then applied butter to my scorched fingers.

My mother's warning was still ringing in my ears, as I put my head on his shoulder. As we left the kitchen, we passed my mother, who was on her way in. It was as though we were a couple of wounded defeated soldiers passing the victor on the battlefield.

Much of my childhood seemed like a battle—my mother and my brother Sal on one side, my father and I on the other. I was three years older than Sal and felt little kinship with him. My father tried to treat both of us equally, but because of my mother's cruelty to me, Father spent an inordinate amount of time consoling me.

Sal was the apple of my mother's eye. He could do no wrong. His room was always cluttered with toys, most of which were either broken or ignored. It seemed as though all of his indiscretions were excused. If he were to break or spill something, it was excused. If he started crying, my mother would comfort him and frequently provide some material inducement to shut him up. This was one of the reasons that his toy box was so well stocked.

I did not feel as though I was a member of the family. I spent most of my childhood away from home, while my brother was allowed to live at home and go to neighborhood schools. I was treated with scorn, contempt, and cruelty by my mother. Even at Christmas, while my brother was showered with gifts, I would only receive a small token gift, a stocking stuffer.

Even my father, who gave all the nurturing that a girl could ask from her father, was hesitant to give me any substantial material gift. I know that he wanted to do more, but I felt that he was intimidated by my mother, and at the time I did not know why.

My mother came from a large family. I was as alienated from them as I was from my mother. During my weekends at home, I would frequently see them, but my contact with them was limited, since they sensed my mother's antipathy toward me.

My father came from a much smaller family. He had only one sister. My first visit with her was not one of my most pleasant childhood memories. One Saturday morning Dad said to me, "Jennifer, I'm going to take you for a ride to meet someone special."

It was a long drive, mostly on wooded back roads. When we finally reached our destination, I was in front of a large gray brick building with bars covering huge square windows. There were people in white clothes moving about. Dad parked near the front door, got out, went around to the passenger side, opened my door, and helped me out. I was frightened, because except for the bars on the windows, this place reminded me of the school, and no matter how bad things got at home, I still felt a sense of security in my home. I was afraid that this was going to be my weekend home. My father reassured me that we were just here to visit, took my hand, and led me inside.

After we went in the front door, many of the people were greeting my father as though he was a regular visitor, and I did not ever recall him speaking about this place. I also noticed many strange things about this place. People were not dressed normally; in fact, some were not dressed at all. There were many people with white uniforms, some were running around in pajamas, and some were running around naked or with sheets wrapped around them. The building had a terrible odor. This was the Fernald School for the Retarded in Waltham, Massachusetts.

We went to a small office where my father spent several moments talking to a nurse. She then led us down the hall to a large set of double doors, unlocked the doors, and beckoned us to enter.

Inside was a ward holding about thirty women. My father walked briskly to a bed where a small dark-haired woman was lying. As we walked down the center aisle to her bed we attracted the attention of the other occupants. They announced our arrival by jumping and screaming as we walked through the ward. By the time we reached our destination at the far right corner of the ward, I was very frightened.

She was sleeping as we approached her bed. Dad gently kissed her on the cheek and whispered, "Connie." Her eyes flew open. She jumped out of bed and hugged my father. Dad then introduced me. She was my father's younger sister. Concetta Vicci had fallen out of a second story window at the age of three, suffered a severe brain injury, and spent most of her life institutionalized.

This may have been my first visit with Connie, but she was very happy to see me. My father had mentioned me to her on his previous visits. She clapped her hands and said, "Come here; let me kiss you." She said it with so much enthusiasm that it scared me, and I hid behind my father.

Connie began to cry and scream and grasp at my father, who hugged her. She was pleading with my father to take her home. Her outburst drew the attention of two attendants who put her back in bed. I found this experience frightening and I told my father that I did not want to come here anymore.

When I recovered from this experience, my father convinced me to accompany him on subsequent trips to see Connie. I would go several times a year, and on each subsequent trip my affection for her would intensify. I grew to love her childish innocence and enthusiasm. She loved music and would frequently dance to the tunes on the radio.

Except for our periodic visits, Connie was a mystery in our house although she was my father's only sibling. If I mentioned her in the house, my parents would shut me up. I just assumed that they were ashamed of an institutionalized relative, so I stopped bringing her up in conversation.

My weekends at home were generally not pleasant, and I gradually began to think of the convent as my real home. My visits with my parents were frequently chaotic, as my mother's cruelty did not diminish, and the fighting between my parents continued.

My mother was a very stylish woman, always well dressed, and she considered a large hat an integral part of her outfit. Unfortunately for me, these hats were fastened by very large pins. These pins became another one of her instruments of terror. She would prick my fingers with these pins, frequently drawing blood, when she perceived that I had misbehaved, after which she would stare at me with a familiar glazed expression. My screams of pain were ignored, and I was left to nurse my wounds in solitude.

The repeated incidents with the hat pins and the stove made me perceive my parents' house to be more of a torture chamber than a home. If it were not for my love of my father, I would never want to come home.

The trauma and chaos at home were offset by the peace and tranquillity at school. Although the curriculum was short on reading, writing, and arithmetic, the concentration on religion and the arts gave me an inner peace that helped me deal with my home life. Sister Maryanne and the other nuns became my surrogate mothers and provided me with the maternal affection that was lacking at home.

I spent approximately ten years with Sister Maryanne in the convent. These were happy years, marred primarily by my mother's sadistic behavior at home. Unfortunately, I developed a health problem that forced me to leave school.

I had developed an asthma condition that slowly worsened during my early teenage years. Our family doctor recommended a warmer climate. So I was shipped out again, this time with no weekends at home. I was sent to live with my cousin and her husband in Phoenix, Arizona, on a naval base.

My formal schooling ended at this point, several years short of my high-school diploma. I missed the convent, but I was excited about the prospect of greater freedom.

My cousin Claudia was twenty, only five years older than I, but she took on the responsibility to watch over me while in Arizona. Claudia and Larry lived off-base in a square stucco house with dirt floors. The accommodations were primitive compared to what I had at home and at school, but I adjusted well. Fortunately, we did not stay here long, since Larry was transferred twice during my nearly two years as their houseguest.

In addition to Arizona, I lived in San Diego and San Francisco. These were formative years for me. I started to date and became aware of my sexuality, which had been repressed in the all-girl school. I was barely five feet tall with long blonde hair. I was not as full-figured as my mother, who wore a 44D bra, but I drew plenty of stares.

Larry would always be bringing guys from the base home to meet me. During this period I received attention that was new to me. I felt like a little girl with carte blanche in a toy store. Since I was attractive and friendly, I easily attracted young men. In addition to the dates Larry arranged for me, I was getting dates on my own. My demeanor was such that strangers would approach me and begin a conversation. I had a date almost every night, but I somehow managed to remain a virgin. The combination of my religious training and the residue of my mother's repressive attitude kept me pure.

Retaining my virginity was not an easy task when my social life was primarily dates with military men. Prior to my extended visit with Claudia and Larry, I never dated or had any real sex education. My sex education consisted of my mother's constant warnings concerning the evils of sex. She pioneered the phrase "just say no." Sex at the convent was not mentioned, not even in a pejorative sense.

I therefore had some interesting times when I started dating. Most of my dates were with teenagers, seventeen to nineteen years old. Boys this age have an abundance of hormones and little self-control.

I found that most of the dates followed the same scenario. First, they would take me to an inexpensive (fast-food) restaurant. Second, they would give me as many compliments as they could think of. Third, they would try to find a secluded spot. This could be anything from a secluded movie balcony to a local lovers' lane. Step four would sometimes get ugly. Some guys would gracefully take no for an answer. With others, I felt that I earned a battle star for keeping my virginity under repeated frontal assaults. What helped was the image of what my mother would do to me if she knew that I had become impure.

After I had spent nearly two years out west, my parents decided to bring me home. My asthma had improved, temporarily at least, and I was looking forward to going home.

CHAPTER THREE

It was a different Jennifer who returned to Boston than the one that left. I left a girl and returned a woman. I had freedom during my life out west that I was not allowed in Boston. I had matured physically and emotionally.

My body had changed and I would spend hours posing in front of the mirror. I had firm breasts, a small waist, and tapered hips, which gave me a nearly perfect hourglass figure. My appearance gave me confidence. It was a confidence that I had lacked when I left home. It is amazing what the attention of dozens of men can do for a teenage girl.

My return to Boston brought a return to my mother's repressive attitude, especially about sex. When I grew bigger than her, the physical cruelty ended, but the mental cruelty continued. She had a primitive view of the woman's role. She told me repeatedly that "only tramps go out at night." Of course, this did not stop me from dating, but my actions only increased my mother's scorn.

Larry had accrued leave, so he and Claudia had accompanied me back to Boston. It was a week before Christmas, and I took them on a tour of downtown Boston.

It was a bitter cold day with a light snow falling as Claudia, Larry, and I walked through the Boston Common. In the distance we could hear the faint sounds of carols being played over a loudspeaker, as we walked down the pathways of the common between the trees heavily decorated with Christmas lights.

Claudia and Larry were holding hands as we were walking through the common. I felt a little jealous and teased, "Gee, I wish that I had someone to hold hands with."

Claudia answered, "Well, why don't you just get someone?"

I responded, "What do you expect me to do, just stop someone along the street?" I did feel lonely and wished that I had someone to enjoy the season with.

As we were passing the statue of some now unknown Civil War general, I turned to Claudia and Larry and said softly, "Do you know that the very first guy that walks by will have the pleasure of escorting me through the common!"

"You wouldn't dare!" said Claudia.

I just grinned and swung my head arrogantly. "Watch me."

Seconds later a handsome man in a uniform passed us going in the opposite direction. As he was about twenty yards beyond us, Claudia taunted, "See! We knew you wouldn't do it."

I accepted the dare. "Hey, soldier, do you want to walk with me through the common?" I was surprised that the words came out so easily. We continued walking, and after several seconds passed, I assumed that he did not hear me, because he was some distance away and there were Christmas noises in the background.

Just as I thought that I might escape my indiscretion, I felt a tap on my shoulder. I turned to find him standing behind me. He stared down at me and said, "I would be delighted to escort you through the common, but I must tell you that I'm a marine and not a soldier."

Even though it was freezing cold, I felt the heat of embarrassment and blushed.

"You're a very attractive girl. Why would you have to pick up a stranger to walk with you?"

I was tongue-tied as I tried to explain my motives. I babbled for a few moments, when he said, "Never mind. It isn't important. My name is Vito Costa. What's yours?"

"I'm Jennifer Vicci, and this is my cousin Claudia and her husband, Larry."

Vito then asked where they were going. When I told him that I was going to see Santa Claus, he asked if I was joking. I replied, "No, why? Don't marines believe in Santa Claus?"

He looked at me with a surprised expression and sighed. "Never let it be said that a marine isn't game for anything." He then approached me and took my hand as if we had known each other longer than two minutes. He told Claudia and Larry that we would be off in search of Santa Claus and we would meet in the same spot in about one hour.

Vito Costa was about six feet, two inches tall, with jet black hair, deep blue eyes, and a clear complexion. I was thinking as to what my mother would think if she ever found out how we met. I knew she would call me a whore and beat me. I had considerably more anxiety over my mother's possible reaction than over my date. Vito's tugging at my hand brought me back to reality, as we started down the path toward the clearing where Santa Claus was holding court in front of a long line of people.

As we continued walking, my thoughts returned to my mother.

Unlike the period that I was out west, here I was under her scrutiny. I thought that she would not like this situation.

I shared my concerns with Vito, who said, "Don't worry, princess; all mothers are like that." The only thing that my mother would like about Vito was his Italian heritage. My mother was ethnocentric and was always telling me to find a nice Italian boy.

We arrived at the spot where Santa Claus was entertaining dozens of children and their parents. I had hoped to relive an earlier Christmas by sitting on Santa's lap and acting greedy. Unfortunately, the line was long and this Santa did not meet my expectations. Rather than my idealized image of Santa as a kindly, smiling old man with a white beard, the Santa before me was an imposter. He had a hassled look, the beard only covered part of his face, and his red suit was badly soiled.

Instead of joining the Santa line, I told Vito that we should take a stroll through the common and the adjoining Boston Public Gardens. The hour passed quickly as we walked around both parks. I was very happy as we walked together. In addition to being very handsome, he was easy to talk to. I told him my life history from the convent to my life with Claudia and Larry. He listened attentively.

As we reached the spot where we were to meet Claudia and Larry, Vito surprised me by asking, "Hey, princess, before I let you go out of my life, can we say our good-byes here? I have to tell you, you're a nutty kid, but I want to see you again. Is that all right?" After a short pause he asked, "May I kiss you goodnight?"

Before I could respond, he wrapped his arms around me and kissed me. It was a long, firm, and passionate kiss. I had not resisted, as I had with previous boys. I felt warm and comfortable in his arms. I had this lighthearted feeling as he held me. Something was different, I was not sure what it was, and I was a little frightened.

It ended too soon. After he released me, he said, "Well, Princess, what's your answer? Do I get to see you again?"

I reluctantly told him that I did not think that it would be a good idea. "My parents are so strict about my choice of friends, and if they were to find out how we met, I would never hear the end of it."

He did not take no for an answer and insisted that he would find where I lived and visit me if I did not give him my telephone number.

I decided that a compromise was in order and asked for his number. He was stationed aboard a ship docked in Boston Harbor, and he gave me the instructions on how to reach him. He expressed doubt that I would call him and even said that I had accepted his number just to placate him. I reassured him that I was sincere and would call him aboard ship when I returned home.

Claudia and Larry were staying with her parents in East Boston. I rode home with them, because I wanted to talk. I had never had feelings like these before, and I felt guilty because they were caused by someone that I had known for such a short time. On the train ride, Claudia gave me an abbreviated sex education lesson. She explained that love at first sight is not an unusual phenomenon and I had nothing to feel bad about. Guys, like Vito, who were tall, dark, and handsome were attractive to girls. His uniform and his relaxed and easygoing personality just added to his desirability.

She told me to be careful because sometimes guys that seemed this good could turn out to be "creeps." She also gave me an unneeded warning to be careful how I handled this situation with my mother.

We reached the Maverick station and said our good-byes on the platform, and I boarded the train for the return trip. On the ride home, her advice was echoing through my mind. My head told me that it was wrong to feel this way for someone that I had known for such a short time and met under such capricious circumstances. My heart was telling me something else. On the walk from the subway, Vito stayed in my thoughts. There were about two inches of snow on the ground, and I felt as though I was gliding through it. I was in dreamland, not Boston.

I arrived home a little after eight. I had told my mother when I left the house that I would be home by six. To most mothers this would be a minor indiscretion. Unfortunately, my mother had a unique attitude.

When I arrived home, my mother was in the kitchen cleaning up after dinner. Whatever her parental shortcomings were, she was perfect in her role as cook and housekeeper. She was an excellent Italian cook. There was always a fresh meal on the table, made from scratch. She never bought canned sauce; hers was made from fresh tomatoes. All her pasta began as flour, which she rolled into dough and cut in the kitchen.

The house was always spotless. When she was not cooking, she was cleaning. We lived in a seven-room, two-story townhouse. Even though she could afford to have help with the cleaning, my mother did it all herself. Even my efforts to help were discouraged. Nobody could meet her standards.

Even though I was not expecting a warm welcome, I was still surprised with my mother's reaction when I arrived home. She was in the kitchen waiting for me to return.

As soon as I closed the front door behind me I heard her shrill tones. "Just where have you been, Jenny? Where do you think you are living, in some boardinghouse, like a little tart? You can be sure you won't leave this house for one week. If I wanted a streetwalker for a daughter, I would have brought you up like one. You're a terrible influence on your younger brother."

I had expected a scolding, but this was too much. "Ma, would you listen to me! It's only eight o'clock. I rode with Claudia and Larry to East Boston." Her response was quick and angry. "Don't you lie to me with a straight face. I'll break your little ass. Now get that little ass upstairs."

I tried to reason with my mother and continued the discourse several minutes longer. The more rational I was, the more irrational my mother became.

She began her admonition in clearly audible English phrases. As I was walking up the stairs her admonition ended in shrill, incoherent Italian.

My father, who frequently refereed these bouts, came through the front door just after I waved the white towel and was heading up the stairs. He just gave me a look that said, "I'm sorry."

My room was my sanctuary. I spent a great deal of time there just listening to the type of music that I had grown to love at the convent. After I locked the door and changed into my nightgown, I remembered my promise to Vito. I grabbed my purse and fished around for the piece of paper where I had written his number. I carefully picked up the extension and listened for any voices on the line. When convinced that the line was clear, I dialed Vito's number, while my heart seemed to be racing out of control.

It only took a few moments to reach him, but the anxiety made it seem like hours. "This is Corporal Costa, may I help you?"

"Hi, Vito; it's Jenny. I just got in. Boy, did I get hell."

"Hey, princess, I really didn't expect you to call me at this hour. How are you doing?"

I explained the reception that I had received from my mother, and Vito was not the least bit sympathetic. "Good, your mother doesn't spoil you. I wouldn't either. She's a good old-fashioned Italian woman, just like my mother. You be a good old-fashioned Italian girl and listen to her."

I wanted to punch his lights out, but I realized that he was unaware of my past problems with my mother. I did not comment on his primitive attitude, but I understood it and respected it.

When the conversation left my mother, I felt more relaxed. I enjoyed listening to Vito talking about life aboard ship. I was not listening to the content of his discourse; I was entranced by his voice and dreaming about his looks. I had a terminal case of puppy love.

I was shaken out of my semiconscious state when he asked for a date tomorrow evening. I accepted before I realized that I was grounded, and then I arranged to meet him in front of North Station. In our house, grounded meant I could not leave the house to have fun, so I had to concoct a convincing lie for my mother.

With the help of Claudia, I came up with a simple and effective lie. I was going to help her pack for her return trip. Fortunately, my mother was not too inquisitive when I told her that I was going to see Claudia. She did give my clothes close scrutiny in order to determine that I was dressed for packing and not for partying. Since I knew that I would have to pass inspection I had to dress down and could not wear the feminine stuff that I knew would arouse Vito's interest.

The next day seemed to drag on endlessly. I could hardly wait to see Vito again. I had the fear that he was not taking the romance as seriously as I was. He had a flippant personality, and it was difficult to tell if he was serious. I was not sure that he would show up, and my anxiety grew as I approached the station.

North Station was the pits. It was a large smoke-filled room with a strong unpleasant but unidentifiable stench. The wooden benches were dilapidated, and the gray paint was peeling off the walls. It was not anyone's idea of a romantic rendezvous, but it had some distinct advantages. Everyone knew where it was, and it was easy to go unnoticed there.

I scanned the area looking for Vito and saw him slouching on one of the benches in the back of the station. I ran toward him and slowed as I approached, not wanting to appear too eager. As I got closer he removed his cap, which had been lowered over his eyes. When I got close enough to get a good look at his face, I knew he was the most handsome man I had ever known.

North Station for all its shortcomings was well lit, and I was able to get a better look at Vito than at the common. His blue eyes were like beacons that drew me toward him. I was so focused on Vito that I did not see a suitcase in my path, which I tripped over.

Vito caught me as I stumbled forward and right into his arms. "Well, you're two seconds late, princess, but I sure love your entrances."

I was embarrassed and weakly replied, "You know how it is. We girls like to keep a guy waiting." He then bent over and kissed me. It was a long and tender kiss, and I experienced a new feeling. I felt lighthearted and warm all over; I never wanted the kiss to end. When it did, Vito gently lowered me to the ground, and I almost stumbled again as my feet touched the station floor.

It took me several seconds to regain my composure and maintain a conversation. We talked about my little deception, and Vito thought it would be best if we went to Claudia's. We walked to a nearby subway station for the ride to East Boston.

Vito and I spent the evening with Claudia and Larry. We played records and danced. Sometimes we would sing along. Mostly we just talked and gazed into each other's eyes.

For the next five months I met Vito secretly. I was very careful, even after my grounding expired. I did not want to do anything that would keep me from seeing him. For fear of my mother I could not take him to my house. Since he was stationed aboard ship, I surely couldn't go to his place. We would meet at romantic North Station and neck under the sign ordering: NO SPITTING ON THE FLOORS. When spring came, we would take long walks along the Charles River esplanade.

Our dates were remarkably sexless considering Vito was a military man and I was hopelessly in love. We would spend a lot of time kissing, but not much more than that. Vito was a gentleman and never gave any indication of wanting to consummate our relationship.

Except for our kissing, our only serious physical contact was his continual rubbing against me. He would wrap his arms around me, and as he kissed me he would gyrate his hips against my body. He would begin slowly but pick up steam as we kissed. When we were finished, I noticed a large wet spot near the fly of his trousers. I would ask him about it, and he would just say, "It's nothing; forget about it, princess." I was fairly innocent as an eighteen-year-old and proved it by asking my mother to explain this phenomenon.

We were having a family dinner and were joined by my mother's sister and Claudia's mother, Theresa. By this time the family knew that I was occasionally seeing someone named Vito Costa, but they knew little else about him.

Mother had asked a fairly innocuous question about what Vito and I did together. After I answered the question I dropped the bombshell. I told her about Vito's wet spot that appeared after he kissed me and asked her to explain it.

After she stared at me for about two seconds, she threw a fit that must have measured a six on the Richter scale. She called me every name synonymous with a fallen woman: slut, tramp, whore, streetwalker, and others that I don't remember. Needless to say, that question ruined dinner.

My father, who was usually my defender in these attacks by my mother, knew a lost cause when he saw one. As her verbal barrage reached its climax, he just stood up and left the dining room. Soon afterward, I slinked off to my room and locked the door.

My sexual naïveté was not limited to this incident. My menstrual cycle began late and unexpectedly. Vito had borrowed a car, and we went for a drive to Cape Cod. During the trip, I felt uncomfortable and noticed blood on my dress. I thought that I had cut myself on some glass or other sharp object on the front seat. I moved my hand slowly on the seat, looking for the offending object, but found nothing. Vito almost caused an accident watching me squirm around. When he asked me what was wrong, I told him that I was sitting on glass. He gave me a puzzled look and pulled over to the side of the road. He saw the red stain on the dress but saw no glass.

I then received a short lesson in sex education that should not be taught by a girl's boyfriend. After an aborted and embarrassing trip to Cape Cod, we returned to Boston.

Vito was restless over our surreptitious meetings. One night he announced, "If you don't take me home to your parents, there will be a surprise for you." I did not heed his warning. One evening while I was listening to the radio in my room, the doorbell rang and I could hear my mother say that she would get it. Several minutes later, Mother was yelling that she would "kill Jenny." I closed my eyes, shut the door, and hoped that whatever caused the outburst would blow over.

To my surprise, things were quiet for about fifteen minutes, when I heard my mother scream, "Jenny, you get down here this instant!" I hurried down the steps and into the kitchen and found Vito sitting at the table with my aunt and mother. My heart sank. Vito stood up, approached me, placed his arm around my shoulders, and sat me down.

Vito and my mother had been talking for fifteen minutes. He had introduced himself as a friend of mine. There had been much small talk. He talked about his life in Michigan, his parents, and his life aboard ship. When I came downstairs, the conversation got serious.

Vito explained his reason for coming by telling me in front of my mother and aunt that he loved me and could no longer bear our secret meetings. He told of our five months together and where we went on our dates. He then walked over to my mother, asked if her could call her "Mom," then bent over and kissed her on the cheek. My mother was speechless. An event that should have been noted in *Guiness Book of World Records*.

The next hour was spent talking and drinking coffee. I was looking at my mother, trying to read some emotion, but could not detect any feeling, either positive or negative. She was conversing in a controlled and calm tone of voice, which was not like her at all. Vito then asked for permission to see me outside, which Mother granted.

Vito took my hand and led me outside, where we sat on a bench in front of my house. We sat in silence for several moments before Vito said, "Princess, I have something for you." He reached into his pocket and produced a ring box. I opened it and saw a beautiful diamond engagement ring.

As I started to cry, Vito took the ring out of the box and put it on my finger. As he slid it on, he said, "Princess, this ring represents my vow to make you my queen. I love you, and I swear before God that you will always be the only one in my life."

I started to cry. "Oh, Vito, I love you so very much, and I want to be your wife. Please marry me now."

"No, honey, when I return from my tour of duty I will marry you. I don't want you to be one of those marine wives that has to wait. I've heard of too many marriages that broke up over wives that could not wait."

I pleaded with Vito to reconsider, but he was steadfast in his decision.

Vito was in the last year of his four-year enlistment. He was scheduled to begin a six-month tour of duty in Japan. He did not believe that a married couple should be separated by twelve thousand miles.

I had known Vito for less than half a year, but I was madly in love. I had never had this feeling for anyone else that I dated. I know we met under unusual circumstances, but my feelings for him grew the more we were together. The initial attraction was due to his being tall, dark, and handsome, but I found his personality traits even more appealing than his looks. He had a relaxed, easygoing personality, and I felt as though I could say anything to him. I felt very comfortable being with him. He also had a great sense of humor. It sometimes seemed like we spent half our time together laughing.

When he said that he wanted to postpone the wedding, I was shaken. It was as though I went from the highest mountain to the deepest valley in a matter of two sentences. When he said he wanted to make me his "queen," I felt exhilarated. I was very disappointed when he wanted to delay the wedding until his discharge.

In many ways I was spoiled. It is not unusual for an engagement period to last a year or longer, but I wanted Vito now, and I wanted an immediate marriage for several reasons.

My life at home was not very good. Although my mother had stopped physically abusing me when I got to be bigger than she was, the mental cruelty continued. I was eighteen and had been working as an electronics assembler since I returned from the West Coast. It was hard to get even minimal respect from my mother. When I approached her about getting a place of my own, you would have thought I was entering a whorehouse. She went into her usual diatribe about how all woman who did not meet her standards were sluts. Regardless of what she did or said, I respected my mother and tried hard to meet her standards, impossible as it was.

Marriage was an acceptable way for a nice Italian girl to leave her parents' home. I did not like my life with my mother, but I respected her too much to move out. I now know that my respect for her was never returned. She said that the only way I would leave her house was in a wedding dress or in a coffin. I considered the former preferable.

I was in love with Vito, and I wanted him totally. He claimed that he respected me too much to have sex with me. I learned years later what the wet spots on his pants meant and subsequently questioned his "respect." He only wanted to marry a virgin.

After our engagement our passion increased. Our necking and petting grew in intensity and duration, but Vito's insistence on marrying a virgin kept our activities in check. I was left unsatisfied. I thought that Vito also was frustrated until I learned that I was a masturbation toy, relieving Vito and not knowing it.

Our dates would always include a lecture on the importance of virginity. Vito would say, "No, princess. You are going to remain a virgin until I come back from overseas, and that is all there is to it."

I felt like a dirty old lady. Although I would not admit it at the time, I was horny. Women have needs, too! I had the need to be physically loved. I wanted to be held intimately, told how much I was loved and how beautiful I was. I wanted hours of foreplay, with the man I loved tenderly kissing and caressing every inch of my body. I wanted it now. I did not want to wait.

Vito and I went into the house and told everyone the good news. My father had come home by then, and he joined in the celebration. Surprisingly enough, my mother was delighted. The family gathered around and wished us luck. After shaking my father's hand, Vito left, promising to call the next day.

I was fearful of how my mother would react to Vito and our engagement, but I was pleasantly surprised at her reaction. I went to bed that night feeling happier than I had ever been before. After I climbed into bed and turned off the lamp, I heard loud talking downstairs.

I listened to my parents arguing. As usual, the first voice was my mother's. "Well, your daughter has finally done the right thing. Maybe now I won't have to listen to people talk about her all the time."

My father just yelled, "Shut up!"

She continued, "He's a nice boy. I think he can do better, if you ask me."

I heard the anger growing in my father. "You got rid of her in the convent. You got rid of her in Arizona. If Jack the Ripper walked into this house and asked for her hand, you would have given it."

Mother countered with anger of her own. "That's right. Stick up for your daughter against me. I should be your life, not her. You always bow to her."

My father responded in a subdued tone, "You never loved that girl, Angie, and you never will. You have never treated her properly."

As usual, my mother got in the final words. "You have chosen her over me. You don't love me; you only love her. You should sleep in her bed, not mine."

There was a short silence; then I heard the front door slam.

I was crushed by what I had heard. I felt that my mother had raised her voice louder than normal to make sure that I heard. I was never willing to accept or understand my mother's lack of respect, which bordered on disdain. This attitude was not limited to me. My father caught as much, if not more, abuse as I did.

My mother was a very jealous and vain person. She would get angry when my father spent time with anyone other than her. Sal was the only member of her immediate family whom she felt close to. It was almost as though my father and I were not part of the family.

It was this dichotomous family relationship that frequently caused disputes. Mother would always remind Father that I was his "little girl." This would sometimes be done in a sardonic way, as it was that night. My father, to his credit, never chided my mother for her cuddling of my brother, Sal. My father and Sal never did the things that fathers and sons do, such as go to ball games or go fishing. Several acquaintances remarked to me that they thought I was my father's little boy and Sal was my mother's little girl.

Due to my father's difficult work schedule, he had little free time. The time that he did not spend with me he spent with his sister, Connie. She was committed to the Fernald institution as a child and had been there ever since. She was allowed "furloughs" if she had an escort. My father took her out for day trips and occasionally took her to New York City on weekends. My father would have liked to take her home permanently to live with us, but my mother did not permit it.

Soon after my first visit with Connie, when I was in the convent, my father told me that he would like to have Connie live with us. He and my mother had discussed it soon after their marriage, but Mother was strongly against it. My mother did not even allow Connie into the house. When Father took her out of the "home," he could never take her to visit with us. Many of the arguments that he and Mother had were caused by my father's visits to Connie. Mother was angered by them. Although Father acquiesced to Mother on so many things, his visits with his sister were sacred to him.

My father worked very hard to support his family. He worked days as a shipfitter at the Charlestown Navy Yard. Evenings and weekends he was a small-time real estate developer. He would buy houses, fix them up, and sell them for a profit. He did most of the work himself, so most of the time that I saw him he was dirty and tired. He was too tired to keep an argument going with my mother for an extended period of time. His hard work brought us an upper-middle-class life-style. Although we had problems in our house, they were not due to penury.

My father was always kind to me and gave me encouragement to achieve. When I was going to school he was always interested in my grades and my achievements. My mother's interest in me was primarily in terms of clothes. I always had an adequate wardrobe. I have since come to believe that I was well dressed in public to be a positive reflection of her, rather than for my own comfort or pleasure.

My mother never worked outside the house after she was married. She was a full-time housewife and had all the technical skills necessary for the position. She was an excellent cook. I may have been abused, but I was always well fed. Also, the house was always spotless.

Approximately one month after Vito met my parents, he received his orders and shipped out about a week after that. We said our tearful good-byes in front of my house. He did not want me to see him off at his ship. We promised to write each other every day. He also promised to send me an allotment check so that we could have a little nest egg to begin our lives together. After a long and passionate kiss, he turned and ran down the front steps without looking back.

CHAPTER FOUR

I stood and watched until Vito was out of sight, then ran into the house, threw myself on the bed, and cried. I was feeling hurt and lonely and was afraid I would never see him again.

In the weeks after Vito's departure, I spent all my spare time in my room writing him letter after letter. I would wait anxiously for the postman's daily visit, hoping to get Vito's responses. I received nothing for about one month. One day as I was walking home, I noticed the mailman making a large deposit in our mailbox. I ran up the stairs and grabbed the handful of letters, most of which were from Vito.

I ran upstairs to my room, sprawled across my bed, and started reading. There must have been close to fifty letters. I must have read each one at least a dozen times. After several hours I gathered them up and held them close to my breast and wept. I was elated. He had kept his promise to write often, writing several letters a day.

Weeks dragged on slowly. I started to receive his letters almost daily, and on the days with no mail I would reread his old letters, some of which were worn at the edges.

I was becoming more and more reclusive. When not working I would be in my room thinking about Vito or reading his letters. I was spending less and less time with my girlfriends. I would get angry when they talked about how they had lost touch with their boyfriends in the service. I did not want that to happen to me.

I was becoming stir-crazy, so one day I took a ride to East Boston to see Claudia. Larry had drawn a tour of duty on Okinawa, and Claudia was staying with her parents. I figured she would understand how I felt and could commiserate with me.

When I arrived, Claudia had a friend with her. Like Claudia and me, Dina James also had a man in the service. Her boyfriend was in the army. Between the three of us we had most of the services covered. The three of us hit it off great. We spent the whole day talking about love, marriage, and loneliness. Those had become my three favorite topics.

Before I left, Dina, after considerable persuading, convinced me to come out of my shell and socialize. I agreed to spend tomorrow with her in Boston, where we would have lunch, shop, and just get better acquainted. Dina agreed to come to my house, and then we would walk downtown.

This was my first social engagement in some time, so I made sure to get dressed up. I put on one of my favorite outfits, a royal blue suit and white blouse. It was too dressy to wear at work, and I welcomed the opportunity to dress up.

When Dina arrived, she was more done up than I was, with heavy makeup. Dina was not a particularly attractive girl. She had a round face with a mole on her left cheek. She was several inches taller than I was but was about fifty pounds heavier.

She led me to a place that I was unfamiliar with. It was just off Boylston Street near the public gardens. It was an ugly storefront with no sign. Inside, the walls were painted bright yellow. There was a large American flag covering one wall. The other three walls had military and patriotic pictures, and the room was filled with servicemen. It was the USO Club.

I assumed that Dina was here to do an errand for her boyfriend, who was stationed in Europe, but I soon learned otherwise.

I had never been in a USO club before and had to ask Dina about it. It was apparent that she had been here many times before because many of the guys knew her. I felt uncomfortable, since most of the men were staring at me. "Come on, Jenny; I'll show you what living is all about," Dina said. This was not what I was expecting when I agreed to spend the day with her.

Dina shouted to a group of servicemen standing next to the jukebox, "Hey, fellas, play me a song! Who's got the first dance?"

One of them gestured in recognition and shouted back, "Hey, Dina baby, how's tricks? Wanna dance, kiddo?" Before I knew it, Dina was off, whirling on the dance floor, leaving me alone and quite embarrassed.

After a few moments, I was approached by a serviceman with a heavy New York accent. He was almost as tall as Vito, but he had blond hair and green eyes and was not nearly as handsome. He introduced himself as Victor Lomax and asked for a dance. This was my first dance of the day.

After about three hours, I felt as though I had danced with every man in the place, twice. I was pooped! After about three hours my energy was drained, but I had just enough strength left to strangle Dina.

I finally got her alone and told her that I wanted to leave. Before we left, some of the guys had her promise to return tomorrow evening and bring "the other cute kid" along. I refused to speak to Dina on the walk home.

Soon after I got home, Dina called me and asked if I was still mad.

31

I replied affirmatively. Dina had a bubbly, friendly personality, and it was difficult to stay mad at her. After we chatted for a while, she asked if I would like to go back to the USO tomorrow night. I said I would think about it. We then said our good-byes.

I did not know that my mother was listening to the last part of our conversation. She asked whom I was speaking to; I explained that it was Claudia's friend Dina. My mother perked up. "That's nice. I hear from my sister that she is a very nice girl."

"She's okay," I replied.

My mother turned to me and said, *"Okay?* She's better than the other trash you used to hang around with, and you would do good to stick around her. Claudia always had better taste in friends than you, anyway."

"Well, she wants me to go out with her tomorrow night. Should I go?"

"Of course you should. It would do you some good to get out of my hair, brooding around this house. You go."

This might seem an unusual attitude for a mother to take, considering that she had never met Dina. But it was consistent with the way the battle lines were drawn in my family. Anything or anyone associated with me or my father was bad. An association with my mother's side of the family was good. Mother's attitude would have been the same if Dina was a combination of Ma Barker and the Boston Strangler.

Dina was a friend of Claudia, who was the daughter of my mother's sister. Since Dina was introduced from my mother's side of the family, she was good. I doubted my mother's theory, but I knew better than to argue. If I told my mother about how Dina was a regular at the USO, I would be the one labeled a loose woman.

I would write to Vito and tell him about my visit to the USO. I knew that he would understand.

The following evening was next in a series of visits to the USO with Dina. My guilt over these visits would diminish as the number of trips increased. This was better than staying in my room yearning over Vito. I began to enjoy the attention that I received from the servicemen.

My correspondence from Vito diminished. His letters became fewer in number and critical in tone. He began to question my activities and wanted to know all the details of my USO visits. I would desperately try to ease his mind by telling him that he was the only man in my life.

My many trips to the USO did not change my feelings toward Vito. I was madly in love, and I expected that soon we would begin our lives together.

Our visits to the USO became routine. Dina could covet the attention of the servicemen, while I tried to avoid it. I was trying to be true to Vito, and I rejected the many requests for dates that I received. My petite good looks and shy personality were very attractive to men. Dina was not as fortunate as I was. It seemed like the guys treated her more like a sister, but she got more attention from men than she would get outside the USO.

At home, Dina's sainthood was wearing thin. My mother's attitude toward her gradually changed. On some nights I would get home after midnight and this would precipitate my mother's anger. She would call us a couple of hookers. I was used to being called such things. I must have been called a hooker, whore, and slut more than any other virgin in history. But it was unusual for my mother to call someone introduced through her side of the family such a thing. Through the trail of gossip, my mother found out that I was going to USO dances. Even though my activities there were limited to dancing and drinking coffee, my mother considered them sinful and started to blame Dina for introducing me to this life of debauchery. She even threatened to write to Vito and warn him of his fiancée's sinful behavior.

If my mother knew the truth about my USO activities, she might not have been *that* upset. She had a distinct double standard. If her daughter was having fun, the devil was at work. If her son was the reveler, everything was fine. I lived under this double standard for my entire life.

The dances ceased to be fun. I was going to the dances to get out of the house. The attention that I was drawing from the servicemen, while flattering at first, became a burden. I enjoyed the dancing, but I did not enjoy the sexual harassment. Of course, back in the mid-1950s, it was not called that. While mild by today's standards, the continual requests for dates and occasional sexual innuendos became a headache. I did not want to spend my evenings at home, and if I went to a place where liquor was served, the guys would occasionally be verbally abusive.

Although most of the guys were gentlemen, a few were obnoxious, and the leader of that pack was the sailor who had first introduced himself to me, Victor Lomax. It seemed as though he lived at the USO. I always saw him there, and he never missed an opportunity to ask me out. I had not had a date since I met Vito and I wanted to keep it that way, but my willpower was weakening.

Victor would continuously goad me into going out with him, even though he knew that I was engaged. "Well, how come you are out having such a good time? If you love your boyfriend so much, why don't you stay home for him?"

"Well, if you must know, I love to dance, and I don't see anything wrong in my being here. In fact, the only thing wrong with tonight is that you're here."

We both had to talk over loud music, so he conveniently ignored my last remark. "Where is your swabby anyway, off dancing with some hula girl in the Pacific?"

"For your information, he's no sailor, he's a marine, and I wish that he was here to shut you up."

Victor started to laugh. "Being in the navy, I don't happen to like marines. I'm going to take you from that marine or die trying."

I told Victor that I had to leave and put my hand out to brush him aside. He grabbed it and looked into my eyes. "Angel, please don't be cruel. At least give my your phone number. There's no harm in that, is there?"

I took my hand back. "Victor, I really must go."

I went to the cloakroom and picked up my coat, and as I was headed out the door, there was Victor standing by the doorway, a cigarette dangling out of his mouth and his cap pushed to one side of his head. He stared at me from the time he let go of my hand to the time I was out of sight.

I was thinking of Vito all the way home. Victor made me angry with his innuendo that Vito was seeing other girls. I did not want to believe it, but we were separated, and I knew the feeling of longing was just as strong in Vito as it was in me. I missed him so much. And more than ever, I wished we were married before he left.

It was late when I arrived home, and the lights were out. I was glad that I did not have to face my mother. When I got to my room, the bed was covered with letters from Vito. All the letters had questions about my current activities and expresssed concern that I was writing him less frequently. He feared that I was ill.

One of the letters contained a check for fifty dollars to start our nest egg. The money was to be deposited in "our bank account" toward a down payment on "our house." After an unpleasant evening, these letters were a welcome relief. I felt as though my life was back on track with the man that I loved.

My euphoria did not last long. My mother had noticed my late arrival the previous evening but waited for the following morning to tell me about it.

Whatever indiscretion I might have been guilty of was magnified by my mother. My coming home late, what would be a misdemeanor in most households, was a felony at my home if I was the culprit. My brother did not have a curfew, although he was three years younger than I. There were times when we would come home the same time and I would be chastised, while my brother would be offered cookies and milk. I would usually get angry and respond to my mother in a nasty and sarcastic manner. She would match my anger.

My father was my protector when I was younger. By the time I was in my late teens, he had given up. My mother had worn him down, and he had the appearance of a beaten man at home. His health was affected, as he developed a heart condition about this time. His contribution was limited to counseling me to avoid Mother.

The following morning I was confronted with my mother's hyperbole. She told me that she could not hold her head up to the rest of the family and why could I not be more like my cousins? My mother's twelve brothers and sisters had at least fifty children between them. It never occurred to my mother that one or two might have stayed out late, and I mentioned that to my mother.

Unfortunately for me, logic was not my mother's strong suit. I was not expecting a Socratic response, but neither was I expecting a slap across the face. I ran out of the house and headed for what had become my sanctuary, the USO.

I wanted someone to talk with, someone who could sympathize with me. I looked around for Victor, did not find him, and asked one of his buddies where to find him. He directed me to a bar on Washington Street.

At a time like this I wished that I had a female friend that I could relate to. Unfortunately, most of my friends were also cousins, from my mother's side of the family. I would get no sympathy there.

I did not feel close enough to Dina to tell her about my sordid relationship with my mother. I would have liked to tell my problems to my father, but my mother gave him more grief than she gave me. I loved him and did not want to increase his burden.

I was desperate for a shoulder to cry on, and I knew that Victor would be more than willing to supply that shoulder. I know now that this was not the best way to handle my anger and frustration with my mother. As an eighteen-year-old girl, I was a bundle of emotion.

When I walked in, Victor was at the bar watching television. "Angel, what a surprise. But I guess I should have expected that you'd come back to me." I was tired and still angry with my mother. I did not answer him.

"What happened? Cat got your tongue? Your eyes are all red. Have you been crying? Don't tell me your boyfriend deserted you like I said he would."

I sat on the bar stool next to Victor. He ordered me a drink, a rye whiskey. It tasted lousy. Although I was well below the legal drinking age of twenty-one, I was never asked for identification, even though I was small and not mature-looking.

After a small sip from my glass, I started to tell Victor my story. I told him that I was upset because of the confrontation with my mother. He sat and listened intently. I then started to slowly pour out my heart to him. I began explaining in a clinical tone about my life in the convent. As I gave him my life story, the emotion and the tears increased. I told him about how I was physically abused as a child and how it had evolved into mental cruelty. I told him about my feelings for my father and how I sympathized with him and how we were powerless against my mother. I told him about my Aunt Connie and how I felt that she was a beautiful person, wrongfully imprisoned. When I finished the whiskey was diluted by tears.

Victor did not say anything until I finished. He held me in his arms and hugged me. He was silent for a few more seconds as though he was surprised with my story. He said my mother "must be the biggest bitch in the world." He also told me that the only solution was for me to leave home.

I had spent most of my first eighteen years away from home. It was not my choice. I was afraid to leave home of my own volition and told him that. The years I was attending school at the convent, I was home most weekends and summers. The idea of leaving home under acrimonious conditions was frightening. In addition, there was Vito. I did not want him to think that I was a messed-up girl that had to run away.

"Are you crazy? Leave my mother and father's home? My father would die. We're very close, and I wouldn't break his heart for anything in the world."

Victor glared at me. "Then you're a crazy broad, kid. I just can't figure you out. Boy, if my parents did that to me, I'd get out of there fast! Well, why do you think I'm in the service? Because I love it?"

I explained to Victor that I was in love with Vito and did not want to do anything to ruin the relationship. Victor did not understand. "Never mind him. If I were you, I'd leave. You're a fool to believe in your boyfriend. In plain English, engagement rings don't mean *shit!*"

I entered the bar looking for comfort, looking to sort out a young but confused life. Like others who enter barrooms looking for similar things, I left in worse shape than I entered. My problem was not due to alcohol, as my first sip was also my last. I knew that running away was not the solution. I had a problem at home and nowhere to turn. I turned to Victor in desperation, and I got a desperate solution.

Dina was my closest friend. Her advice was similar to Victor's. She also thought I should leave home. Ironically, Dina was part of the problem. Many of my late evenings were spent carousing with her.

Dina's family situation was not like mine. Her mother gave her considerable freedom. She did not have a curfew. Her family was not as affluent as mine. Her father worked as a janitor and could barely support Dina and her three younger brothers and one younger sister. Many times Dina told me that she went on dates just to get a good meal.

Dina lived near Claudia across the harbor in East Boston. She did not like me to visit because her mother was not a good housekeeper. Her place was always a mess. Dina felt guilty having me over because she knew how clean my mother kept our house. Her mother had to work part-time, and she could not keep up with her domestic chores. Dina and her sister, Cheryl, did their best to help, but it was not enough. It was therefore understandable that Dina would consider running away such an attractive option. She wanted to do it herself!

Victor and Dina became my closest friends. I began seeing Victor on a regular basis but always platonically. We would go to movies or go dancing. He would pay attention to me and say nice things. I needed that. I needed someone to help me pass the time pleasantly. I worked 7:30 to 4 in the electronics assembly plant, but without someone, the nights and weekends were long and lonely.

When I was out with Victor, my thoughts were with Vito. I could not wait for him to get home so that we could start our life together. My dream was similar to those of most young girls of my generation: marry the man I loved, have a family, and live happily ever after. I soon learned that there is a fine line between a dream and a nightmare.

My life at home was unpleasant and becoming unbearable. I was coming home from my dates with Victor at a reasonable time, well before midnight, but my mother's invective continued. It got so bad that I decided to stay home nights and count the days to Vito's return. He was due in about four weeks.

I was in my room shortly afterward when the phone rang, and when I answered it, I heard Victor on the other end. I had not given Victor a very good explanation as to why I had stopped seeing him. On our last date, I had mumbled something about wanting to be left alone for a while, and he did not question me then. He called to question me now.

"Victor, I told you not to call me at home," I said.

He just laughed. "Why are you hiding from me? I love you and want to see you."

I felt nauseous. "No, Victor, I can't ever see you again. Don't call me here at my house anymore. Just forget that you know my number." I slammed the receiver down.

Moments later the phone rang. It was Victor. "Look, angel; don't do that to me again. If you don't see me, I swear I'll make my next call to your mother and tell her that another man wants to marry you. Would you like me to do that?"

I was scared. "No, Victor, please. I promise I'll meet you. Don't do that to me. If you cared, you wouldn't threaten me."

He raised his voice. "It's because I love you that I'm doing it. You're too dumb to see who you're really in love with. Meet me at the USO in one hour. You'd better be there!"

The nausea was accompanied by fear. I needed an excuse to leave the house, where I felt like a prisoner. I went downstairs and found my parents with my Aunt Theresa at the kitchen table.

My mother spoke first. "Sit down and have a glass of milk and a piece of cake." Food was the last thing on my mind.

I decided on the simple approach. "No thanks, Mom. I'm going out for a short walk, okay?"

My mother overreacted to my request. "Oh, no, you're not! You're going to go out with us, young lady. What do you think this is, a boardinghouse? You happen to have a good family, and you are going to start being a part of it again."

I turned to my father. "Dad, can I go? Please! You're just going to visit someone I hate. Please, Dad. I promise I'll stay in the rest of the week."

He looked at me with a weak smile. "Well, honey, it's up to your mother. I'm not going to say anything. You never go anyplace with us anymore. Don't you think you could put yourself out, just this once?" Then he stood up and left the kitchen.

It was then my mother's turn. "I'm ashamed of you, Jenny. Not one of my sister's kids is like you. They are good to their mothers and fathers. All you want to do is paint your face and walk the streets like some tramp. Well, you won't do that to me, because I'll break your back. When I was young, I respected my parents, and that is why God has been good to me. Your father didn't marry any tramp. Look at your cousins—"

I could not take it anymore and had to interrupt. "Nice cousins! You must be kidding. I don't care about them. Why should you? I'm not them; I'm me. I've never been good enough for you!"

Her rebuttal was biting and typical: "You're goddamn right, they're not like you. They're clean, not filth like you."

It was extra embarrassing because my aunt was present, but at least I got in the last word. "Is that right! Well, I don't care what you have to say; I'm going out. I don't have to sit here and argue this nonsense with you, Ma." I stood up and ran out the back door.

38

I was eighteen years old and a virgin. Since I was five years old, I had been called every synonym for whore that my mother knew. I was probably cursed at a younger age, but I cannot remember much before my fifth year.

As I ran out of the house, my head was spinning. I was confused and upset. Why did my mother always refer to me in a sexually pejorative way? I had only one true love in my life, and I would marry him. I liked to go out at night and dance. I liked to dress well. Contrary to my mother's opinion, I didn't stay out late. I was usually home well before midnight, much earlier than other girls my age. I'd never slept with a man . . . I almost wished that I had. My mother was obsessed with sexuality.

I wanted to keep Victor from speaking to my mother. If Victor told her that I was engaged to him, *bigamist* would become one of her favorite words. She did not need more ammunition.

Victor was sitting in a dark corner of the USO drinking coffee. His face lit up when he turned and saw me. I wanted to punch him in the mouth. "Hi, doll. You're a little late. I was just about to call your mother to see if you'd left yet."

"Victor, you're lucky you didn't and you're also lucky I don't own a gun. You asshole! You threatened me!"

Victor giggled at my anger. But he was somber when he responded, after a short pause, "Angel, I've got to admit that what I did was blackmail, but I had to do it. I love you. Dammit! Don't you see that I can't eat or sleep because of you? I want you to be my wife, and I'd do anything that I could to have you. Anything! Your damn marine is out screwing all that slanted pussy in Japan. Can't you see that? He is not faithful to you. I'm a sailor. I know how it is. Grow up and face reality."

I just glared at him. "Shut your mouth, Victor. He's not like that. I know better. He sends me presents; he sends me money. If he were out screwing around would I get his money? Would you send your check to a girl that you did not love?"

Victor responded, "You go on. Live in your world of make-believe. Let's just talk about us, okay? I want to marry you."

"No, Victor! I don't love you. I'm going to be married to Vito. I'm going to get a big church wedding. I'm going to walk down the aisle in white."

"Okay," Victor replied. "Marry me and you can have your big wedding. If you don't, I'm going to tell your parents you don't deserve to wear white."

This exchange was wearing me down, and I was starting to come apart. "No, Victor, please don't do that. I don't love you. Why do you want someone who doesn't love you? Please, Victor, leave me alone."

"Why not, doll? You hurt me, so what the hell is the big difference?"

"There's a big difference, Victor. I told you from the start that I was engaged to be married. Why make trouble? You knew what you were getting into. Can't you bow out gracefully?"

His face was turning red. "Well then, you have forced my hand." He reached into his pocket and started to jingle his loose change.

I panicked. "What are you going to do?" I screeched.

"I'm calling your old lady, kid," he answered.

I was at the end of the line. I did not want to face my mother under these circumstances. I knew I was being blackmailed, but like many victims, I felt helpless. I could not go home if Victor made the call. I was subjected to abuse for little or nothing. If Victor were to call my mother with this story of how he wanted to marry me, life at home would be unbearable. I could not marry Victor for two reasons: first, I did not love him; second, I loved Vito.

I was young, emotional, and irrational. So was my course of action. I decided to run away from home. The emotion of the moment forced me to make a bad decision. The action that was unthinkable a few moments ago was now my chosen course of action. Like so many others, I thought that I could run away from my problems.

As I reached into my purse, Victor asked, "What are you doing?"

I triumphantly said, "I'm going to run away, sailor boy." I headed for the pay phones, placed a call to Dina, and told her to pack. I told her where I was and what I was going to do. I knew she was crazy enough to go along.

Victor was shocked. "Look, angel; you can't do it. The cops will pick you up in a minute! You're a minor."

I felt like I was in a high-stakes poker game. "If you promise me that you won't call my mother, I won't run away."

Victor sank back in his chair, heaved a long, breathy sigh, and called my bluff. "Boy, you must love that guy. I never thought that you would go this far. Dammit! I wish to hell that I never laid eyes on you, but I'm not backing down. If you leave, angel, I'll follow you. I'll go wherever you go."

Shortly thereafter Dina came into the club, dragging two large suitcases. She wanted to know what was going on. I told her that my options had been narrowed. When I told her that I was leaving home her eyes widened and she broke out into a huge grin. At that moment I knew that she was crazy!

This was a tough and painful decision. I was choosing the lesser evil

(I thought). I was not doing this for excitement. I was doing this because my mother had pushed me to the brink. I could not relate to her in a normal mother-daughter relationship. I could not even relate to her as one human being to another. I feel more comfortable with strangers.

After eighteen years of physical and emotional torture, I had reached my breaking point. The thought of my mother's reaction to Victor's disclosure was horrifying. I was not going to take any more abuse. I was tired of being treated like dirt in my own home. I had done nothing to deserve being treated that way. I was a normal eighteen-year-old girl. I had not done anything to be sorry about.

I had made a mistake with Victor. In my mother's eyes, I could not make a small mistake. She would consider this a capital offense.

I knew running away was not the answer. It would only allow me to delay dealing with the problem. But it was the best that I could do.

CHAPTER FIVE

Dina and I planned our escape. Between us we had fifty dollars, which would get us a train ride to Newport, Rhode Island, an affluent town on the coast, and we believed we could find work there without much difficulty. I chose Newport because I had taken a weekend trip there with my parents and enjoyed the shoreline and the stately mansions that one did not see in the north end of Boston.

At the time, Dina and I ignored some of the other necessities of life in our "planning." Things like food and shelter were not accounted for. Being teenage girls, we were interested in planning for the important stuff, like what to wear.

I felt apprehensive about leaving and not telling my family, but considering the way my mother felt about me, I would not be missed. I was worried about how my father and Vito would react. I hoped they would understand.

While Dina and I were planning our escapade, Victor was also making plans. He excused himself and went to the phone booth. He placed a call to one of his shipmates and had him come to the USO.

Thirty minutes later a tall, gawky sailor with a pockmarked complexion came into the USO. Victor waved him over to us and introduced him as "My good buddy Joe Mooney."

As Joe approached our table, he produced a huge wad of dollar bills from his shirt pocket. "Well, Victor, here's the most that I could raise on such short notice."

I watched as Victor started to count the money. Dina and I were out the door as Victor occupied himself with the cash. I should have known why Victor wanted the money.

Between the time that I decided to run away and the time Joe arrived, Victor was continually trying to talk me into staying. Victor said if I could not be convinced to stay, he wanted to go with us. For this reason Dina and I made our destination a secret, or so I thought.

The USO was only about a quarter of a mile from South Station. With each of dragging a huge suitcase, the walk seemed much longer. We arrived at the station about ten minutes before the train departed.

Running away was my first major insubordination. I had been away from home before, but at my parents' behest. All kinds of fears were going through my head. I was afraid of what my parents would do. I was afraid of what Vito would think. I was afraid that the police would be notified. I was a bundle of nerves as Dina and I took our seats in the train. But I began to relax as the train pulled out of the station, and I paid the conductor for two one-way fares to Newport.

After about ten minutes I put my head back on the seat and tried to get some rest. I closed my eyes and one image came to mind. Vito! I started to daydream about him. I was dreaming about our wedding in the Sacred Heart Church. Walking down the aisle with my father, I was dressed in a white gown with a long train. Everybody was standing, and the organ music was playing in the background. Just as we reached the altar, I felt a tap on my shoulder. I opened my eyes and saw Victor standing over me.

"What the hell are you doing here? This has got to be a bad dream. Victor, you just can't do this to me!"

Victor only smiled and motioned to Dina. "Hey, Dina, do me a favor. Why don't you just go sit in the back of the car with my buddy and gab for a while, okay?" Dina quickly got up and scurried toward the back of the train.

Victor sat next to me. "Look, doll; I can fix everything with my superiors. My ship is sailing from Boston to Newport tomorrow. I can join it there. Newport is a navy town, and you girls can't be by yourselves. You don't know your way around. Besides, fifty bucks is no money, so I came well prepared." He then flashed his wad of bills.

I just scowled at him. "I'd call a cop if I knew there was one on this train. It looks as though I'm stuck with you. I guess I'll have to make the best of it."

This situation was getting further out of control. Victor was smothering me, and I did not know what to do. After our initial exchange we sat silent for about a half hour. On occasion I turned around and looked at Dina, who seemed to be having a ball with Joe. They were laughing and chatting and seemed to be having a good old time.

After I had turned around to watch Dina for about the tenth time, Victor finally said something. He told me that Dina was handling the situation properly by not worrying, just having a good time. He told me that Dina was a good sport and I should be one, too. My animosity toward Dina was rivaling what I felt toward Victor.

After about two hours, the train arrived in Newport. It was not as I remembered it. From the station I did not see the beautiful large houses. It appeared to be a small hick town with wall-to-wall sailors.

We met Dina and Joe on the platform. The sheepish attitude that

43

Dina had had at South Station had disappeared. Dina and the guys were treating this like a pleasure trip. I felt like a party pooper.

Victor recommended that we all go for a cup of coffee and talk things over. We went to a small restaurant across from the station. It was like no restaurant that I had ever seen. It was filled with sailors, many of them here to sober up with strong coffee. Others were sobering up the easy way, by passing out while seated at the counter. The jukebox was blasting an Elvis tune. People were screaming to be heard over the music.

It was midafternoon. I wondered what this place must be like in the evening. We found a booth in the back near the rest rooms.

I was getting very nervous. "I don't want to stay here. Let's go," I said.

Victor tried to be supportive. "Look, angel; let me and Joe find a room for you girls. What are you going to do, roam the streets?"

"Don't worry your little head over us, Victor. I got us this far, and I don't need you to help out."

Victor was losing his cool. "Okay, be pigheaded, you little fool. Joe and I will be at the YMCA. When you need us, just call. Have a ball!"

Victor and Joe left, leaving Dina and me alone at the table.

"Nice going, Jenny! They have the money. What are we going to do now? We're both strangers in this town."

I was still mad and showed it by growling at Dina, "Dina, don't worry that stupid little red head of yours. We'll take care of ourselves. We don't need them. Maybe you need Joe, but I want no part of Victor."

We stayed in the restaurant several hours after Victor and Joe left, spending what was left of our fifty dollars on coffee and doughnuts. It was evening when we left, with no place to go. We dragged ourselves and our suitcases to a nearby park, where we spent the night on a wooden bench. We were both too scared to sleep, so we spent the night talking and staring into a cloudy autumn sky.

The evening got progressively colder. Dina and I were both shivering. Neither of us had a coat warm enough for this occasion. It was four-thirty in the morning when we decided that this park bench would not be our savior. We needed human help. Our only human help was staying at the YMCA.

We easily found the building, as it was only a block from the park. The lights in the lobby were brightly lit as we walked up to the desk clerk and asked if Victor and Joe were there. He explained that they had checked in but left their room soon afterward. We decided to wait in the lobby for them. The chairs in the lobby were softer than the park bench, and the lobby was well heated. We found it easy to fall asleep here.

It seemed as though I had only been asleep for a few minutes when I felt someone tugging at my sleeve. "Angel, angel, wake up! It's me, Victor. What are you doing here?"

I was groggy when I answered, "Victor, where are we? What time is it?"

"It's after ten o'clock. How long have you girls been here? Did you sleep here all night?"

Although I was sleepy and disoriented, Dina seemed fully conscious. She and Joe were getting reacquainted. She was giggling as he knelt beside her, whispering in her ear. I did not understand how she could be so oblivious to our problems.

"While you girls were out goofing off, Joe and I rented a place for you to live in. It's in Middletown, a small place just outside of Newport. Come on; we'll take you there. We think you are going to love it."

For once Victor was right. Dina and I fell in love with the cottage, which was dark brown with white trim. It was on a street with many similar houses, all separated by high shrubbery.

The inside was as pretty as the outside. The furniture was polished, and there were lace doilies on the tables. The windows were decorated with white lace curtains. In many ways this place reminded me of my parents' home.

"Look, girls," Victor said, "the landlord is a nice guy; he told us that he would stop by later and we could get introduced to him and his wife. I told him that Joe and I needed a place for us and our wives. Now remember, we are all in this together; play your parts."

I began to get nervous when Victor said this. "What do you mean, play our parts? You two are not going to stay here with us. Get that out of your head, Victor. I do not intend to sleep with you in exchange for rent. That is not why I ran away!"

Victor looked at Joe and they began to chuckle. "Hey, doll, don't get shook up. I didn't mean that at all. This place has two bedrooms. One for you and Dina. One for Joe and me. Okay?"

I did not like this arrangement. I did not like lying to the landlord. I did not trust Victor. Unfortunately, I did not have many options. I could tell that Dina liked this situation by the way she was getting along with Joe, and she would not mind playing his wife. I was unsure, and my insecurity was reflected in my answer. I just told Victor that "we have to think about this before we give an answer."

"Joe and I are going to the store to pick up some food," Victor said.

When the door shut behind them, I breathed a sigh of relief. I just wanted to be rid of Victor.

After the boys left, I went into the bedroom and turned on the radio.

45

I always relaxed to the sound of popular music. In 1955, popular music was relaxing. The rock and roll era was just beginning, and it was still possible to listen to modern music where you could understand the lyrics. An Eddie Fisher song was playing as I closed my eyes and tried to forget my problems.

Dina was not nearly as anxious as I was. She was looking on this as a great experience, an opportunity to exert her independence. While I was lying in bed listening to Eddie Fisher, she was singing joyfully as she unpacked in the other bedroom. I felt like a scared little rat. I was feeling the guilt over leaving home and the fear of a strange situation.

Just as Eddie was finishing, I heard a loud knock at the front door. I jumped out of bed and ran into the hallway, where I met Dina.

"Who do you think it is, Jenny? The boys are gone. It can't be them, can it?" This was the first time that I had seen Dina nervous.

"I don't know, Dina, and I don't have any intention of finding out either. You go and answer the door. Maybe it's the landlord. After all, Victor said that he was coming over."

Dina answered the door, with me standing beside her. I was afraid that Dina would say something that would identify us as runaways, so I decided to introduce our aliases.

"Hi! My name is Jody and this is my sister, Lee."

The landlord and his wife were both short, stocky, and sixtyish. "Hi, girls! My name is Ed Greenlaw, and this is my wife, Eleanor. We own this cottage. We just dropped by to meet the new tenants and to make sure that everything is all right."

The door chain was still latched, and Dina and I gave no indication that we wanted company. I told him that everything was fine and we would call him if there was any trouble. We kept him and his wife standing in the doorway for a few minutes while we exchanged small talk about Newport. They finally understood that we wanted our privacy and left.

"Phew!" Dina exclaimed. "I'm sure glad they left. But did you have to make it so obvious that we didn't want company?"

I ran over to the couch and collapsed. "Shut up, Dina! If it wasn't for me, you would have given us away. By the way, where are those two guys? Did they leave us stranded?"

A few minutes later our two sailors came through the door, each carrying a bag of groceries. We rushed over to them to tell them about our visitors. Joe was amused, but Victor was not.

"You know, angel, sometimes you are very stupid. You don't know how to lie." Victor told me that my nervousness with the landlord and not letting him in probably had created suspicion. He spent about five minutes telling me that I had made a mistake and I needed him to protect me from future mistakes. I was not in the mood for a marriage proposal, and I told him that. I blamed him for this predicament, and I got progressively angry as I recapitulated the events of the past two days. After several minutes of my ranting, Victor ran out the door, followed closely by Joe.

Dina was disappointed, because she liked Joe and my quibbling with Victor was spoiling the budding romance between her and Joe. At that time romance was not on my mind. After the boys ran out, Dina spent about an hour telling me about her tender feelings for Joe and how my dispute with Victor was ruining things for her. Just as I was beginning to see things from her perspective, there was someone knocking at the door. I answered it alone and saw the familiar face of Mr. Greenlaw.

"Hi, Jody. I'd like to speak to you and your sister right away. Is it all right for me to come in the house this time?"

I was embarrassed, since it is not my nature to refuse entrance to my home. I slid the chain off the bolt and opened the door.

Mr. Greenlaw smiled as I invited him in and asked him to be seated. He plunked his bulky frame in the biggest chair in the house.

"Look, Jody; I'll come right to the point. In addition to owning real estate, I am also the town's police chief. I've been getting bulletins from the Boston police regarding two runaway girls. My previous visit here made me suspicious. I want to know if you are really sisters?"

I started to panic and looked to Dina for help. She appeared to be as shaken as I was. She had a wide-eyed, vacuous expression that told me she did not have a response either.

Fortunately, before I could say something foolish, I heard voices at the front door. Victor and Joe had returned just in time. They were smiling and laughing as they came through the front door. Their mirth ceased when they saw Mr. Greenlaw.

"Oh, come in, boys. I was just talking to your wives about a missing persons bulletin that I received from Boston. It seems as though two girls, who bear a remarkable resemblance to your wives, ran away the other day."

Victor and Joe sat on the couch as Greenlaw proceeded to give Dina and me the third degree. I could tell by his smug grin and arrogant attitude that he was convinced that we were the runaways. We stuck to our marriage story as the game of cat and mice continued for several minutes. I was getting increasingly nervous as the lies were growing. I finally excused myself to go to the bathroom.

As I was leaving the room, Greenlaw shouted, "Oh, by the way, Jenny, how long are you planning on staying?"

I turned and said, "About six months, as long as the guys tour at Gitmo." As soon as I got the words out, I realized that I had made a mistake, answering to my real name. I started to sob, "Oh, Mr. Greenlaw! What are you going to do?"

His attitude softened. He gently smiled and said, "Nothing, honey. All that I'm going to do is send you and Dina back home to your parents. After all, they must be worried sick."

Victor tried to comfort me. "Don't cry. I'll go back with you, okay? We can face your parents together."

Victor was rubbing my head as he was hugging me. I knew that he was trying to be nice, but I just didn't want him. "No, Victor, you just don't understand. I can never go home again. My family will believe that I did something sinful. Things will be worse than ever."

My protestations were in vain. That night, escorted by a policeman to the station, Dina and I boarded the train for Boston. Greenlaw was waiting there for us and told us that our parents had been notified and the Boston police would be waiting for us at South Station to take us home. Great! All I needed now was police protection to keep my mother from killing me.

Victor and Joe rode with us to the Newport train station. They told us how sorry they were and that they wanted to see us again. The cops gave us a few minutes alone on the platform, but nobody had anything much to say. The boys gave us their apologies on the trip to the station.

Dina and I boarded the train for what was to become the longest ride of my life. It was also one of the quietest. Dina and I hardly spoke. We were not looking forward to our reception.

My mother finally had real ammunition to use against me. I knew that she had some sadistic surprise waiting for me. I never believed that she would be glad to see me and welcome me with open arms.

When the train arrived at South Station, I recognized our reception committee. There were two policemen waiting on the platform, and another was waiting by the exit.

When the train stopped, Dina and I picked up our suitcases, walked to the end of the car, and climbed down the two steps to the platform. The two policemen recognized us immediately and escorted us to a waiting squad car. It appeared as if all the commuters were staring at the two fugitives from justice with the police escort.

Dina and I climbed into the backseat, as the officers watched us. With the siren blaring, we were able to make the trip from South Station to my home in the north end in about five minutes. Five very painful minutes. Dina and I scrunched down in the seat to avoid recognition.

When the car stopped in front of my house, the driver told us that both Dina's parents and my parents would be waiting at my house. The officers took our suitcases out of the trunk and carried them to the front door. They then wished us luck, returned to the car, and took off. We were left standing by my front door awaiting our double execution.

I rang the bell and the door was answered by my Aunt Theresa. She hugged me and Dina and directed both of us into the living room, where Dina's mother and my parents were waiting.

When we entered the room, Dina's mother ran to her and showered her with hugs and kisses. They embraced and cried. Dina started to apologize, but her mother stopped her and told her that all was forgiven and she was happy to have her daughter back again.

My mother was seated in a big overstuffed armchair. Her gaze was fixed on our eighteen-inch Dumont television set. She acted as if nothing had happened. She never moved.

I ran over to her and knelt at the right side of the chair. In a halting, sobbing voice I said that I was sorry. Just after I began my apology, she stood up, giving me a stare that would melt granite. She then gave me a slap that knocked me from my kneeling position and put me flat on my back. She strode to where I was lying, looked down and snarled her first word: "*Trash!*" She turned around and walked upstairs.

After my mother had left the room, Aunt Theresa rushed to my side and helped me into the kitchen. Her soothing voice helped assuage the pain. "Honey, your mother is a proud woman, and in her eyes, you have disgraced her. Please, for your own sake, go to your room, stay there, and wait for your father to come home. Now say good-bye to Dina and her mother and then go upstairs."

When I reached my room, I found several letters from Vito. One of the letters gave the date of his arrival in Boston, one week hence. I became very concerned over what Vito would think about my adventure. He would never forgive me for what I had done. He was an old-fashioned Italian like my mother. I knew that he would think the worst of me.

I was facing another dilemma. I wanted to run away again, only this time I had no place to go. As much as I loved Vito, I did not want to face him.

My father put in very long days. After he finished his regular shift at the shipyard, he would spend many hours fixing up the old houses that he had bought. This would be an especially long day for him.

As soon as he walked through the door the assault began. My mother began screaming immediately. She had only spoken one word to me, but my father was getting considerably more. She blamed him for my running away. He was accused of not being firm enough with me. She said, "You should have beaten Jennifer's brains out long ago." I was called by my familiar nicknames, hooker, slut, and cheap trash. I was sorry for what I was putting my father through.

Shortly afterward, my mother calmed down and I heard a knock on the bedroom door. It was my Aunt Theresa. "Jenny, I'm sure that you heard what was going on downstairs. Your mother wants you to do something to put her at ease. She wants proof from a doctor that you did not sleep with anyone. She really loves you. Do this for her."

I flew into a rage. "I would not do that for the pope! She should know that I would not do anything to disgrace my family. Why is she so obsessed with my sexuality? She was not concerned about my welfare. She was not glad to see me. She only wants to know if I was getting laid. What is wrong with that woman?"

I did not feel comfortable after I said that, but that was what I believed. I did not like the idea of screaming at my Aunt Theresa, but she was the messenger for my mother and I had to take my anger out on someone.

Aunt Theresa remained calm. "But what about Vito? He will ask you the same questions. You still love him, don't you?"

"Of course I do! He should love me enough to trust me."

Aunt Theresa then told me that she was sure that I would "do the right thing." After that she grabbed me by the hand, pulled me to her, and hugged me. After a forced smile, she left the room.

I was disappointed and very angry. I realized that I had made a mistake by running away for a few days, but I had paid for my mistake. My experience in Newport was not pleasant, and I did not do anything shameful.

I was jealous of Dina's warm reception. I wanted my family to receive me the same way. The closest show of affection was from Aunt Theresa, but even that was tainted.

My mother's reaction, although cruel, was expected. I was eighteen years old and at the time did not understand my mother's sexual obsession. I knew virginity was important, but it could not be the only important thing.

She had beaten me and abused me throughout my childhood. The abuse was accompanied by name-calling, utilizing every synonym for prostitute. I wanted her to be like Dina's mother, accept me for who I was, be glad to see me. I was tired of my mother seeing everything that I did in sexual terms. That was one of the things that I was running from.

I was hoping that my father would at least give me a warm reception. I needed someone to love me. I knew if my father could, he would tell me that he loved me and he was glad to see me. After he came home from work and received my mother's tirade, I was sure he was in no mood to incur more of Mother's wrath by visiting me. I loved my father, but he was pussy-whipped.

I called Ships' Information in Boston to confirm that the arrival time that Vito had mentioned in his letter was correct. His ship was indeed arriving in about one week.

I was afraid that Vito's love for me was conditional. He was in love with the image of the pure, virginal Italian girl. I felt that his response to my escapade in Rhode Island would be similar to my mother's. When he found out that I had gone to Newport with a couple of guys, he would think the worst. I did not want any more scorn. I wanted unbridled, unconditional love.

I was mad, and when I was mad I usually did something irrational. I picked up the phone and dialed the number of Victor's ship. When I finally got him, I told him to come and get me and I would marry him. He was delighted and said that he would come and get me the next day.

I did not love Victor. I was just running away again. By getting married I was expecting to get acceptance. I was hoping to be treated like a mature woman and that my mother's name-calling would cease. I wanted a life better than the one I had with my parents. I was getting married for all the wrong reasons.

I had always dreamed of a big Italian wedding with a wine toast to the bride. I wanted all the joys of planning and preparation, picking out the rings, the white gown, and the bridesmaids' dresses. I wanted the wedding in a big church with the rich organ music. Most important of all, I dreamed of getting married to the man I loved. This would be substituted for with a quickie wedding before a justice of the peace, to a man that I did not love. I cried myself to sleep that night.

Early next morning I heard Father calling me to come downstairs, that I had a visitor. I ran downstairs, saw nobody in the living room, and went immediately to the kitchen. Victor was there talking to my mother and father. I was fearful of fireworks when they met, but they were holding a civilized conversation.

I had not told my parents of my decision to marry Victor. They would get a big surprise as Victor had not told them yet.

As I entered the kitchen, Victor was telling my parents how much he loved me and that nothing mattered to him except me. The three of them were sitting at the kitchen table. I took the fourth seat, next to

51

Victor and across from my mother, who stared at me with her familiar scornful look.

She contained herself until Victor was finished. "Look, young man; I know my daughter very well, and I'm telling you that she does not love you. She is engaged to another boy. What are you trying to do? You're not our kind, and the two of you will never have anything in common. At least Vito is Italian, like us. I'm sorry, but I could never accept you as a son-in-law, and I know Jenny will never be happy with you."

She then turned back to me. "And you, don't just sit there, young lady. I want you to tell this boy the truth. What the hell do you think you're doing? You can't just go around hurting all these men. Someday you'll get hurt, too! Now, tell him!"

"Mom, I'm going to marry Victor, and that's all there is to it."

The anger was growing in my mother. Her face was turning red as she stood up and faced me. "Vito will be home this week. You will kill him if you do this."

She then turned to Victor, who was growing quite pale. "I don't think you are a man if you can hurt Vito like this. I hope that someday you will know how it feels to be hurt like this. Now get out of my house!"

My father glanced apologetically at Victor and said, "I think you'd better go, son."

I accompanied Victor outside, and in the quiet of the chilled night air we made our plans to wed. He gave me a long kiss on the lips and left.

When I went back into the house, I met total silence. My parents both gave me an icy stare, without saying a word, although I believed there was so much to talk about. I returned the silence, going upstairs to my room.

The next day, I got my blood test and went to City Hall for the marriage license. After finishing my chores, I went to my room to await my wedding.

My solitude was broken when I went downstairs and encountered my Aunt Theresa in the kitchen. She motioned me over to the table to sit with her. "Jenny, can I talk to you?"

I responded sharply, "No! No one can talk to me about all of this. I'll sit with you, but we must not talk about this mess, okay?"

Aunt Theresa agreed not to talk, but I had lied; I really wanted to talk about "this mess." I bared my soul to Aunt Theresa. I told her that I was not getting married for love. I told her that I was getting married because I expected more respect as a married woman than I was getting now. I desperately wanted my mother's respect.

My aunt nodded as I spelled out my reasons for getting married. I could tell by her pained expression that she realized I was making a mistake, but she did not comment; she just let me talk.

After I finished, she said in a hushed tone, "Jenny, go upstairs. Lie down and try to take a nap. Dream good dreams during your last hours in your mother's house."

I did just that. I dreamed of Vito all afternoon.

The wedding was scheduled for six-thirty at the residence of the justice of the peace. It would be a civil ceremony, not the grand church wedding of which I had dreamed. I stayed in my room until about four o'clock, when I went downstairs.

The house was empty. My father had left a note saying that he and my mother had gone to pick up my aunt, who had gone home right after our talk. Those three people would represent my side of the family at the wedding. My mother would not even let my younger brother, Sal, attend. She was very protective of him and did not consider him old enough to handle the shame. Victor would be the only representative from his family.

Shortly after I put down my father's note, the phone rang. It was Victor saying that he would be around in about one hour to pick me up.

I ran upstairs and took a bath. There was a brand-new white dress that I had been saving for Vito. I decided against wearing it. I chose a pink chiffon dress instead. I wanted to wear a black outfit, because Vito had made me promise that if I married anyone but him, I should wear black.

I had the strangest feeling. I knew that I was making a mistake that I felt powerless to prevent. My religious training asserted itself as I prayed while I dressed. I asked God to forgive me. I also asked for a miracle: I prayed that this marriage would be successful.

After I finished dressing, I heard noises downstairs. My family had returned and was waiting in the living room. All eyes were on me as I entered the room.

My father put his arm around me. "Honey, if this is truly what you want, then I want it. If it isn't, please tell me now. It's not too late."

I kissed him as I squeezed his hand. "It's okay, Dad; I'm fine."

My mother, who was sitting on the couch, could not contain her anger any longer. "It's fine, huh! Well, I'm not going to go to this mockery, and neither is your father. If this is what you want, then you do it *alone*."

Aunt Theresa came next to me and said, "I'll be there with you."

The atmosphere was tense. Mother did not want any of the family members to accompany me to the ceremony. This set off an argument between my mother and father. My father usually deferred to my

53

mother's wishes, but he put up a fight this time, saying that he would go because it was the least that he could do for his only daughter.

The sound of the doorbell stopped the arguing. It was Victor. I was to ride to the ceremony with him. My father would accompany my aunt.

I made one last plea to my mother. "Ma, I'm going. Please come."

She did not answer. She sat stone-faced in the chair with tears streaming down her face.

CHAPTER SIX

On the way to the chapel, Victor was singing a cheery rendition of "Here Comes the Bride." I was glad that he had something to be happy about. I was approaching this with much trepidation. I could not wait for it to be over with.

It was important that Victor wanted this so badly. He had to have desire for two. I knew that Victor wanted me. I was not sure about Vito, and I was afraid to face him.

We arrived at the justice's house and met him. He was short, fat, and balding. What hair he had was filled with dandruff, the overflow covering the neck of his rumpled black suit.

Victor was eager to get started.

"Well, here's the happy couple. Are we all set to start?"

I looked at my father and started to cry. Victor gave me a tender look and said, "Don't cry, honey. I know you'll be happy."

I could not believe that Victor could be so blind. He knew that I did not love him. He knew that this was a marriage of convenience. He was either very stupid or very horny or was denying reality. In any case, I was in trouble.

The service lasted barely ten minutes. Victor cheerfully took his vows; I solemnly took mine. I did not feel married. I had dreamed of the romance of the wedding ceremony, the large packed church with everyone formally dressed, the music, the bridesmaid, the rice, everything! I never thought that I would be married in a civil ceremony to a man that I did not love, with the service performed by a dirty little man with dandruff.

When we were outside the justice's house, my father handed me my suitcase and kissed me on the cheek. He shook hands with Victor and wished us both luck. Aunt Theresa hugged Victor and me; then my father helped her into the car and they drove off.

Victor had planned our honeymoon. He picked a small motel on Route 1 in Saugus, which is several miles north of Boston. Most of the light bulbs in the motel's name had blown out, so I could not make out the name. I stayed in the car as Victor checked us in. The motel had about thirty units, all on one level. When Victor got into the car he drove to the far left-hand side of the building. Our "suite" was the second from the end.

Victor did not even carry me over the threshold. After he got out of the car, he struggled with the lock to the unit. He then grabbed me by the hand and pulled me into the room.

Our bridal suite was a single room with a double bed, a lamp, and a chair. That was it! There was no phone or television set. This was not where I had expected to spend my honeymoon. This seemed like the type of motel that rented by the hour.

I was still wearing my pink wedding dress with a sweater. Victor nonchalantly told me to get undressed while he went into the bathroom. I followed his orders and then climbed into bed. I lay naked under the sheets looking around this grubby room while Victor was running water in the bathroom.

I lay still for about five minutes waiting for Victor. I was faintly optimistic that this honeymoon could be saved. In my dreams, my wedding night was spent in a fancy hotel suite. I was wearing a long black nightgown; my husband was in silk pajamas. There was a chilled bottle of champagne and a toast before retiring. The remainder of the evening would be spent kissing and caressing. The sexual climax would be after hours of tender foreplay. We would then lie in each other's arms and talk until dawn.

Just as I was finishing my daydreaming, Victor came out of the bathroom. He was naked, with a large erection, and still wet from his shower. He gave me a half-smile and told me that I would be in for "the time of my life." He was correct.

He jumped on the bed and tore back the sheets. I tried to squirm away, but since Victor was so much bigger than I was, he was easily able to pin me down. He grabbed both wrists and held them against the mattress, over my head. He then gave me a sloppy wet kiss that I was not ready to receive. All he managed to do was smear some leftover toothpaste that was on the side of his mouth onto my cheek. That was the extent of the foreplay.

I started to scream, "Victor! Victor! No!"

It was useless. His face was turning red, and he had a wild look in his eyes. He just yelled back, "Shut up!"

After those tender words, he spread my legs with his knees and thrust inside me. I screamed again. This time it was a piercing shriek. I felt myself tearing. Victor continued to thrust, and I continued to scream. It couldn't have lasted for more than a minute, but it felt like an hour.

When Victor had satisfied himself, he climbed off me and rolled to the other side of the bed. There was a puddle of blood under my hip, and I felt as though I were torn in half.

After I saw the blood, I ran into the bathroom and locked the door. Just after the lock clicked, I leaned over the toilet bowl and vomited. After my stomach settled, I used a washcloth to wipe off the blood. Fortunately, the bleeding stopped quickly, but I spent the rest of the evening in the bathroom.

I had been very conscious about saving my virginity. My mother had taught me that virginity was a sacred thing. Except for Vito, I never was tempted to lose it. I had expected that my wedding night would be a beautiful thing and my virginity would be a gift to the man that I loved. Rather, I would always associate it with rape, blood, and vomit.

The following morning Victor got up about six o'clock, put on his uniform, and left. He had to report to his ship in Newport. He hardly said a word to me; he just threw me out of the bathroom so he could do his morning toilet. My condition improved just after Victor left.

When I was alone, I paced around the room saying aloud, "I don't want to stay here. I don't want to stay here."

I still had Vito on my mind. I called Ships' Information to get the arrival time for Vito's ship. It had arrived yesterday. I wished that I could have been at the dock to greet him. I wanted to run away again, this time from Victor.

At about ten in the morning, I received a call from Victor saying that he would have to pull extra duty aboard ship tonight. This was good news. The bad news was that I would be alone in this seedy motel.

I decided to clean up the room, and I started by throwing the soiled sheets into the trash can. I was going to go out for something to eat when there was a knock at the door.

It was my Aunt Theresa with my mother standing behind her. I began to feel faint. My aunt brushed past me into the room with my mother following closely. Neither said a word until they were both standing in the center of the room.

As my mother slowly scanned the room, I asked my aunt, "What is it, Auntie? What's wrong?"

My aunt spoke first. "Jenny, call room service. Order us some coffee. We hit heavy traffic getting here."

The motel had a small coffee shop attached. I called the office and asked for three cups of coffee. The man at the desk grumbled before agreeing to bring the coffee to the room.

When I hung up the phone, I tried to break the suspense. "For God's sake, Mom, tell me what is wrong. I know that you have a reason for coming here."

She still had her back to me. "Jenny, I want you to tell me the truth. Do you still love Vito?"

I walked around the room to face her. "Ma, please. I don't even want to hear his name. The mere thought of him makes me feel empty inside."

She became angry. "Well, you're going to hear his name, young lady. Vito came to the house last night. I told him what happened, but he thinks that we are not being serious with him. That boy loves you with all his heart. There still might be a chance for Vito. I'll have the marriage annulled. You have to make a decision right now. I told Vito that I was going to see you. You can come back to Boston with Theresa and me right now. This might be your last chance."

Moments later, three cups of coffee arrived. After paying for them, I gave one each to my mother and Aunt Theresa. After taking a sip, I said, "Mom, I'm so confused, I'm going to have to think about this. I'm going to the drugstore across the road to get a pack of cigarettes. Let me alone for these few minutes so that I can sort things out." My mother nodded her agreement, and I left.

On the way to the drugstore, I thought about my dilemma. In the next several minutes, I would be making perhaps the biggest decision in my life.

I loved Vito. I had always loved Vito. I had married Victor because I did not want to face Vito. I got into this mess by running away from my responsibilities. All this running caused more trouble. I was getting a chance to correct my mistake.

My painful first night with Victor was probably an indication of what I could expect from my marriage to him. He only wanted his pleasure; when he had it, I was discarded. I was pushed aside to spend the rest of our wedding night bleeding and vomiting. He gave me much sweet talk and kindness until I was in his bed. At that point he only showed selfishness and brutality.

The decision became easier; I would return home with my mother and aunt.

I asked my mother and aunt to wait outside as I placed the call to Victor's ship. I had to wait on the line about ten minutes before I could reach him. I told him that I was afraid and homesick.

After about a five-second silence, he stammered, "Wha-what's wrong? Let's talk before you do anything."

I told him that I was sorry, but I had made up my mind and I was going home to my parents. I hung up before he could respond.

My mother and aunt waited in the car as I scampered around the room collecting my things. I was packed and ready to go in about twenty minutes. I threw my things in the trunk and climbed in the backseat. I felt relieved as my mother started up the car and we headed back to Boston.

On the trip, my mother and aunt talked solely in Italian, to keep their discussion private. I was not conversant in the language, only knewing several words and phrases. The one word continuously coming up in their chat that I recognized was *Vito*.

When we got home I understood why Vito's name kept coming up in their discussion. He was standing in front of our house. As my mother parked the car, I felt my heart race. I wanted to jump out of the car and run to him, even before my mother finished parallel parking. Whatever my feelings for Vito, I was still married to Victor. This marriage that was not even twenty-four hours old was inhibiting my welcome for Vito.

Vito stood by the front door as we parked. When I got out of the car he swept me into his arms and gave me a long, passionate kiss. He was about a foot taller than I was, and my feet were dangling in midair for what seemed like ten minutes. When he finally put me down, I needed a few moments to catch my breath. I was feeling warm and happy. I had waited and dreamed so long for this moment. It was as though no one were on the street except us.

My mother had taken my suitcase out of the trunk and put it on the sidewalk. Vito took the suitcase in one hand, put his arm around me, and led me into the house. We did not say a word until we were in the house.

After we were in the house, Vito asked to borrow my mother's car. When she gave him the keys, he looked at me and said, "Come on, Jennifer; we have to go out and talk."

He looked tired. He was normally bright-eyed, energetic, and enthusiastic. Today he seemed to be dragging. I understood why. He opened the passenger-side door and helped me inside. We sat silently as we headed toward Revere Beach, which was about a fifteen-minute drive from my home.

I was getting extremely nervous. I knew what Vito wanted to talk about. I knew what his questions would be. I was praying that I had the answers. If Vito could accept a "soiled" woman, I would utilize my mother's offer to get the marriage annulled. If he would not accept me, I could go back to Victor or I could still get the annulment and try to start over. It was a very scared and confused teenager riding along Revere Beach.

Vito found a parking spot and pulled in. It was high tide, and the waves were rising up to the surf in a fierce and foamy anger. Vito turned to me and pulled me into his arms. He kissed me with all the passion that had been present in his earlier kisses.

"For God's sake, Jennifer, tell me *why*. I have been torturing myself with that question. Now tell me!" He was shaking me as he was talking.

I started to cry. "Vito, I don't know why. It made sense to me when I did it. But now I don't know anymore."

We both calmed down and I proceeded to explain the whole story to Vito. When I was finished, he leaned his head over the back of the car seat and sighed.

I was surprised at his response. "Well, I blame that pig Dina. This whole thing was her fault. Your mother told me about her, but I had to hear it from you. Oh, Jenny, after all these months of planning my life with you, I have to come home to a married woman."

I stared at his face as I wiped the tears from my eyes. He looked so troubled. I owed him more than this heartache. "Don't worry, Vito. I'll have this marriage annulled. I can still be your wife."

His face turned red with anger. His words were harsh and direct. "That's just great! Did you forget that you had sex with that guy? You're not a virgin anymore. Can you annul that?"

There was silence. We both stared at the surf. As it was a brisk autumn afternoon, the beach was deserted except for a few people walking their dogs and some stray members of the Polar Bear Club.

I felt sick and wanted to say something but couldn't. I realized that I had made a mistake, actually a series of mistakes, but couldn't understand why we were being denied this chance at happiness.

The problem was virginity! My mother was obsessed with it. Vito was obsessed with it. Their attitude reflected their Italian-Catholic heritage and the times. In the 1950s morality and tradition dictated sexual attitudes. Even then, I was something of an iconoclast. I wanted to question that tradition.

I had lost my virginity the previous evening. The only significance to me was in the pain. My mother and Vito considered virginity to be a sacred state. I never truly understood. I just kept it until my wedding night. Was I such a different person because I had lost about one half-pint of blood during sexual intercourse? What about me was different? I was the same person that Vito loved. Why didn't he still love me? Why was my loss of virginity so ugly, painful, and passionless if it was such a sacred state?

It was important for a girl to be "pure" on her wedding day. What about the man? What sexual tradition must he follow? Was Vito a virgin? Should I know as much of his sexual history as he knew of mine? All I knew was that the fun of sexuality rests with the man and the guilt rests with the woman. I sat there in my mother's car with Vito at Revere Beach feeling like dirt. If I had sinned, I should have at least enjoyed it.

60

I had loved Vito and had sex with Victor. I wanted both with one man, Vito! I realized that I had made a mistake in running away and beginning the chain of events that led to this dilemma. If Vito loved me as I loved him, he would accept me. If I were in his place I would have forgiven me. If he had come home and told me that he had gotten married, realized it was a mistake, and wanted me back, I would have behaved differently. After I gave him hell, I would have taken him back. I would not have asked how marriage had changed his genitalia. I would be concerned with emotion and feeling. I would want to know if he loved his wife and if he still loved me. Even at the tender age of eighteen, I realized that marriage is more an emotional bond than a sexual one.

Unfortunately, men are preoccupied with the physical and women with the emotional. This irreconcilable difference denied me my first great love.

After about fifteen minutes of staring at the waves, Vito started the car. "I'm taking you back to your mother's house. She will be waiting for you. I want you to know that if I ever see that swabbie, I will kill him. Your mother has been through a lot, too. I love her as if she were my own mother."

Vito and I did not speak during the ride home. My parents would be expecting a happy ending. They wanted Vito and me to get back together.

When we arrived back at my house, Vito got out of the car first, walked around to the other side, and opened the door. My family was waiting for us in the kitchen. Mother, Father, and Aunt Theresa were sitting at the kitchen table when we arrived.

My father stood up and shook hands with Vito. Vito then went to each woman and kissed them. He acted as though he were part of the family.

My mother and aunt scurried around the kitchen making coffee and preparing a snack. Vito and I did not touch any of the food; we just stared at each other. My mother and aunt sat down and started to make small talk, something about the prices at the local food market. They did not ask about how Vito and I had made out. They were apparently waiting for us to make an announcement.

Both Vito and I were feeling anxious. He asked me to take a walk with him. We excused ourselves and left. This time I decided that I should speak first. This would be my last chance.

"Vito, I just want to say one thing. I love you with all my heart. I'm sorry for what I have done, and I don't know what else I can say. All I ask is that we give it a second chance. *Please!*"

"Oh, Jennifer, I love you, too," he replied as he turned to me. "I don't know what to do. Maybe if I talk to my family, they can help me sort things out. Now, I'm going to take you back to your house. Please, this time wait to hear from me before you do anything else."

He walked me back to my house, and we said good-bye on the front steps. There was no passionate kiss this time. He just turned and started walking down the street.

When I returned to the house, my parents were eagerly awaiting the news, expecting a positive response. The best that I could give was an inconclusive one. I just told them that Vito wanted more time to think about things. They knew that this was a delicate subject and did not press for more details.

It was early evening. I ran upstairs, undressed, and went to bed to dream of a happy ending. I would be hearing from Vito the next evening. I was hoping that his family would be more forgiving. I wanted them to convince him that I was worthy of a second chance.

The next day passed slowly and anxiously. Victor called twice, and both times my mother told him that I was sleeping. Even though Victor was my husband, I spent the day thinking of Vito and awaiting his final judgment.

Finally that evening, when the doorbell rang, I rushed to answer it. Vito arrived about seven o'clock. I put out my arms to embrace him, but he just walked past me into the living room. I took this for a bad sign.

When my parents saw who had called, they dragged my brother, Sal, away from the television set and the three of them went into the kitchen, leaving Vito and me alone in the living room. He gestured for me to sit down on the couch. He sat on the armchair across the room.

Thirty-five years later, I can hear his words as clearly as I did then:

"After I left you yesterday, I went back to the ship and placed a collect call to my parents. We have an extension, so both parents were able to talk to me at the same time. I asked them what I should do. They thought that I deserved to marry a virgin. Any girl that did all the crazy things that you did could not be trusted. They did not think that you would make a very good wife. You belong to someone else now. That is the way that it should stay. I have to agree with them. I really wished that things could have worked out as we had planned. You made your decision; you are going to have to live with it."

Whatever hope I had, had vanished since yesterday's ride to Revere Beach. I had prayed that Vito could overcome the myth of virginity. I did not know his parents, but I had hoped that they would be liberal-minded enough to give him a broader perspective.

Virginity was good; loss of virginity before marriage was sinful—

Vito's parents appeared to share my mother's simpleminded beliefs concerning sexual morality.

I was usually emotional and cried very easily. Now I surprised myself, because I was very unemotional after Vito told me of his decision. I walked over to where he was sitting and kissed him on the forehead. I then got his cap from a table in the vestibule and handed it to him. As I gave him his cap, I told him that I had decided to return to Victor and try to work things out.

Vito had a surprised look on his face. He could see that the control of the situation had shifted. As long as I was the emotional, lovesick girl, awaiting his decision, he had power. I am sure that he expected me to break down, cry, and beg him to come back to me. He was wrong. I had shown enough weakness, this was a time for strength.

I was holding his engagement ring in my hand. I had kept it with me all day, hoping that he would place it on my finger after he "forgave me." I handed it to him as we were saying good-bye at the front door. He refused to take it. He had to have the last word.

He smiled as he spoke to me for what I thought was the last time. "Keep the ring, princess. It wasn't our love, just a symbol of it. You know, diamonds are so hard, they can last forever. Too bad love is not as eternal as diamonds."

He turned and ran down the front steps and walked briskly out of my life. In my heart I wanted to chase after him, but my legs knew better.

My rational self was telling me that it was over and to get on with my life. My emotional self did not want to let go of my first great love. A woman gets into trouble when the emotional self wins too many battles. I stood at the front steps and watched him until he was out of sight. Heavy tears stung my face and blurred my vision of Vito.

I wanted to get down on my hands and knees and beg Vito to come back. Fortunately, my pride and common sense made me do the right thing. I did not have what he wanted. I had to let him go.

After Vito left, I called Victor's ship and told him to come to Boston and get me. He seemed very happy as I spoke to him. He did not know the details of why I had left him and did not seem too concerned with them. He kept saying how glad he was that I had made the right decision. I started to feel better because I knew that at least someone wanted me.

I informed my parents of my decision to return to Victor. I did not have to tell them how things had gone with Vito. They could tell that Vito had rejected me. They could see that my face was still red from crying and tried to console me and protect me from making another mistake.

They reiterated the annulment option, telling me that my lack of feeling for Victor would cause me trouble in the future. I was only eighteen and could easily start over. My parents spoke with one voice. I should have listened.

CHAPTER SEVEN

The following morning Victor arrived to pick me up. He was happy, cheerful, and optimistic about the future. He did not ask any questions about my activities of the last two days. I did not volunteer any information.

Victor drove me to Newport, so that we could finish our honeymoon near his duty station, the USS *Essex*. On the long trip from Boston to Newport he told me that he would be leaving on a seven-month cruise. His ship would be sailing in six days.

I had this feeling of déjà vu. It was a six-month tour of duty that had precipitated the disintegration of my relationship with Vito. After Victor and I had only been together for a short time, he would be gone for a similar period of time. This was one of the problems of military life. But there was a difference now: I loved Vito and did not want him to go. I did not feel the same way about Victor.

Victor asked me to stay with his family in New York while he was at sea. He was probably afraid that I would get in trouble if I remained in Boston. I would have rather stayed in Boston and wait for Victor, but I reasoned that I would feel "more married" if I stayed with his family. It would probably be better to start a new life in a new place.

In addition, Vito's ship was scheduled to remain in Boston for several months, and I still did not trust myself to be that close to him.

Victor arranged for the completion of our honeymoon at the Star Motel, which was about a ten-minute drive from his ship. This place was similar to the motel where we had begun our honeymoon, except this one had a television set. In addition to the TV, the "suite" had a large bed, a desk and chair, and a phone. The bathroom was tiny. It was barely large enough for my five feet and ninety pounds.

My wedding night had been grisly. I was not looking forward to six more like it. I hoped the worst was over. Except for his actions in bed, Victor was a nice guy, if a bit pushy. He was friendly and enthusiastic. I wanted to be in love with him, but my feelings for him did not approach my passion for Vito. I just did not love Victor.

We arrived at the motel about noon. After lunch at a local greasy spoon, we took a tour of Newport. Victor showed me around the waterfront, pointed out his ship, and introduced me to a few of his shipmates that we met on the dock.

We then drove around the area of Newport that had the fancy mansions. As we drove, Victor told me more about his family and where they lived. He said that he was from Tuttle, a small town on the eastern end of Long Island, near Montauk Point. I knew where Long Island was, but I had never heard of his hometown or Montauk Point. He talked about his father and how much I would enjoy meeting him. Victor's father owned the biggest nightclub on Montauk Point and was also an occasional singer at the club. Victor talked about growing up on the fringe of show business and meeting celebrities.

Prior to our marriage, he did not talk very much about his family and home life. Now it was as though he was trying to make me comfortable. He knew that I had run away from him, and I think he was trying to prevent a recurrence.

We returned to the motel about 7:00 P.M. We stopped for hamburgers on the way back; I ate too much and was stuffed. We had been riding around for about twelve hours. I was looking forward to a peaceful evening, after a very tiring day.

I brought some bedclothes with me and changed into a long blue nightgown and climbed into bed, while Victor was in the bathroom. I was hopeful that our love life would improve, if only because it could not get much worse than our wedding night.

I was anxiously waiting to see how our second night together would be. I wanted to make our marriage work, even though I did not have any love for Victor. The bedroom was a good place to build a marriage, or so I thought. I wanted Victor to show me tenderness and affection. I was willing to write off the wedding night as an aberration.

When Victor came out of the bathroom he was naked. He slowly walked toward me, told me to relax, and pushed me backward toward the bed. I fell onto the bed, and he quickly followed. He unceremoniously lifted my nightgown, tearing the hem. The bottom of the nightgown was over my face, so I was not able to see what he was doing.

I may not have seen it, but I sure felt it! I lay there with the nightgown over my face and my eyes closed. He was able to satisfy himself in about the same amount of time that it had taken on our wedding night. On the remainder of our "honeymoon," I don't think the sex act ever lasted more than two minutes.

It was a lot easier for me this time. There was no blood, and I did not have to vomit. All I had to do was wash myself. I figured that I was building up an immunity to sex.

Our honeymoon evenings followed a similar routine: Victor got his pleasure quickly and rolled over. I considered myself fortunate that Victor had no endurance. I was not enjoying sex; I was glad that it was ending quickly.

When our honeymoon ended, we went back to Boston so that I could pack more things for my extended stay in New York. I also wanted to see my family before I left.

My parents were not happy to see me leave. They thought that I could wait for Victor at my home. But I was married and I thought I would feel more like a married woman if I stayed with my husband's family.

I did not feel close to Victor; I did not love him. If anything, our honeymoon had driven a wedge deeper between us. I had had an image of a romantic honeymoon and had been looking forward to sex. My seven nights with Victor had shattered that image. Victor treated me like something that was there to give him his nightly orgasm. I did not feel like I was part of the act. I just spread my legs, counted to fifty, and washed myself. I did not feel loved.

I wanted to run away from Victor, but I had no place to go. Maybe, I thought, my image of marriage was unrealistic. Maybe my experience was normal. I had never spoken to anyone about this aspect of marriage.

My mother was no help. She just told me that if the man "wanted to put his thing" anywhere but in my vagina he was "sick." I did not know where else he would "put it." She told me that the day before my marriage. That was the extent of my sex education.

I needed a break from my past, a chance to show independence. Even when I was away from home in the past, I was dependent on my parents. They always determined where I went and how long I stayed. I was an adult and could take care of myself.

My parents drove me to Logan Airport. From there I would catch a plane to La Guardia Airport, where Victor's father would pick me up for the long drive to Montauk Point.

I was apprehensive about meeting Victor's family. Victor was not close to them and did not tell me much about them. But I was looking forward to the new experience. From what Victor told me, his family led an exciting life.

I arrived at La Guardia expecting a welcoming committee or at least meeting Victor's father. Victor had said that his father had my description and flight arrival time and that he would be there to meet me when I deplaned.

When I reached the terminal there was no one there to meet me. I sat on one of the long benches and waited. It was about ten-thirty. I had not had any breakfast, and I was getting hungry.

I was in the terminal about thirty minutes when I was approached by a stocky man with gray hair and a craggy face who looked like a boxer who had taken too many punches to the head. He introduced himself as Jake Ramsey, a partner of Victor's father in the Magnolia Palace. Jake hailed a porter and told him to carry my bags to the terminal entrance.

There we were met by a black Cadillac limousine. The porter put the bags in the trunk, while Jake and I got in. Jake handed the porter a ten-dollar bill through the window. Seconds later, we were on the highway.

It was about a two-hour ride from the airport to my new home on eastern Long Island. In that time, Jake told me about my new family. I had known Victor was not poor, but I did not know that he was rich. According to Jake, I would live on easy street for the rest of my life. I did not ask for any financial details. Although this was a pleasant surprise, I wondered why Victor was not more open with me.

Jake also told me about other branches of the family tree, specifically one of Victor's uncles whom the family considered eccentric. This uncle claimed that American automobile manufacturers were building junk and he had the design for a new-quality automobile that would put the American manufacturers out of business. He had a prototype and was about to begin production. I never heard about this uncle again. I assume that he moved to Japan.

By the time Jake had finished with all the family scuttlebutt, we arrived at the club. Victor was right—it was enormous. It had large glass windows around the perimeter of the building. It was a one-story structure, and unless you looked closely it looked to be all glass. There was a garden about two yards wide that circled the entire building. I was impressed.

It was about one o'clock and the club was not open to the public, but there was a small crowd inside. Most of the people were sitting at a hundred-foot-long bar, being entertained by a singer onstage. I sat at a table with Jake at the foot of the stage and listened to the singer. When he finished his song, I asked Jake who he was. "Why, honey, that's your new father-in-law, Eric Lomax."

Eric Lomax was tall and well built, with fair skin and reddish-blond hair. He was wearing a dark blue tuxedo. When he was finished with his set, he introduced himself.

"Well, Jennifer, I just can't believe what good taste my son has. You are a beautiful young lady. I can certainly see why my son has fallen in love with you."

I began to blush. Eric just laughed. "That's great, just the way a proper Bostonian should act."

He helped me from my chair, and we walked toward the front door. He turned around and told Jake, "I'll be back for the first supper show. Take it easy." He took me by the arm as we left the club.

"C'mon, honey; you have an awful lot of people waiting to meet you, and I want to see the looks on all of their faces. Oh, by the way, please feel free to call me Eric. I hate the thought of being called 'Dad.' It's much too old for me." I nodded in agreement.

When we were outside, there was a limousine waiting for us. This one was blue, the color of Eric's tuxedo. I was overwhelmed with all this opulence. I climbed in; Eric followed me. When he settled in, he told me that I would be getting a "little tour of the family." The chauffeur closed the door and walked around to the other side, and in a few seconds we were off.

I told Eric that Victor was sketchy with the details of his family life. He sighed, "I'm sorry that my son has told you nothing of our family." He went on to tell me that he was divorced from Victor's mother and had since remarried.

He showed me the home where Victor's mother lived and he showed me the house that he shared with his second wife, which was twice as large as the first. We did not stop at either house. We then went to see Eric's mother, who lived in a small apartment in Tuttle. She was a friendly gray-haired lady with a pronounced limp. We stopped here for about fifteen minutes, to introduce me as her new granddaughter. I wondered why we did not stop to visit with either Eric's present or former wife.

I had a great afternoon. After we left his mother's apartment, we went to a small, dimly lit restaurant and spent an hour talking over drinks. I began to understand where Victor got his attitude. Eric was very charming, but boastful. He reminded me of his success in the nightclub and entertainment business. He did a lot of name dropping, but I could not believe people like Bing Crosby performed at his club.

After we left the restaurant we went shopping. We went to Feingold's Department Store and bought out the place. He bought me a new wardrobe. I had never bought so much clothes at one time before. I was beginning to suspect an ulterior motive.

The afternoon flew by and as we headed back to the club, Eric gave me its history. He told me that fifteen years ago it was just a barroom, and through his efforts it became a plush supper club.

As we reached the club, night had fallen, and the nightclub was lit up like a Christmas tree. The club's marquee was ablaze, and there were people everywhere. The car swung around to the back of the building. We left the car and entered the club through a small private entrance.

The atmosphere of the club had changed. Earlier in the day it was relaxed and informal. Now it was electric. The place was packed. The dance floor was teeming with life, and there were waiters rushing around everywhere.

Eric led me to a large table that seated about twenty people. "Everybody, I'd like to present my son's wife, Jennifer." I looked at Eric and he had a huge grin. He was proud as he introduced me to my new family.

I was warmly welcomed, as I received wellwishes, hugs, and hand-shakes from the whole family. The crowd included Eric's present wife, Sylvia, and ex-wife, Margaret, who had declared a truce to meet me.

After I was introduced to everyone at the table, Eric got up to sing. He had a deep voice and sounded a lot like Frankie Laine, especially with his rendition of "Mule Train." He was not the type of singer who just stood there and crooned. He was very animated and moved around the stage. He even dedicated a song to me at the end of his set. I was getting a little tipsy and cannot remember the title; I only remember his big white teeth as he sang it to me and smiled.

Margaret noticed my intoxication and suggested that I leave and stay with her. I agreed, and before we left, Eric handed me an envelope and told me not to open it until I was alone. I nodded, got my things, and left with Margaret.

Margaret was a tall, buxom woman about forty-five years old. She was very loquacious and did not stop talking on the fifteen-minute ride from the club to her home. Most of her conversation centered on her unhappy marriage to Eric and his philandering. She seemed bitter from the experience. I hoped that my marriage would turn out better.

Victor had a younger brother and a younger sister. Both were living at home with their mother. They lived in an eleven-room Victorian home that sat on about two acres of land. It was a gorgeous estate.

The inside of the house was immaculate. It contained lavish draperies, rooms covered with Oriental rugs, and a large collection of antiques. The hallways were lined with oil paintings of Victor's family tree. It seemed more like a museum than a home.

Margaret's daughter, Kerry, was as talkative as Margaret. She kept me up late with her adolescent rambling about her latest romance. I was only two years older than she was, but before the evening was over it felt like twenty. When I could not take it any longer, I excused myself and went to bed.

I was tired and did not get up until eleven. Just after I awoke, I found a note on the pillow from Margaret telling me that she had gone to work and would be home about four-thirty.

As I was getting out of bed, the phone rang. It was Eric. "Hi there. How's my little daughter-in-law this morning? How about joining me for lunch at the club today? I'll send the car for you."

I told him that I should call Margaret and tell her where I was going. He did not think that it was necessary. "Oh, Jenny, you're such a baby. I'm your father-in-law. Doesn't that count for anything?"

He sounded hurt and I acquiesced. "Okay, okay. You talked me into it. I'll need an hour to get ready."

As I was getting dressed, I noticed on the dresser the envelope that Eric had given me the previous night. It contained a $500 bill. I could not believe it. This was the most money that I had ever had. I stared at the bill for about fifteen seconds before I folded it carefully and hid it in a secret compartment of my wallet.

I did not feel comfortable taking the money. I was not a gold digger. I did not know why I was given the money. It had to be returned to Eric.

I heard the horn of the limousine just as I finished dressing. I ran out the door toward the driveway. Eric was in the backseat wearing a blue blazer with his hair slicked back.

As I approached the car he whistled at me. "Wow, you're a gorgeous doll. No wonder my son lost his heart to you." I just smiled. "Jennifer, I am going to take you to lunch first. Then we'll do some more shopping and I'll show you around—"

I stopped him. "Eric, I can't take the money." I took the bill out of my wallet and started to hand it to him through the car window.

He refused to take it. "I can tell you're a proper Bostonian. You're going to keep the money. If you like, you can earn it by working at the club."

I agreed to work at the club, without asking what my job would be. I was only here for a day, and I was getting bored. I liked the idea of getting back to work, especially in a nightclub.

Eric and I spent the afternoon riding around the small town. It appeared as though everyone knew and liked him. Afterward we went back to the club, because Eric wanted to rehearse a few numbers.

Sylvia was there when we arrived back at the club. She was seated at the bar beside a large adding machine and a pile of receipts. Eric went over to see her as soon as we went through the door. He leaned over and kissed her on the cheek.

Eric looked over to me and winked. "Ah, the big businesswoman. She's always thinking about the club. She's so afraid of losing a buck."

Eric started to laugh, but Sylvia just looked up at him and replied, "Yeah, I'm afraid of losing a buck." Then she turned to me. "And I'm afraid of losing you, too, Eric."

Eric pulled the both of us next to him and with his infectious smile said, "Boy! How lucky can one man get? I've got two beautiful girls, and Jake has none." I did not know what he meant, but Sylvia sure did. She burst out laughing.

Sylvia and I sat at the end of the bar nearest the stage while we waited for Eric to change. I noticed that Sylvia appeared to be much younger than Eric.

"Hey, Sylvia, I hope you don't mind my asking, but is Eric a lot older than you?"

Her answer was expressionless. "He's a lot older than me, baby, but age isn't important, is it?"

I felt guilty asking the question and looked at the stage as I responded, "I guess not. Not if you're happy together."

Sylvia's speech was becoming slurred. "Besides, the older they are, the better they are. Do you get what I mean?" She started laughing.

When I asked her about her drinking, she confessed that she began at ten in the morning. I also asked her what Eric meant when he said, "I've got two beautiful girls, and Jake has none."

It was a longer explanation than I was expecting. She explained how Eric and she had met about three years earlier on a plane headed for New York. She was a singer and was fortunate to work in small clubs. At the time she was married to Jake Ramsey. He had owned a small nightclub in Long Island City. He was a big gambler and lost the club and his savings.

Before the plane landed, Eric had offered her a job at his club. The relationship between Sylvia and Eric became intimate, and he wanted her to leave her husband.

The marriage between Jake and Sylvia was disintegrating before she met Eric. Sylvia welcomed the opportunity to divorce Jake, but he was not so eager to dissolve the marriage. He wanted a financial settlement to assuage him for his lost love.

Eric offered Jake a percentage of the club in exchange for his consent to divorce Sylvia. I would have liked to ask Sylvia what percentage of the club she was "traded" for but decided that I had asked enough personal questions.

Eric came onstage and began to sing, and Sylvia ordered another round of drinks. I was a cheap drunk. My first drink made me tipsy, and I did not touch the one that Sylvia ordered.

Sylvia drank like a fish. After she took a large swallow from her glass she gave me a personal appraisal. "You know, I like you, Jenny. You're an okay kid. It's just that you are a little green. You will learn. You seem unaware of your sexiness. I'm sure that you have no trouble getting boyfriends but have lots of problems being friendly with girls. Am I right, honey?"

I was not going to argue with a drunk, so I just nodded my agreement. She continued, "You bet I'm right. I bet you hooked Eric's kid on the first dance, right? You like to dance?" I nodded. "I thought so. You look like the dancing type. He likes to dance, too." She gestured toward Eric. "Eric's a good dancer. You have to try him out sometime. Be careful, though. He likes to blow in your ear."

She tried to suppress a giggle but couldn't. After several seconds she got to the point. "Jenny, I hope we get to be good friends. I don't have a friend, or at least a friend that will not try to steal Eric. I worked hard to get him."

I thought that her situation was sick. Her first husband had traded her for a percentage of a nightclub, while he continued to work alongside her. She was insanely jealous of her current husband, for reasons that I did not understand at the time.

When Eric finished his set, he joined us. After I told him how much I enjoyed his show, he offered me a job as the hat-check girl. Since I had been paid in advance, I graciously accepted. I would start work the following evening.

Sylvia congratulated me on my new job. She seemed genuinely happy that I would be working in the family business. She took my hand and gave me an extensive tour of the club, spending extra time in the hat-check room. When the tour was finished, she called for the chauffeur and ordered him to drive me to Margaret's house.

I enjoyed my new life. As Eric and Sylvia became more confident in my abilities, my responsibilities expanded. I was spending less time in the hat-check room and more time in the business office. I was taught the intricacies of hospitality management. They showed me how to do the bookkeeping, the purchasing, cash management, and personnel management. I competently handled my assignments, and my confidence grew. My previous experience had been limited to menial positions, and I appreciated the opportunity to assume additional responsibilities.

For the first time in my life, I felt confident in my abilities. I was grateful that Eric and Sylvia gave me this chance. I did not want to disappoint them. I worked very hard and learned as much as I could.

I became immersed in my work and did not immediately notice how Eric's attitude toward me changed. I considered Eric Lomax to be my boss and father-in-law. He thought that there was an additional dimension to our relationship.

I was very naive. When Eric continued buying me expensive clothes,

I thought that it was fatherly generosity. But he bought me things that fathers-in-law don't buy for their daughters-in-law, things like sequined gowns, mink stoles, and seductive lingerie.

In addition to the exotic stuff, he bought plenty of things that I could wear on a daily basis. After only several months of working for Eric, my wardrobe of dresses and sweaters had tripled. It seemed that every day I had a new outfit.

Eric was not my idea of a father-in-law. My stereotypical image was of a grumpy, disheveled old man. Eric dressed, looked, and acted like a playboy. He was youthful, attractive, and vibrant.

Margaret knew Eric better than I did and was upset with my new life-style. I continued to live with her, and every day when I returned from the club she would ask me pointed questions about Eric. She was very interested in the relationship between Eric and Sylvia. She wanted to how they were getting along, if they were arguing, where they were going, and what they were doing.

She also became very critical of me. She thought that it was wrong for me to accept the gifts from Eric. She wanted to know if Sylvia was aware of Eric's generosity. She thought that Victor would not allow me to work in "an environment like that."

I had not spent much time thinking about Victor. He was thousands of miles away, and I did not miss him. We had spent very little time together, and most of my memories of him were not pleasant. I did not confide this to any members of his family, but since I rarely spoke of him, I'm sure that they were aware of our fragile relationship. If the marriage gave me a career opportunity, I did not consider it a total loss.

Margaret tried to warn me about Eric. She said that Eric's generosity was not without its price. Eric's friendliness was a facade. I thought that this was jealousy. Eric and Sylvia had a lavish life-style and seemed to be an ideal couple that shared a successful personal and professional life. I became very upset with Margaret's innuendos.

After her repeated badgering, I threatened to move in with Eric and Sylvia if her nagging did not end. Margaret relented, and her inquiries became less caustic. I continued to live with her, but our relationship deteriorated. I spent more and more time at the club, and I only went home to sleep.

On one rainy evening, I was in the office reconciling the bank statements. Sylvia was home with the flu, and business was slow. On busy nights, I had to balance my administrative duties with my responsibilities on the club floor. I enjoyed the quiet night so that I could relax and concentrate on one thing.

Just as I was making progress with the bank statements, Eric walked into the office and broke my concentration. "Hey, Jenny, forget all that bullshit. I want to dance."

I saw that he had been drinking heavily. "Sure, Eric. Are you going to teach me a new dance?"

He grinned. "Yes, honey. I think it's about time that I did."

He grabbed my hand and led me out to the dance floor. When we were in the middle of the floor, he put his arms around me and we started dancing. The band was playing a slow dance, which was fortunate for Eric. He could not move very fast in the shape that he was in. Fortunately, the dance floor was nearly deserted.

After a few steps, it was apparent that he wanted more than just a dance. He wanted to talk. He was very complimentary. He told me what a good job I was doing and how pleased he was with my performance. He appreciated the many functions that I was handling and how difficult it was to find someone as versatile as me.

He then told me that I was attractive and how I seemed very mature for my age. After the second dance, my head was spinning. I had never been so lavishly complimented. I had an inferiority complex due to my mother's constant criticism. It was almost "cured" after two dances with Eric.

After another dance, Eric said that he was tired and asked if we could finish our conversation in the office. He told me to go first and he would meet me there in a few moments. I went inside and sat at my desk. A waiter brought in a bottle of champagne with two glasses. As the waiter was leaving, he passed Eric, who notified him that we were not to be disturbed.

Eric filled the two glasses and pulled up a seat on the other side of the desk. He had a very dour expression. "Here, I know you are not much of a drinker, but it will do you some good. At least it will help with what I have to tell you."

I became nervous. This was a contrast from his extravagant praise on the dance floor. I did not know what I was being set up for.

"Look, I know you're not in love with my son. I can tell by your attitude toward him. You hardly mention him, and I know that you do not write to him. Before he left, he told me about your brief history together. I know that your relationship is not a marriage. I don't understand why you got married.

"You're too mature for Victor. He ran away and joined the navy because he did not want to face his responsibilities and learn the family business. He wanted to run away. He just wanted to get laid and get high. I hope the navy is making him grow up, but I doubt it. My son does not deserve you.

"When you first came here, I just looked at you as my daughter-in-law. In the months that you have been here I have come to look upon you as much more. I have become very fond of you. More than that, I fell in love with you.

"Until now, I have been too embarrassed to say how I felt. I have to know if you feel the same way about me."

I just sat there and stared at him in disbelief. After about ten seconds I managed to speak. "No, no, I don't love you. You have been kind to me, and I appreciate that kindness. I am grateful for the opportunity to work here. I like you, but I don't love you."

"Well, young lady, am I wrong in thinking that you don't love my son? We never discussed your feelings toward him, and I think that now is the time to do it."

I stood up and faced him. "No, Eric, I don't love Victor. I never have, and I don't think that I ever will. Maybe I should go home. I feel that I have caused too much trouble." I turned and started to leave the room.

As I was walking toward the door, he grabbed me by the shoulders and started shaking me. While he was shaking me, he started talking irrationally.

"I have money; I can easily get you a divorce. Victor won't care. He's probably screwing someone else right now. I need you, Jenny. Change your mind!"

I was given a reprieve when the telephone rang. It was Sylvia wanting to know why Eric was late. He told her that he was doing some bookkeeping. He also told her that he was finishing up and would be right home, after she volunteered to come out of her sickbed to help him. When their conversation ended, Eric slowly hung up the receiver. He gave me a quick glance and hurried out of the room.

I was forced to deal with my feelings toward Victor. At the same time, I knew that it was not my vocational talents that interested Eric. I had thought that I was secure here and was finished running. I was wrong.

I lay awake all night thinking over the situation. I was confused but finally realized that I had to do two things: I had to go home, and I had to get a divorce.

In the morning, I told Margaret everything. We cried on each other's shoulders. I then packed my bags, wrote a farewell note to Eric, which I asked Margaret to deliver, and called for a cab to take me to the airport.

The local airport did not have any direct flights to Boston. The plane made five stops, which gave me plenty of time to come up with an explanation for my parents.

I did not call ahead to tell my parents that I was coming home. I hoped that my parents would understand, but I was expecting lots of "I told you so's."

I knew that I was probably doing the wrong thing by running away again, but I could not control my impulse. I had felt as though I was settling in with Victor's family, but it was a false sense of security. I was too immature and naive to recognize Eric's motives. If I had understood what was happening, I might have been able to control the situation.

In many respects, I had regarded Eric as a substitute father. I assigned to him the same qualities as my father. But my father was a kind, trustworthy gentleman. Eric was a lecher.

CHAPTER EIGHT

I had to think of something to tell my parents. I expected to catch hell, or at least a million "I told you so's," from my mother. I expected my father to be compassionate.

My sense of security grew as we circled over Boston. I felt safe in my hometown. I just did not feel safe confronting my mother.

I decided against calling home from the airport. I just took a cab and went home. When I approached the house, I could hear the Italian music playing. I was shaking as I rang the doorbell.

My younger brother, Sal, answered the door. He put his arms around my neck and gave me a big hug. My mother followed behind Sal. When she saw me she turned a pale white.

"Jenny, what are you doing here? What happened?"

"Nothing, Ma. I just felt homesick, and I wanted to come home. There's nothing wrong with that, is there?"

"No, but I know you, Jenny. You wouldn't be here if there was nothing wrong. Did you eat? You look like you've been starved to death."

My mother saw food as the answer to every problem. Even though she did not know what was wrong, she knew that food would solve the problem.

She led me into the dining room, and I sat at the table while she warmed up the pot of minestrone that was sitting on the stove. While it was warming up, she cut a large slice of French bread, put it on a plate, and placed it in front of me. She then placed a bowl in front of me and poured the soup.

When all was done, she sat at the table across from me. I never touched the soup. I just sat for several seconds and looked at my mother before she spoke.

"What is it, Jenny? What happened? Did anyone hurt you? Tell me!"

I tried to remain under control, but I failed. I started crying. "Oh, Mom, I'm sorry, but I can never love anyone but Vito. I don't love Victor. I know that I made a mistake. I want a divorce. Please, Ma, help me. I'll go crazy if I have to stay married to Victor. I'm sorry for everything that I have done."

I was afraid that my mother would explode in anger. She surprised me, saying, "You go to bed after you eat. We'll talk in the morning." She left the table and went upstairs.

I stayed in the dining room and stared at the lima beans floating in the soup until I heard my mother close her bedroom door. I then went upstairs to my bedroom. I stayed in bed with all my clothes on, thinking of Vito.

In New York, I had been kept busy, plus I had tried to suppress my thoughts of Vito. I wanted to believe that Victor could replace him. I was married to Victor and wanted to be loyal to him. I tried not to think of Vito.

Eric's advances toward me were a catalyst. They burst my bubble of illusions. I realized that I was living a lie, and I responded in typical fashion: I ran.

I finally fell asleep. Fortunately, I did not dream. When I awoke in the morning, I was very nervous and sick to my stomach. I went to the bathroom, and when I returned, my mother was sitting on my bed waiting for me. She told me that she and my father wanted to speak to me downstairs. She left my room. I dressed quickly and joined my parents in the dining room.

There was a bacon and scrambled egg breakfast waiting for me on the table. The rumblings in my stomach precluded my eating. My father came over and kissed me on the cheek. "Honey, I don't know what we're going to do with you. Your mother told me that you came in out of the night crying and asking for a divorce. Why? What went on in New York? Why are you bringing up Vito? That should be finished. You should be beginning your new life with Victor. He loves you. You can learn to love him in time."

"No, Dad, I can't. I can't go back to Victor or his family, never!"

"Well, his father called here this morning while you were sleeping. He was very worried. It seems that you forgot to tell anyone that you were leaving. You can't do those things, Jenny. You act first and think later. That will only get you in trouble."

I did not tell my dad that Eric was only worried about losing a piece of ass. "What did you tell his father, Dad?"

"I told the truth: you came in and said nothing and went to bed. What did you want me to say, that you love someone else? I did not want to hurt them. Listen to me, Jenny. What you felt for Vito was puppy love. You have to get over it!"

"Maybe you think I will, but I won't."

My father temporarily dropped the issue.

It was as though Victor and his family never existed. Eric kept trying to call me, but I refused to come to the phone or to answer Victor's letters.

Vito was again fresh in my memory. The months of working for Eric were forgotten. Vito occupied my thoughts. I became obsessed with my love for Vito.

Torturing myself, I was getting a physical reaction from my anxiety. There were headaches and a tightness in my stomach. My parents took me to a doctor who talked to me in great detail.

Dr. Solomon spent a great deal of time talking to me about my condition, both physical and emotional. He provided two prescriptions: an antianxiety pill and a divorce.

This was 1956 and nineteen-year-old divorcées were uncommon. They were even more uncommon in a traditional Italian family. When Dr. Solomon brought up the possibility to my parents, my mother thought that he exceeded the scope of his responsibility. After all, a medical doctor should only deal with the physical condition of his patients.

My father was more open-minded. That evening, my parents had a spirited debate and decided that I should get a divorce. I was glad that they reached that conclusion and was thankful to Dr. Solomon for his input.

When my parents reached that decision, they moved quickly. Through the family network, they contacted a divorce lawyer in Boston. Mr. Corvino had assisted one of my aunts in getting a divorce and a healthy alimony settlement.

My mother took me to see him at his office on State Street. I sat quietly while my mother explained the situation. They spent about a half hour discussing the matter. I sat quietly and said nothing. Mr. Corvino concluded that I would be "free" in about a month. I went home feeling relieved.

Mr. Corvino drew up the papers and brought them to my home several days later. I quickly signed them without reading them. I just wanted to get this over with.

Victor was notified aboard ship that he was being sued for divorce. He agreed to waive his military rights so that the divorce could be granted quickly.

Servicemen have rights that can make divorce proceedings more difficult. I was a little disappointed that Victor waived these rights without a fight or even an inquiry. I believe that he also realized that the marriage was a mistake and welcomed the chance to end it. The divorce came through about forty-five days after my mother and I first went to see the lawyer.

I spent the next several weeks as a recluse. I do not easily recover from disappointment, and this was no exception. I felt embarrassed being a nineteen-year-old divorcée and did not want to go out in public.

I did not get over Vito. I kept thinking about him. He was my first true love, and I kept imagining various pleasant scenarios. I dreamed about what it would be like if I had waited for him and we had married. I was lost in a fantasy world.

My parents left me alone to dream. Even my younger brother recognized my problem and was less obnoxious than usual.

I had been divorced about two weeks when I read that Vito's ship was docked in Charlestown and would be there for several weeks before going on a Mediterranean cruise. I knew that I had to see him.

The next day, I got dressed up for the first time since I left Tuttle. I felt better immediately. I was finally going to do something about my frustration. I was going to see Vito.

I was hoping that Vito had changed and become more open-minded. I was divorced now. I was free, but my virginity was gone forever. But I was hoping that his priorities had changed.

I was dressed to kill as I prepared to leave the house. The prior evening, I had washed and set my hair and ironed my favorite blue dress. I put on enough makeup to make me appear much older than my nineteen years.

I was quietly tiptoeing down the stairs when my mother caught me. "Where are you going, Jennifer?"

"Oh, I don't know, Ma. I'll just look around the stores for a while, I guess. It's such a nice day. Too nice to stay in the house."

"Well, maybe I'll go with you."

"Oh, no, Ma. I feel like going alone."

"Look, Jennifer, I know that you're not all dressed up to take a walk, especially since you have been locked up in your room for so long. I wish that you would go hunting for a job. I hope that you are not looking for trouble."

"Oh, Ma, please don't start. I'll be back later."

I was lucky to get out of the house without additional interrogation. I took the bus to the Charlestown Navy Yard. The bus let me off about one hundred yards from the main gate. The closer that I got to the gate, the more nervous I became.

What if Vito would not see me? If he did agree to see me, how would he react to seeing me? I was hoping that he had changed and would accept me now. My feelings toward him had not changed.

There were two marines standing outside the guardhouse by the main gate. One was tall, well over six feet, and rugged-looking, the other several inches shorter, with a smooth complexion.

I approached the taller one and told him that I wanted to speak to Vito Costa, a marine serving on the USS *Bagwell*. He responded with a broad grin and a wise remark.

"Sure, honey, I'll get him for you, only if you'll see me tonight." The little one started to laugh.

I was not in any mood for this crap. I repeated my request with a very stern expression. He took me seriously this time and told me to have a seat inside the guardhouse while they contacted Vito. I followed his instructions.

He followed me into the guardhouse, walked up to a phone on the counter, and called the ship. It took him several minutes to contact Vito. When he did, he told Vito that he had a visitor waiting at the main gate.

Bill, the tall marine, told me that Vito would be here in about ten minutes. I was nervous and could not sit still. As I was pacing around the main gate, Bill continued to hit on me.

With a very straight face, he said that he was going to marry me. I told him that I was in no mood to kid around. He paid no attention to my request and continued to harass me.

"Hey, who's this jar-head that you had me call? Are you going with him? I can find out. I know most of the jar-heads that come through these gates, so why don't you tell me and make it easier for me? Why do you want to see this guy when you can have me?"

I responded in a loud, angry voice, "Look! Leave me alone! I don't want to have anything to do with you."

Just then Bill grabbed my right arm. I struggled, but he would not let go.

As I was spinning, trying to escape, I saw Vito approach the main gate. His eyes were glued to the spectacle of Bill and me doing our strange dance near the guardhouse.

Vito did not appear happy to see me. He grabbed me by my good arm. "What are you doing here? Who's that guy that had his arms on you? Well, princess! What *are* you doing here? Going around like a tramp? Is that what your husband did for you? If you had married me, you would have worn white. Now, you will always wear black." Vito walked a few steps, turned his back to me, and stared at his ship.

I could not hold back the tears. Vito was so cruel. I was both angry and disappointed. I was sorry that I had attempted this reconciliation.

Bill was watching this scene with great interest. Just as Vito started walking away, Bill approached me and asked, "Look, miss, can I help you?"

I responded while sniffling, "No thank you; I'm fine."

"Yeah, you look it."

Bill turned and walked toward Vito. Bill said something to him that I could not hear, but I saw Vito take some paper out of his pocket and show it to Bill. Bill nodded and then came back to me.

He stood before me and in a voice loud enough for Vito to hear said, "If you need me for anything, I'll be right here at the gate."

Vito's face was turning red. It was apparent that he did not believe that I had just met Bill. He turned and walked back toward his ship. My final picture of Vito was of his red face, scowl, and gritted teeth.

Tears were now streaming down my face. Bill told me that I could use the bathroom in the guardhouse. I went inside and found a small washroom in the corner. I looked at my reflection in a cracked mirror. As I wiped the tears from my face, I considered my current situation.

I wondered about my love for Vito, I was angry about how he had just reacted, but I knew I loved him and I desperately wanted to be with him. But for some reason we were not meant to be together, though I did not know why.

That day's encounter between the three of us was so similar to my introduction to Victor. It was a case where a casual and unwelcome advance messed up the chance for me to be with the one I loved. I should have been mad with Bill and/or Vito for the way that he reacted. Instead, I blamed myself!

As I was standing in the small guardhouse bathroom, I was not analyzing the situation: I was feeling sorry for myself. I could not believe my bad luck. After about five minutes, I had used up my Kleenex and regained my composure.

Bill had a cup of coffee waiting for me. "I hope you don't mind, but I thought that you could use this."

I accepted his offer. "I'm a long way from home, and am I ever homesick," he said.

I began to relax a little as we had our coffee. Bill told me that he was off-duty in about an hour and he would be glad to drive me home.

We spent the hour talking about ourselves and our families. Bill was interested in Vito, but I avoided the issue. I talked about my parents and Sal. I told Bill how I thought my brother was a spoiled brat. I told him that my mother was a great cook and that my father liked to restore decrepit houses. I told him about my Aunt Connie and how much I admired her courage. I gave him personal information, but not the *really* personal stuff.

Bill told me about himself. He had been raised on a farm in North Carolina, an only child who joined the marines to get off the farm. I was surprised over his southern heritage, because he hardly had an accent. What accent there was seemed more midwestern than southern.

The hour passed quickly. When Bill was relieved at his post, he drove me to a market on Hanover Street. I told him I had to pick up a few things before I went home. I could not let him take me home. I could not risk my mother's reaction.

I began to feel comfortable with Bill and conveniently forgot how we happened to meet. I accepted when he offered to take me to a movie the next night, and we agreed to meet at 8:00 P.M. in front of the Paramount Theater on Washington Street. I got out of his car and walked toward the market. When Bill's car was out of sight, I turned and headed home.

When I opened my front door, my mother was waiting for me. When she asked me where I had been, I told her the truth. I was in no mood to lie and told her about Bill and how I met him. I did not want to worry about any cover-ups and was willing to risk my mother's wrath.

My mother had never gotten over the shame of having a divorced daughter, even though she was more than willing to help me get the divorce. On more than one occasion she would explain how embarrassing it was to have a teenage divorcée as a daughter. Her twelve brothers and sisters were not a kindly or forgiving bunch. I overheard her dear sister Yolanda say, "If I had a daughter like Jennifer, I would kill her. She is just a spoiled brat and a tramp."

The attitude of Mother's other siblings was similar, but not as vitriolic. They enjoyed telling my mother that their children were not like me, they never had the same problems with their offspring that my mother had with me. Many of my female cousins were married and, according to my aunts, were living ideal lives. None had the stigma of divorce. . . . yet.

All of my girl cousins had walked down the aisle in white gowns. My aunts forgot to mention that several had spent their honeymoon in the maternity ward. I was the victim of their hypocrisy and was very angry that my mother made no effort to defend me. I made a mistake, but I did nothing to be ashamed of.

My mother not only neglected to defend me; she joined in the lynching. She constantly referred to me as "that whore" or "my little tramp." I thought that she had forgotten that my name was Jennifer. She had never treated me with much respect, but my divorced validated her scorn.

During her mellower moments, my mother tried to rationally warn me of the consequences of dating. "You are going to be hurt. Mark my words, you haven't grown up yet. As a divorced woman you will be the target for every whoremonger in the city."

I thought that I had learned my lesson. I would not be as vulnerable as I had been before. I told my mother, "I am never going to love a man again. I am just going to use them; I will never be vulnerable. I will never be hurt again."

The double rejection by Vito left a permanent emotional scar. My love for him was shaken but not destroyed. I wanted to build a wall around myself to avoid getting hurt again.

The wall had holes in it, and Bill sneaked through one of these holes. I did not heed Mother's advice. I met Bill the following night. I thought that I was emotionally strong and would just use Bill to help me leave my self-imposed exile and reestablish a social life. I could not spend more time in my room fantasizing about Vito.

I met Bill the following night. We saw a movie. It was one of those things about the Roman Empire starring Victor Mature, not my favorite genre, but I was just glad to get out for the evening.

I liked Bill. Bill was not aggressive like Victor or Vito. Our first encounter at the Charlestown Navy Yard did not reflect his real personality. He was quiet and polite. I could relax with him.

We dated frequently. He spent most of his off-duty hours with me. As soon as he found out that I loved to dance, we spent most of our dates in the Boston dance halls. Bill was a very big man, about six feet, four inches and two hundred and thirty pounds. I was just five feet and about ninety pounds. We were a sight on the dance floor. Bill was not a good dancer, and that made things worse. I was fortunate to escape without any broken toes.

Bill became infatuated with me. I could tell by the way he held my hand and looked into my eyes. Another indication was that he ended every date by telling me that he loved me.

The feeling was not mutual. I enjoyed Bill's company but was not becoming emotionally involved. I wanted to use him as a vehicle to forget Vito. I was fearful of being hurt again. The wall that I built was too thick for any man to penetrate.

Bill introduced me to many of his friends, and we all got along. When Bill had duty, his comrades would call me up for dates. I did not consider Bill my steady, so I saw no reason not to visit the dance halls with others. Since most of the guys were better dancers than Bill, I considered this a wise decision.

I was having fun again. I was out almost every night. I enjoyed dressing up and wearing makeup. I was reestablishing my social life and putting my bad experience behind me.

My fun was innocent. I would just go dancing and afterward get a quick bite to eat, then go home. Although many of the guys made sexual advances, the most they ever got was a goodnight kiss.

I had been going out for several weeks without any comment from my mother. I was hoping that she had mellowed and was willing to accept my behavior. This was a bad assumption.

She cornered me one night. "Jennifer, we're going to have a talk. I've been getting phone calls about you. People have been seeing you with all kinds of different men."

"So what, Ma! I'm not doing anything wrong. What do I care what they say? I know that I'm doing nothing wrong, and that's all that matters! Don't you agree?"

"No, I don't! When you act like a whore, you'll be called a whore. You are acting like the biggest whore in town!"

"Well, that's great! You are always worried more over my image than over me. You don't give a damn for my welfare, only what your friends and relatives think about me. I have only been going dancing. You react as if I have been screwing everyone."

"Don't talk to me that way, or I'll slap your face! As long as you live under my roof, you'll live by my standards."

"Well, don't push me or I'll move out, Ma. I'm not a kid anymore."

My father heard the argument and came downstairs. As soon as he reached the bottom step, my mother presented her side of the story. She explained how I was embarrassing the family by being seen around town in the company of different men. I was just a teenage divorcée on the loose.

She told him, "You should try and talk some sense into her, since it will take me a long time to live down the terrible reputation that she has acquired."

My father put both hands on her shoulders and tried to calm her down, since by this time she had worked herself up into an eye-bulging anger. He was unsuccessful. His pleas to "calm down, Angie" were for naught.

She continued her pathological rage, at times sinking into periods of incoherence. Her screaming mixed the Italian and English languages. I was called tramp, whore, and slut in both languages. I was used to her insults, but this display was worse than most. For the first time I realized that my mother was crazy.

She stormed away from my father and started walking back toward me, keeping her invective intact. She drove me over the edge.

When she was several feet in front of me, I lashed out. "Go to hell, Ma!"

Just as the word "Ma" was leaving my mouth. I felt a slap across my face. I turned around and ran up the stairs crying. I was more hurt at having told my mother that than at her assault.

I was tired of having to live up the hypocritical standards of my mother's family. I was supposed to be happily married not for my happiness, but for my mother's. She wanted to be on equal footing with her sisters, whose daughters were happy little housewives, not whores. It did not matter that many of them had become happy little housewives because they acted like whores. They got knocked up by their boyfriends, and in the preabortion era they had to get married.

I only had sex when I was married. I was only with Victor for a week. That week gave me a fear of sex. The sex act disgusted me. I thought that it was filthy, and yet I was called a slut!

I tried but could not communicate this to my mother. She had an old-world mentality that I could not shake. She was more concerned with appearance than with fact. If I had many dates, I was promiscuous. It did not matter that those dates were innocent.

I did not move out, and my mother's attitude did not change. We had an uneasy truce.

Except for the shaky relationship with my mother, things were going well. I began work as a trainee at Cannon Electronics as an assembler.

Bill's attitude toward me had changed. When we first started going out he was easygoing. As time went on he became more possessive. He started to consider me "his girl." I did not welcome this change in attitude, but I did not think that it was dangerous. He knew I was dating others, and his protests were mild.

One Friday evening, I was sitting in the Wonderland Ball Room with a couple of marines that shared the sentry duty with Bill. One of them, Burt, was short and stocky, with red hair. He was a terrible dancer, but he had a good sense of humor. He was fun to be with.

We were sitting at the table, talking, when Bill came in. He walked over to our table and matter-of-factly said, "What are you guys doing with my fiancée?" Bill had neglected to tell me that we were engaged.

I responded accordingly. "You'd better not tell anyone that. You know that it's not true. What got into you?"

Bill turned into a madman. He reached over the table and grabbed my arm and pulled me from behind the table and threw me onto the floor. A man standing nearby saw what was going on, put his arms around Bill, and wrestled him to the floor. People started screaming and running over to see the action.

I was still sitting on the floor when Burt bent down, grabbed my arm, stood me up, and hustled me out of the ballroom. "Come on, I'll give you a ride home, before you start any more trouble." I gladly accepted the offer.

Before going home, I had to use the rest room of a nearby restaurant to compose myself. On the way home Burt was inquisitive. "What the hell is going on? Are you going to marry Bill, or is he full of shit?"

I told him that I was just dating Bill, there was nothing serious between us. Burt did not believe me.

"You should tell him that you are just friends." He went on to tell me that Bill had told all the guys in the barracks that we were engaged. "They just laughed at him. They knew that you did not love him, that you were just dating him."

Burt and I tried to account for Bill's misconception. We kicked around different ideas, from lovesickness to an overactive imagination. We stopped for a cup of coffee at a shop near my home to continue our analysis.

We arrived at my home about an hour after leaving the ballroom. Burt stopped the car and told me that he was sorry that the incident had ruined the evening.

Just as I was turning to exit the car, the door was ripped open and I was pulled out. Bill grabbed my arm for the second time that evening, and I fell to the sidewalk. Unlike our encounter at the club, he did not let go. He lifted me up and started to yell at me. His face was bruised, and he had dried blood at the corner of his mouth.

While this was going on, Burt jumped out of the car, ran around the front, and shoved Bill, who released my arm. Burt was a lot shorter than Bill, but he was powerfully built, and the force of his shove threw Bill against the fence in front of my house.

Bill came storming back and within moments fists were flying. I tried to stop the fight, to no avail. I was dumb enough to step between and play referee. I received a punch to my right eye. I thought my head was broken. My crying in pain did nothing to stop their fisticuffs.

Both marines were fighting and yelling and making quite a commotion. That, together with my crying, created quite a sight and sound. Within moments, the whole neighborhood was awake.

My mother was the first one on the scene. When she saw what was going on, she ran into the house for my father. Moments later they both came running out, my mother carrying Sal's baseball bat, my father in the process of getting dressed, buttoning his shirt as he descended the steps.

My mother added to the cacophony by standing on the sidewalk screaming, while my father attempted the impossible task of stopping the fight, quieting my mother, and providing first aid for me.

My mother ran into the house and called the police. By the time the police arrived, it looked like a full-scale riot. Several of the neighbors had joined the fray, in a peacemaking capacity, but they were just adding to the uproar, as their yelling did not placate any of the participants.

My mother, after phoning Boston's finest, ran back out of the house, invigorated and eager to join the fray.

I was standing to the side, crying and holding both hands over my right eye. I must have been a juicy target to a sadist like my mother. She ran over to me as fast as her stumpy little legs could carry her. She stopped and screamed, "This whole mess is your fault!" and started flailing me with both of her arms on the side of my head.

I ran back to the front steps of our house and had turned to see if my mother was following, when I heard the police sirens and saw the flashing lights.

Two police cars stopped in front of my house. By this time most of the neighbors had left their houses and were gathered around the fray.

Two policemen emerged from the first squad car on the scene. One grabbed Burt; the other grabbed Bill. The police had no trouble pulling them apart, because they were quite winded from their battle. The policemen stood between Bill and Burt, while the cops from the second car dispersed the sizable crowd that had gathered.

There should have been a third patrol car, since my mother did not consider the battle over. She saw where I was standing, grabbed me by the hair with one arm, and hit me with the other. Finally one of the cops who was dispersing the crowd stepped between me and my mother.

My mother continued swinging, hitting the policeman. I'm sure the cop would have pressed charges, except it might seem silly for a six-foot policeman to press assault charges against a middle-aged woman standing four feet, seven inches.

When the cop with the sergeant stripes started to question Bill, he blurted out that he had caught Burt fooling around with his fiancée. His angry diatribe had continued for about thirty seconds when the cop turned to me and asked me what was going on. I told him that I had never seen either of the two men before.

The sergeant knew that they had a screwed-up situation, but an innocuous one. He said that he was taking Bill and Burt to the station and I would also go along to make a statement. The fighting and screaming had stopped, and the situation was calming down. This was unacceptable to my mother! Her arms may have been tired, but her voice was in good form. She screamed, "Lock them all up, especially my troublemaking daughter! Don't forget to throw away the key!"

We were fortunate that the sergeant had a sense of humor. He tried to suppress a smile when my mother started to scream.

Bill and Burt rode in one car, I in the other. When we got to the station house we were also separated. The sergeant directed me to a little room near the front door and told me to have a seat in a wooden straight-backed chair. He stood over me and broke into a huge grin.

"You should know enough to go out with only one guy at a time. If you are messing around with a bunch of guys, you should be smart enough not to get caught."

I did not admire his sense of humor and asked him when I could go home.

"Well, I don't know. Your mother told me to lock you up and throw away the key. If I release you, could you stay away from our fighting men and be a good girl?"

"Very funny! You missed your calling. You should have been a comedian."

He gave me a stern look and pointed toward the door. As I was walking out he asked, "Are you worried over what is going to happen to the guys?"

"Hell, no! I'm only worried over what's going to happen to me when I get home."

CHAPTER NINE

I took the bus home. I was in no hurry to face my mother. When I got back to my house, my mother and father were waiting for me at the kitchen table. My little brother, Sal, stared at my black eye. He said that he had never seen one on a girl before. Mother promptly chased him from the room.

"What a disgrace! The whole neighborhood will be talking about the brawling Italians that live here. I'm so ashamed. I will never be able to hold my head up because of you. My sisters never went through any of this with their children. You're lost bread; that's what you are," she began. "Look at you! You're worse than a streetwalker. If anything ever happens to me or your father, you can blame yourself. I'm going to light a candle to Saint Anthony for you to break both of your legs, so that you can't run around anymore."

My father told my mother to calm down; then he turned to me. "I suggest that you go straight to bed. You had better dream about finding one man and settling down. There are plenty of nice guys out there."

"Sure, Dad. It's not as easy as you think."

My mother had been quiet long enough. "You should go straight to the crazy house. That's what you should do. Maybe you'll meet a nice doctor. Now, go to bed before I break your back!"

A black eye was bad enough. I did not want to risk any additional parts of my anatomy. I went straight to bed.

I continued to get many phone calls asking for dates but did not go out because of my black eye. Unfortunately, Bill did not spend much time in jail, so he was my most frequent caller. He called at least three times a day. Burt was also a frequent caller, but he was able to take no for an answer.

For a two-week period I only went from home to work and back. I constantly wore sunglasses and was very reluctant to explain how I was hurt.

At the electronics factory I had a corner bench where I did my assembly work and had minimal contact with other employees. I told my story to a couple of girls that I became friendly with, but that was the extent of my socializing.

At home, I stayed in my room as much as possible. If I was downstairs and guests arrived, I fled to my room. My mother was very ashamed of what I had done. If a family member or friend was unaware of what had happened, my mother explained my absence by saying that I had the flu.

Bill was becoming a bigger pain than my sore eye. He continued calling, professing his love for me and saying that he would "make everything right" by marrying me. I still liked Bill, but not that much.

After about two weeks, the swelling and discoloration around my eye was disappearing and I was looking forward to resuming a normal social life. I stopped hiding from visitors. The first visitor to see me with a nearly normal right eye was my Aunt Theresa. She was a frequent guest at our house, chatting in Italian with my mother when I was present. I never figured out why their gossip should be such a big secret.

The doorbell rang and I went to answer it. There were two deliverymen from Sears Roebuck saying they had a delivery for Jennifer Vicci. I checked the manifest, because I had not purchased anything. It had the date, name of the store, delivery address, purchaser, and item purchased.

The last two categories caught my attention. Bill had bought me a hope chest. I was shocked. I felt like I had received another blow to the head. I told the deliverymen not to take it inside, that I would not accept it. I then shut the door in their faces.

My mother and Aunt Theresa were standing behind me in the living room as I had my conversation with the deliverymen. My mother wanted to know what was going on, who the men were, and why I shut the door in their faces. I told my mother what was being delivered.

"I thought that you told us you weren't engaged to him. What the hell is going on!"

"*I'm not!* How am I supposed to know that he was going to send me a hope chest?"

"Well, he has got to be a nut to send that to someone that he is not engaged to marry. As usual, you probably led him on and the poor sucker thinks you will marry him."

"Look, Ma, I know that you won't believe me, but I turned down his marriage proposal. He won't take no for an answer. What can I do about it?"

"Someday, young lady, they will find you dead from some crazy jealous man."

"Oh, Ma, please leave me alone; I don't want to talk about it anymore."

My Aunt Theresa acted as peacemaker. She walked over to me and softly told me to drop the subject and not provoke my mother. I took her advice and quietly went up to my room.

I was in my room for about a half hour listening to records when the phone rang. It was Bill calling to ask me how I liked the hope chest.

The anger that was left over from my confrontation with my mother now had an outlet. "You shouldn't have sent that thing. *WE . . . ARE . . . NOT . . . ENGAGED!* I had it returned to the store."

Bill returned my anger, saying that he was going to have it sent back to my house. I pitied the poor deliverymen who had brought it.

I lowered my voice and explained to him that sending it back to me would only create more trouble. I told him how angry my parents were with him and me. I tried to be rational. I explained that I just wanted to be "left alone."

When our conversation ended, I did not think that I made any progress in getting him off my back. He would call constantly. After a while, I would not speak to him. If I heard his voice on the other end, I would just hang up.

When I refused to talk to him, he would drive over to my house and park across the street. He spent many of his off-duty hours keeping my house under surveillance. Bill's jealousy was getting out of hand. He stopped this latest prank only when the neighbor called the cops.

I knew that I had to do something when the neighbor told me that she had called the cops on my "suitor." The next day I went to the Charlestown Navy Yard. I was fortunate that Bill was not on-duty. I told the marine on-duty that I wanted to speak to the commanding officer of the base. When he asked what my business was, I told him that it was personal. He then asked for my name and phone number. I just gave him my name.

He went into the guardhouse and emerged a minute later with a little piece of yellow paper, which he handed to me. As he was opening the gate, he smiled and pointed the way to the headquarters building. I thanked him for his assistance and headed straight for the base CO.

The headquarters building was an old three-story brick building about fifty yards from the main gate. The reception area was empty except for a sergeant sitting at a wooden desk. When he asked me my business, I told him that I wanted to see the base commander and gave him the yellow paper. He handed the paper back to me and told me to have a seat, while he went through one of the half-dozen doors that circled the reception area.

After several minutes he came back out and escorted me through the same door. I assumed that this was the base commander. There was a young marine sitting at the desk in a dress green uniform, behind a desk plate that said LIEUTENANT HAYWOOD. I later found out that marine lieutenants do not command naval bases.

He was very friendly and put a wooden high-backed chair next to his desk and told me to sit down. He then asked me to explain my problem. I told him all about Bill and how I thought things were getting out of hand. I told him the whole story, from the incident at the main gate when I met Bill to his staking out my house.

When I finished, he got up, walked to the door, opened it, and called for the sergeant to get two cups of coffee. He turned slowly and returned to the desk. Just as he was sitting down, the sergeant brought in two cups of coffee on a plastic tray and placed them on the desk.

We both picked up a cup and took a sip. He then asked me what he wanted me to do about Bill. Before I could answer, he gave me his analysis of the situation. He said that I could make out a formal complaint, the marine equivalent of a sexual harassment charge. Bill could then be subject to an "Article 15," which is not a court-martial, but an administrative procedure that could lead to punitive action. I could also request that Bill be transferred to another base. My third option would be for Bill's CO to "just talk to him." This third action was the most benign and could not guarantee a solution to the problem.

I would have liked someone to give Bill a direct order to "leave me the fuck alone." When I told this to the lieutenant, he just laughed and told me that was not a possibility. I did not want to hurt Bill; I just wanted him to stop bugging me.

I decided on the transfer. I wanted Bill transferred to another base and told this to the lieutenant. I spent another half hour in the lieutenant's office, putting my story on paper and signing forms. As I was leaving Lieutenant Haywood's office, he told me not to say anything to Bill about our conversation.

For the next two weeks, things with Bill remained the same: he was still pestering me. Then I finally got the call that I was waiting for. Bill called to tell me that he was being transferred to Camp Lejeune.

We talked about the transfer, which came as a total surprise to him, since he had expected to spend a year in Boston. He was here barely six months when the papers came through.

Bill was from some small town in North Carolina—Autryville, I believe. I told him how glad I was that he was going home or at least to the same state. He told me that he would be stationed about a hundred miles from his hometown and then started to talk about the geography of North Carolina. If I did not feel guilty about initiating the transfer, I would not have listened to his babble.

When he finished talking about North Carolina, he started to talk about us. He told me how much I meant to him, how much he loved me. He wanted me to marry him and move to North Carolina with him. I wished the geography lesson had continued.

I was honest with him. I told him, for what seemed like the hundredth time, that I did not love him. After my bad experiences with Vito and Victor, I did not want to get involved with anyone.

Bill would be leaving in three days. He asked to see me for one last time. I turned down this request, saying, "There should be a clean break. It will be less painful that way." He finally accepted my point of view and we said our good-byes. When I hung up the receiver I thought that I was through with Bill.

Bill left and I did not miss him. I went about reestablishing my social life without the danger of Bill intruding. One of my favorite places was Gerard's on Washington Street, what is now called the Combat Zone. During the 1950s, Boston's red-light district was Scollay Square, which was several blocks away.

The bartenders at Gerard's got to know me quite well. They usually teased me. I was not much of a drinker and usually ordered ginger ale, which was fortunate, since I was not twenty-one. They sometimes threatened to call the cops if I ordered something stronger than my customary soft drink.

Even after two traumatic experiences with Vito, I could not get him out of my mind. I still loved him. I frequented Gerard's, not because the place had anything special, but because I knew that it was Vito's favorite place.

His ship was docked in town, and I was praying for a miracle. I would find a table near the door and check out every marine who entered, hoping to see Vito.

Vito had rejected me twice before, but I put that out of my mind. I was still love-struck and unrealistic. I wanted us to start over. I wanted him to come through the door, put his arms around me, and pretend that everything that had happened since our initial walks through the commons had not happened. Vito never came through the door at Gerard's, but I continued to dream.

In the mid-1950s it seemed like Boston was saturated with service-men, most of whom made a pass at me at one time or another. Most of my dance partners were marines. That was the closest that I could come to Vito.

Even though I always had male companionship, I was lonely. In affairs of the heart, as in other things, quantity is not a substitute for quality. I was walking around with an empty feeling.

I would reminisce about the time that I had spent with Vito. About our walks through the commons, our visit to Saint Anthony's Church, our visits to Revere Beach. We never had a glamorous date, such as going to see a stage play or to an expensive restaurant. We enjoyed being together, just talking about our families and exchanging stories about our Italian culture.

Everything seemed so natural with Vito. I could relax with him. I did not have to put up a front, like I had to with other men. He had a great sense of humor. I could say anything to him. I missed him so much. I usually cried when I thought of our times together.

If I could not reunite with Vito, I looked for him in other men. I looked for tall, handsome men with coal black hair.

It seemed as though the more I went out, the lonelier I became. Although I spent many evenings dancing with Vito lookalikes, they were no substitutes for the real thing. My female hormones were acting up, with no acceptable outlet.

Bill did not give up. He kept calling me from North Carolina. It had been months since he was transferred, but his ardor had not cooled. He wanted me to marry him and move to North Carolina. I kept telling him that I did not want another marriage.

I remained dissatisfied with my social life. I was becoming bored and restless. I kept looking for Vito and not finding him.

The loneliness was exacerbated by my divorce. I did not fit in with the "singles" or the married crowd. Most of my friends and relatives who were my age were married or engaged. I was a misfit.

My job kept me busy during the day, but the nights were lonely. It appeared as though there was a caste system and a young divorcée was an outcast.

After a while, I stopped going out at night. I faced the fact that I would not see Vito come through the door at Gerard's. It was very frustrating to wait for someone who never came. I was also getting annoyed at the advances of the people that I was dancing with at the club. Optimism turned to despair, and I spent my evenings at home.

My evenings at home were not as peaceful as I would have liked. My mother was incessantly nagging me. She never lost an opportunity to tell me that my female cousins were happily married and starting families. I almost felt sorry for her when she related "the burden of being the mother of a slut."

She had me believing that I was a hopeless sinner. My early training at the convent left a permanent impression on me. I accepted guilt very well. My mother was very good at dispensing guilt. It was as though I had left a permanent scar on her. Intellectually, I knew that I had done nothing wrong. Emotionally, I yielded to my mother's vitriol. I kept quiet and took it.

She would berate me for my evenings at Gerard's, as well as my divorce. I could not take it anymore. I just wanted to go away. I had a problem and was receiving no support, not from my peers, not from my family.

My mother was terrible; I avoided her whenever possible. My younger brother, Sal, was a spoiled brat, with as much compassion as my mother. He told me that the guys in his class offered him five dollars to fuck his sister. He was born to be a pimp.

My father was the only member of my family to whom I could relate. He never gave me grief about my personal life. I would tell him my problems; he would smile and tell me, "Everything will be okay." But when I asked him for help in getting my mother off my back, he would wither. He would not confront my mother.

On top of everything else, I was laid off from my job. A recession caused the company to lay off about one hundred people, and since I was one of the last hired, I was one of the first to go.

I felt very alone. I wanted to run away. At that moment, there was one place to run: North Carolina!

I called Bill and told him that I would accept his invitation to visit him in North Carolina. He was very happy. The way he was screaming on the phone, I thought his clothes were on fire.

He said that I could stay with his mother, who was now living in Wilmington, which was a short drive from the base. He would send me the plane fare immediately, and we would be seeing each other in a matter of days.

I did not tell my parents anything until I received the plane fare, three days later. My mother's reaction was expected. She did not want to hear my reasons or that it was just a respite. She saw it as another reason to verbally pummel me.

"You are not satisfied whoring around the city; you're going national! You are just going to get into more trouble and come back home with your tail between your legs. Why are you always coming up with something new to bring shame to your family?"

As usual, I could not answer her; I could just run. I felt obligated to take my mother's abuse. When she was through, I went upstairs and packed. Within an hour I was packed and in a taxi on the way to Logan Airport. There were no good-byes, not even from my father.

I arrived at New Bern, North Carolina, at about 5:00 P.M. I called Bill, and he was at the airport in about an hour. I had almost forgotten how big he was. His clothing and his hair were disheveled. He gave me a big bear hug, lifting me off the ground, when he saw me.

I was not as glad to see him. Rather than making remarks about him, I made sarcastic remarks about North Carolina. I told him that "the bus stops in Boston are bigger than the New Bern Airport."

As he drove to Wilmington, I made nasty remarks about the wooden shacks that we saw along the way. It looked as though someone had just nailed a few pieces of wood together and moved in. I asked him if he could tell the difference between the outhouses and the shacks that people lived in.

Bill was so glad to see me that he ignored my sarcasm. Between my caustic remarks he was telling me how much he loved me and how happy he was that I decided to come south.

I was nervous, doubting the wisdom of this trip. I knew that I could not run away from my problems. I should have faced them in Boston and lived my life, regardless of what others perceived my image to be. I was very sensitive to what others, especially my mother, thought of me. I knew that I was making a mistake, but I felt helpless to do anything about it.

Bill's mother lived on the outskirts of Wilmington. I was very surprised when I saw her house. It looked like the shacks that I had been laughing at.

We got out of the car and walked to the front door. Bill opened the door and called for his mother, who was not at home. Bill took my suitcases and put them in what was to become my room.

Although the place looked terrible from the outside, the inside was very neat and orderly, but very quaint. The newest piece of furniture must have been fifty years old. I thought that I was in a museum. Bill reassured me that if I married him, we would not live in a place like this. I nervously laughed.

Bill told me to make myself at home while he made coffee. Just as he was bringing out two cups of coffee, we heard someone on the porch. A moment later, the front door opened.

Bill's mother was very tall, almost as tall as Bill. She had short, dark brown hair and was very well built. Bill introduced us. "Jenny, I want you to meet my mother, Nancy Hanlon."

Nancy smiled at me and said in a barely understandable southern drawl, "Nice to meet you, Jenny; you left quite an impression on my son."

I responded in my Boston accent, which must have been just as foreign to her, "I'm happy to meet you, Mrs. Hanlon."

It seemed that Mrs. Hanlon had recently married. Bill made another cup of coffee, and we sat around talking family stuff.

I did not want to talk about my family, so I directed the conversation to Bill's. He told me that he was an only child and a bastard. His father was a soldier who left his mother in a family way and disappeared. His mother had only recently married for the first time, to a sailor, who would be coming home on leave this evening.

Bill pointed out of the window and explained how he had worked the cotton fields as a boy. He was no good in school and dropped out after the ninth grade. He did not want to spend his life in the cotton fields, so he joined the marines.

He explained how much he would like to have a home of his own, with a wife and children to share his life. Bill said that when he got married, he would not live in a place like this. He said that he had seen many cute homes near the base, in one of which he would house *his* family.

Bill took me for a ride around the neighborhood while his mother cooked dinner. Unfortunately, all the housing in the area looked like Nancy Hanlon's house.

Then Bill took me into downtown Wilmington. Although it looked nothing like Boston's Back Bay, the housing at least looked like it could withstand a good rainstorm. There were no skyscrapers; the tallest building was four stories. The town had none of the sights of Boston. The main attractions were the movie theaters.

After Bill gave me the grand tour, we went back to his house. Dinner was ready. We sat down at the table, and Nancy put a plate in front of me. The plate had a thick piece of meat covered with fat. There was also something that looked like Cream of Wheat. The third delicacy appeared to be a distant relative of spinach.

Bill and Nancy were chowing down with enthusiasm. I tentatively sampled the white stuff, since I like Cream of Wheat. Whatever it was, it was not Cream of Wheat. It tasted like gravel. I did not want to make a bad impression, so I closed my eyes and swallowed.

Nancy asked me if I liked the grits. I told her that they were delicious, but the plane ride had given me an upset stomach and I didn't think that I could finish my meal. Nancy said that she was sorry but would put the plate in the icebox so that I could have it later. I sat and drank my coffee while Bill and Nancy finished their meal.

After dinner the three of us sat around and talked. This time I had to tell something about my family. Before long we had a visitor. A very young sailor opened the front door. He was not much older than I was. Nancy jumped up, ran to him, and threw her arms around him.

Bill introduced him as his stepfather, Terry Hanlon. The shock must have showed on my face, as Bill dragged me out the front door and onto the porch. He explained that his mother had married when he was stationed in Boston and that he was just as shocked when he met his stepfather. His mother had never told him that she was twenty-two years older than her husband.

It was a whirlwind romance. They only knew each other several months before they got married. Bill said how unhappy he was because of this, but he was getting used to it. He was sure that I would feel the same way. I did not respect Mrs. Hanlon and tried to stay away from her.

I had fun with Bill. We went swimming, dancing, and picnicking. Time was moving swiftly and I began to relax. I was almost getting accustomed to southern cooking.

Several days before I was scheduled to return to Boston, Bill confronted me at a weak moment, saying, "Look, Jenny, you have been happy here. Why go back? Marry me, and I promise you that it will always be like this."

I believed him and said, "Yes." It was not an enthusiastic "yes." It was a resigned one. Marriage was the lesser of two evils. Again, I was getting married for convenience, not for love; *again!*

If I went back to Boston, I would return to my own personal twilight zone. I would not be accepted at home or have much of a social life outside my home. I was not looking forward to more lonely nights at Gerard's. I wanted to be a part of a family. I wanted the social acceptance that belongs to a married woman.

The pugnacious attitude that Bill had displayed in Boston was not evident in North Carolina. He seemed more relaxed in his neck of the woods.

Whatever romantic illusions that I had of marriage had disappeared. I grew to like Bill, but I never loved him. He was madly in love with me. I hoped that was enough.

CHAPTER TEN

Bill and I were married by a justice of the peace in Wilmington. It was a no-frills affair, just Bill, me, and his mother. It was a Saturday, and the justice of the peace was busy. His waiting room was filled with military men and their brides. They all seemed very happy. I felt out of place.

I called my home. My mother answered the phone. When I told her what I had done, she seemed happy. She said that I needed to be married, and she wished me happiness. I was surprised. I had expected a caustic response. I told her that I would be visiting her the following summer and I would write often. I also gave her instructions on what clothing I wanted shipped south.

The day that Bill and I had become engaged, I had called and told her that I would be spending a little extra time in North Carolina. I did not give her the specifics, for I was fearful of her response. Now I was happy that I was starting married life for the second time with my mother's blessing.

Bill rented a small five-room house near Camp Lejeune. I was happy that it was nothing like the place where his mother lived. It was a pretty little white, two-story frame house on about a half-acre of land. It was surrounded by a three-foot-high chain link fence.

Since Bill lived on the base, he had no furniture or fixtures, so we bought what we could and rented the rest. Neither Bill's mother nor my family gave us any wedding presents. I guess they figured that their blessings were enough.

I was not looking forward to my second wedding night. I had vivid, unpleasant memories of the first. Prior to our marriage, Bill and I had necked a little, but nothing more serious than that. I was easily able to put off any serious advances. He respected me and did not push things.

Most of the rented furniture arrived before the wedding day. I knew that Bill and I had to save up to buy the stuff, because the cost to rent the furniture was almost as much as the house rental.

The day before the wedding, I went shopping and loaded up on all the little things that go into setting up a household, everything from paper plates to bath mats.

I was very meticulous in measuring the windows for the curtains. I always considered curtains the single most important furnishing. A house is not a home without Priscillas.

We did not have a honeymoon. After the ceremony, we went to a cafeteria for lunch. Nancy had lunch with us. I just had a tuna sandwich and coffee. She had one of those disgusting greasy southern meals.

After lunch, Nancy returned to her shack and her boytoy, while Bill and I went home. I felt very uncomfortable about the prospect of another wedding night. The only consolation was that this one could not be any worse than the first one.

When we arrived at our new home, we realized that there was much work to do. We could not jump in the sack like other couples home from the ceremony, because the sack was not put together.

Until this moment, I was living with Nancy and Bill was living at the base, so the rented furniture and other furnishings were deposited in our house in no particular order. The first thing that we did was assemble the king-size bed. After that, we organized the other stuff as best we could. I paid particular attention to hanging my pink Priscillas.

By ten that evening, we were both very tired. Bill took a shower and I took a bath, after which we faced the moment of truth. I had on a long pink nightgown and he had pajama bottoms when we finally climbed into bed.

Unlike Victor, Bill tried to be gentle. He kissed me softly on the lips, while he used his right arm to slowly remove my nightgown. After a few kisses on my naked nipples and several "I love yous," he was ready. After removing his pajamas, he positioned himself on top of me.

I closed my eyes and gritted my teeth, expecting the same searing pain. It was painful, but not as bad as before. Like Victor, Bill finished quickly and rolled off to the side. I relaxed when I knew that Bill's weight was no longer on me.

I rushed into the bathroom and inspected myself. I was expecting blood but was pleasantly surprised. I washed myself thoroughly. That stuff that men deposit inside you looks and feels awful. I treated it like a disease and did not feel clean until I washed it away.

When I left the bathroom, I grabbed my nightgown and put it on. Bill looked at me and asked if anything was wrong. I told him that everything was okay. I got into bed and we both quickly fell asleep.

Our sex life was never pleasant, but it was never horrible either. Bill required sex nearly every night. The act became very routine. The only difference was that the foreplay diminished over time. I was thankful for that, because I just wanted to get it over with as quickly as possible.

I began to think that it was natural for a woman not to enjoy sex. I had never had a real "facts of life" discussion with my mother. Our discussions of sex were usually limited to her telling me, "Don't do it until you're married."

I acquired some knowledge from my friends and some surreptitious reading. It was mostly the mechanical stuff. It didn't say whether or not a woman is supposed to get anything from the act except a clammy vagina.

Bill bought me a dog to keep me company during the day. It was a female black chow puppy with a miserable disposition. I named her Chin because I did not know many Chinese names. Although she was paper-trained, she was not housebroken. She ate everything but dog food. I was glad that the furniture was rented.

Bill and I settled into a routine. Bill would leave early for the base; I would do the housework and shopping. This was the first time that I had to do my own cooking. I was getting good at it. Bill developed a taste for lasagna and meatballs. I refused to cook that southern junk.

Bill told me that he had had his dependent allotment check transferred to me. His mother had been the recipient, but since she had married, Bill felt that she did not need it.

After we had been married for about a month, I was visited by a Marine Corps lieutenant. He had a briefcase under his arm, and he resembled Lieutenant Haywood. He introduced himself as Lieutenant Wojtanek.

I invited him in, told him to have a seat, and offered him a cup of coffee. He declined the coffee. He asked me if I was Mrs. Garrison. I responded in the affirmative. He inquired if I knew that Bill had requested a change in the allotment. I told him that I did. He then asked to see my marriage license. I got up, went to the cabinet where it was kept, and brought it to him.

As he was examining it, I asked him, "What the hell is going on?" He told me that when Bill put in for the change in the allotment, the bursar's office received a letter from Mrs. Hanlon saying that her son and I were not married. This would invalidate any change in the allotment, since it must go to a dependent.

I felt sick. I did not like Nancy Hanlon, but I did not think that she would sink this low. I thought she would be content with an allotment check from her husband.

I told the officer how confused and disappointed I felt. He looked up at me, smiled, and said, "I haven't given you the punch line yet." He proceeded to tell me, "Mrs. Hanlon is *not* Mrs. Hanlon. She is still Miss Garrison. She never married the young sailor; they were just living together. She therefore is not entitled to an allotment from the sailor. She just wanted to keep the one that she was getting from her son."

He told me that it appeared that the allotment was rightfully mine. He would do a little more investigating, but as things appeared now, I would be getting my check promptly next month. I thanked him and saw him to the door

I was red-hot. I called Miss Garrison. As soon as she answered the phone, I yelled at her for trying to cheat me out of my allotment, "You cheap bitch, why did you lie about me and Bill? Just to steal my allotment!"

"Look, Jennifer; Bill's check is mine. I need it to live on. I don't get shit from Terry. No damn Yankee is going to take what is mine."

I ended our brief conversation by calling her a "thievin' whore" and slamming down the receiver.

I had to tell Bill what had happened. The lieutenant had said that Bill had not been told. I was in the kitchen when Bill came home that evening. The phone rang soon after Bill came through the door.

Bill answered it. His mother was on the other end. After he greeted her with a "Hello, Ma," he just held the phone against his ear for several minutes, with an angry expression on his face.

Nancy was telling him about our conversation earlier in the day. She told him how I had insulted her and called her a "whore." She did not tell him the reason for the insult. She conveniently forgot to mention the matter of the allotment check. She also did not give Bill her correct marital status.

When Bill hung up, he walked toward me, yelling, "Why did you insult my mother? I know that you don't like her, but you could at least be civil. Why the hell did you call my mother a whore?"

I tried to explain, but Bill would not listen. I could not outscream him. The last time that I saw him this angry, he was in a fistfight. He called me everything from a "spoiled brat" to a "fuckin' Yankee bitch."

I had enough! I picked up a plate and threw it at him. Unfortunately, I missed. I ran into the bedroom and locked the door before he caught me. He banged on the door for several minutes before he gave up. Our first fight was a dandy!

He slept on the couch and left for the base early the next morning. I was nervous all day. I did not want to spend another night in combat.

When he came home the following evening, he looked like a whipped puppy. Lieutenant Wojtanek had had a long talk with him and told him all about his mother's escapades.

Bill was very apologetic. He put his arms around me and told me that he was sorry. He was embarrassed because his mother had lied to him. He was more embarrassed that his mother supported a swabby.

Bill's mother would not give up. Even though we knew the truth about her, she continued to call requesting the allotment. This woman had no shame!

She regularly called me telling me that I was young and did not need the money. She also tried to talk Bill into changing the allotment. We were both getting sick of her.

I was not only getting sick of Nancy, I was getting sick of North Carolina. I was not making many friends, and I never felt comfortable in the small-town culture. Five months was more than enough time to spend here. I wanted to return to Boston!

When I told Bill that I wanted to go home, I was expecting a big fight. Instead, he told me that he thought that was a great idea.

Bill had about one month remaining on his four-year enlistment. We planned to move to Boston when he was separated. Moving was easy, since everything was rented. We just packed our clothes and our Priscillas and headed north.

Soon after I moved to North Carolina, my mother and father sold their one-family house in Boston and brought a three-family house in Malden. It was a city of about thirty thousand people five miles north of Boston.

It was a large dark brown frame house with a little front yard. My mother, father, and brother lived on the first floor. A nurse rented the second-floor apartment. The third floor was vacant. Bill and I rented it sight unseen. Whatever faults my mother had, she was immaculate. I knew that Bill and I would be getting a clean apartment.

I was glad to be reunited with my family. My father was especially glad to see me. When he first saw me, he hugged me for about five minutes.

My mother and I sat at the kitchen table and talked for about two hours. We had rarely spoken on the phone because of the toll charge between Boston and North Carolina. She caught me up on all the gossip of her new neighborhood. She had spent her whole life in Boston's Italian north end and was slowly getting used to Malden.

My little brother, Sal, was not so little. He had grown quickly and was now taller than I was. He had turned sixteen while I was away, but he was still the spoiled little brat that I had left behind. He wanted to know if I had brought him any gifts from the South. I would have loved to give him a bucket of grits.

It was a pretty little four-room apartment. Bill and I furnished it in a haphazard manner. My parents and relatives contributed some pieces,

105

Bill and I purchased some from the Salvation Army, and we bought other things on time. I enjoyed decorating, and when I was through, we had a cozy little home.

I settled into a comfortable routine with Bill. He got a job at a machine shop in Somerville. I found a job at an electronics company in Cambridge. We were both working within a fifteen-minute commute of our home. I was fortunate that my job was on the bus line, since Bill took the car.

I felt that my mother was accepting me more now than before I went to North Carolina. I had a husband, an apartment, and a job. I was now a respectable woman. The monthly rent check that we were paying to my mother also did nothing to hurt my status.

My married status gave me a place in the social structure. I was now socializing with other couples. When my mother had visitors, she frequently invited me over to meet them. I was also invited to more functions now than when I had been divorced.

Things went along smoothly for about a year. My mother treated me well. Bill's mother wrote to him about once a month. Bill and I were both happy with our jobs.

Our personal life settled into a dull routine. We would get up, go to work, come home, and have dinner and watch television. Our sex life was a one-sided affair. I would climb in bed and assume the position. Bill would climb on; moments later he would climb off. He would then fall asleep, while I would wash away his pleasure.

Although sex was not painful, it was not pleasurable. It was a dull chore, but still a chore. I tried to talk to Bill about it, but as soon as I approached the topic, he changed the subject. I got the impression that if I told him that I did not enjoy sex with him, I would be challenging his masculinity.

He was a big, burly man. Although he was not violent, I did not risk his reaction if I made an all-out assault on his manhood. I, therefore, did not tell him that he was "a lousy lay."

My own innocence was also an inhibiting factor. I did not know what good sex was. I only knew that I was not getting any pleasure from it.

I had just celebrated my first anniversary working at Whitestone Electronics by splitting a pizza with some of the girls from work. I felt sick on the bus ride home. I thought it might have been the pizza. I only had one slice, but I could not think of anything else that could cause the nausea.

When I woke up the following morning, the nausea was accompanied by dizziness. I felt a little better when I got up, took my bath, and prepared for work. This was a Thursday morning. The condition persisted on Friday, but I did not change my routine.

I told Bill, but he just told me to "take some aspirin and you'll be okay." My mother was a little more sympathetic. She recommended that I go to her doctor for a checkup, since it had been about two years since I had a medical examination. I told her that I would make an appointment for the following week.

On that Saturday, I went shopping by myself in Malden Center. After about fifteen minutes of window-shopping, the symptoms came back. The nausea returned first. I felt as though I wanted to throw up. This was followed quickly by the dizziness. I felt light-headed, then very weak. A minute later, I was unconscious.

I awoke in the Massachusetts General Hospital emergency room. The attending physician told me to relax and lie still and that my mother has been notified of my hospitalization. My mother was very excitable. I expected her to be panic-stricken.

About ten minutes after I had regained consciousness, my mother and Aunt Theresa came charging into the emergency room. Even though Aunt Theresa had ten children to take care of, she could be counted on to be there in a family crisis.

My mother asked me what happened. I told her that I had just awoken and was still shaking out the cobwebs. I told her and my aunt that I was just window-shopping when I felt faint and collapsed.

A nurse walked in and told me that Dr. Charles would be in to see me in a moment. Dr. Charles was a friendly, cherubic young man. He asked me how I was feeling; I told him that I felt better. He then gave me the results of the tests that they had taken while I was unconscious. He told me that everything seemed fine, but all new mothers had to be careful. I almost fainted again, this time from shock. My mother and Aunt Theresa just stared at me with their mouths open.

"Me, a mother?" I laughed. "You must be wrong, Doctor. A child!"

My Aunt Theresa was already a grandmother several times over, so this was a routine matter for her. This was to be my mother's first grandchild. She seemed pleased at the thought of becoming a grandmother. She grabbed and hugged me.

I did not know that the symptoms could have meant that I was pregnant. I had no sex education, which meant no birth control. Bill and I had never talked about having a family. It was a subject that neither of us wanted to deal with, so we just ignored it.

My mother and other family members inquired about my plans for a family. I did not feel ready to deal with the question, so I just changed the subject.

107

The doctor discharged me and advised me to see my family doctor for prenatal care. My mother drove me home. Aunt Theresa sat in the front seat with my mother, while I sat alone in the backseat.

As I sat in the backseat on the way home, I was still in a state of shock. All kinds of crazy things started to run through my mind. I was afraid that I would put the diaper on the wrong end.

I knew nothing about caring for a baby. I did not know what babies ate. I was frightened that I would do all the wrong things. When I relayed my fears to my mother and Aunt Theresa, they just turned around and laughed at me and told me that everything would come naturally. I did not know what they meant.

I also had fears that I did not mention. I feared for my appearance. I was petite, a perfect size 3. I was afraid of how I would look in a few months. I was only two months pregnant. The physical distortion would start shortly. I felt a little guilty that I was more concerned about my dress size than my baby.

I thought that it was unusual that I was not thrilled at the news. The baby was obviously not planned. I was thinking how the baby would impact my appearance and my life-style. My immaturity was showing.

I was concerned how Bill would take the news. He was out at some ball game on Saturday and did not get back that night until after I came home from the hospital.

Bill came home in a good mood, partly because his team won, partly due to the beer that he had consumed celebrating the victory. As soon as he came through the door, I sat him down on the couch and sat next to him. I took his hand and slowly explained to him what had happened to me that day.

He was thrilled when I told him that I was pregnant. He jumped from the couch, pulling me with him. He grabbed me and hugged me. This was the happiest that I had seen him. He noticed that he was more excited than I was and asked me if anything was wrong.

"Oh, nothing. I'm not sure I can handle this. I just don't think that I'm ready for this."

"Well, it's too late now, dear, and if you must know, I'm crazy about the idea. Just think, Jenny, it might be a pretty little girl, just like you."

"Well, that's a hell of a thing to wish on an unborn child."

I was as sick that night as I had ever been before. But at least I knew what was causing the discomfort.

My mother came up to see me the first thing in the morning. I was in the bathroom splashing water on my face when she arrived.

"Well, now you will know the pains of being a mother. Dress up, and I'll make you a nice breakfast. You have to eat for two now, you know."

I was not a big eater before I was pregnant. Now I did not feel like eating anything, never mind eating for two!

I was very sick. I could not get dressed without vomiting. I had to quit my job, as I could barely walk without feeling sick. I spent most of the week following my hospitalization in bed. I was very weak and not getting any better.

My mother knew that this was not an ordinary pregnancy. She took me to Dr. Piscatelli, the family obstetrician. He had delivered all of my cousins' children, and my mother had confidence in him.

After his examination, he ushered my mother and me into his office and explained that there was a complication that was causing my problem. He believed that it was toxemia, which was caused by poisons absorbed by my system. A few days later, tests confirmed his diagnosis.

I was put on a very rigid diet and given pills. Dr. Piscatelli explained that I could go into convulsions and lose the child if I did not follow his instructions.

It was a painful pregnancy; I was sick for the duration. I spent most days downstairs with my mother. She did not think that I should be left alone.

I would get many visitors. Many of them were my mother's relatives. Her sisters were frequent visitors. They usually stopped by to give me advice, since they were experts on pregnancy. Each of my mother's nine sisters had at least five children. Most were grandmothers several times over. Some of them were nice, but a few were really obnoxious. My Aunt Anita was probably the worst. She was always bragging about her family. One of her daughters had had a baby boy six months ago. Aunt Anita boasted about how much she had bought for the baby, how cute the baby was, how smart he was. She spent the afternoon she visited me bragging about her grandson. I could understand grandmotherly pride, but this was ridiculous. When she pulled out pictures of the little darling, I went upstairs. Fortunately Aunt Anita was not a regular guest.

My mother was not the greatest companion either. She was always pointing out things that I was doing wrong, and she relished doing it. If I lit up a cigarette, she yelled that it was no good for the baby. If I was sitting with my legs crossed she yelled that the baby could not breathe.

I was hoping that the pain would subside as I got closer to term, but it did not. The pills were not much help. I went to see Dr. Piscatelli regularly, but he was not much help. He said that much of what I felt was the baby kicking. Every day I had a new pain; I could not distinguish the baby pains from the regular pains.

One day, as I entered my ninth month, I felt a little better because the baby stopped kicking. After nine months of dancing around, I figured it was due for a rest.

I had a little dinner party that evening. I had invited six of my female cousins. My mother and I cooked a ten-pound roast beef, along with a chocolate layer cake. My cousins raved about my cooking, saying my new family would be well fed.

After dinner we went into the living room for some more girl talk. We sat around and talked for about fifteen minutes, after which I went into the kitchen to bring out the coffee and cake.

I was pouring the coffee when I felt a convulsion. I became faint, and within moments I was unconscious. I woke up in the emergency room of Mass General.

Dr. Piscatelli was there when I awoke. He said that he was going to induce labor because I had too much fluid. I was very frightened as I was wheeled into the delivery room. I was so scared that they gave me a general anesthetic.

When I woke up, there was a nurse beside me telling me that I had a beautiful baby girl. The nurse then brought me a little bundle wrapped in a pink blanket. I peeled back that blanket and saw that the nurse was right.

My daughter had a mop of jet black hair. I took inventory; she had ten toes, ten fingers, two eyes, two ears. Everything seemed to be there. I held her close. I fell in love with her immediately. She was all mine; she was like my toy. I promised her that I would treat her like a little princess.

I decided to call my daughter Robin. Bill and I had kicked around a number of names but never decided on a boy's or girl's name. That name came to me the first time that I held her. No one in the family had that name; it came to me spontaneously.

That night my family came to see me. In addition to Bill and my mother, father, and brother, many of my aunts and cousins stopped by. My father seemed the most excited. He was like a big kid, talking to the baby for the whole hour that he visited. He told me that he was "so happy to have another girl in the family."

When Robin and I came out of the hospital, my mother decided that it would be best if we moved downstairs with her. Since she was an experienced mother, she could watch better over Robin, and I could learn the art of motherhood.

I felt that I could take care of my daughter by myself, but Bill agreed with my mother. The baby's crib, diapers, formula, and other stuff were all put in my mother's first-floor apartment. I frequently slept on the couch to be near the baby. My mother acted like she was the baby's mother and I was the maid. My mother would feed the baby, change her, and hold her in her arms while she walked her around the apartment, singing Italian songs. My mother did let me clean the apartment and do the dishes. It was as though I traded my baby for a cleaning job.

About two weeks after Robin came home, we faced our first crisis. Robin was a noisy baby and seemed to cry twenty-three hours a day. On this day she started to cry like she had never cried before. It was a painful, wheezing cry. After a few minutes the crying stopped, and I ran over to the crib.

Robin was lying there, blue and unconscious. I picked her up and started to shake her. My mother ran to me, saw the limp baby, and screamed, *"She's dead!"*

Fortunately, my father was home. He ran into the living room and tried to take the baby away from me. I was in a panic and crying uncontrollably. I held Robin as tight as I could.

My father finally managed to wrench the baby away from me. He put her on the couch and applied artificial respiration. After about a minute she regained consciousness. Her natural color returned, and she started to cry.

My mother was so upset that after she pronounced the baby dead she had run screaming out to the street for assistance. By the time she had induced some of the neighbors to help, Robin was back in her crib resting comfortably.

My father remained calm, called the doctor, dressed Robin, and told us that he was taking her to the hospital. I went to the hospital with my father and Robin. My mother was still in a semipanic and was reliving the scenario with the neighbors.

When we got to the hospital, we explained what had happened to the admitting physician. He proceeded to do the routine tests. Dr. Piscatelli came just as he was finishing. The preliminary tests did not detect the problem, but Dr. Piscatelli recommended that Robin be admitted for observation and further tests.

Robin spent a day at the hospital. The doctors could not find anything wrong. They sent her home and told me to watch her very closely and bring her back if there were any other problems. My father drove us home. As I held her bundled up in the front seat, I wondered if I could have done anything wrong to induce her condition.

Soon after we got home my mother took charge . . . again. She did not want me to be near the baby. If I picked up Robin, my mother began to scream at me. I backed off, because I thought that I may have caused Robin's problem. My mother did all that she could do to exacerbate my guilt. It was a combination of this guilt, my insecurity, and my respect for my mother that prevented me from confronting her. She was constantly telling me that I was a bad mother and that "you know nothing about a baby."

Before Robin's hospitalization, I had performed some motherly duties. I was "allowed" to hold and nurture her, to feed and change her. Now my mother considered the baby to be totally hers. I was forced to spend more time in my third-floor apartment and less time with Robin.

Bill was working as much overtime as he could to support us. He was not aware that his mother-in-law had usurped my role. He was working six days a week and was not home much. On Sundays he usually went bowling or to a ball game. He was happy that the baby was well. When I tried to explain what my mother was doing, he was glad. His reasoning was that since my mother was taking care of Robin full-time, I could return to work. He did not understand my dilemma. I wanted to strangle him!

I felt very frustrated in having my role of mother diminished. I still had the role of housewife, and I immersed myself in it. I was a cleaning fanatic. I kept my apartment spotless, in addition to helping out with my mother's apartment. I made sure Bill always had a hot meal when he came home, and because of the baby, I had to do at least two loads of wash a day.

One day, when Robin was about four months old, I was in the basement doing laundry. Bill was a machinist and his clothes were always filthy; he was also leaving all sorts of things in the pockets. I always went through his pockets thoroughly, because the washing machine did not react favorably to small tools.

In going through a pair of his pants I found a crinkled piece of paper. I opened it up and read it:

Dear Bill,
   I enjoyed our night out together and look forward to seeing you again. Call me when you can.

Love,
Lydia

CHAPTER ELEVEN

I was shaken. I did not believe what I had read. Bill did not spend his overtime working at the machine shop. He spent it working on "Lydia."

In the first few minutes after I read the note, several different emotions ran through me. The first was anger. I wanted to kill Bill. I worked very hard at being a good wife. I kept his home spotless. I made sure that he was well fed. I took care of our child as best as I could. I was doing the best that I could. I felt betrayed and I was mad.

I experienced other feelings. For the first time, I felt empathy for Vito. I could understand Vito's feeling of betrayal when he found out that I was married to Victor.

I wondered if I could have done anything to drive Bill away. He gave no indication of being unhappy. He seemed very content. I knew that we talked less as time passed, but I thought that was a part of marriage.

I finally considered the core issue: love! I had married Bill for many of the same reasons that I had married Victor. I married him for social acceptance. Marriage was a vehicle with which I could run away from my problems. I got married because I was insecure. My life had no direction. Marriage gave me direction and a role, the role of wife.

Vito was the only man that I truly loved. Victor and Bill were surrogates for Vito. Whatever attraction that I had to Bill was that he resembled Vito. They were both tall, dark marines. I was not mature enough to know that love could not be easily transferred.

I did not love Bill, and it was apparent that he did not love me either. I wondered if he loved his new girlfriend or if she was just another "piece of ass."

I was sure of two things: I could not tell my parents what I had found out and, second, I would give Bill hell when he came home.

I went crazy when Bill came home that night. As soon as he walked into our apartment, I threw the crinkled-up note at him. As he picked it up and read it, I gave him all the expletives that had building up in me all day.

"Who is this fuckin' bitch that you are seeing? Is she worth breaking up your family over? Is she better-looking than me? Is she a better lay? Get all your shit and get out, or I'll move out."

Bill just stood there and said nothing while I ranted on. When I cooled off, he admitted to the affair. He said he was sorry and would have no further contact with Lydia. He begged me not to leave him. I promised him nothing. If it hadn't been for Robin, I would have left him.

Our life together was forever changed. Bill and I never slept together again. I slept on the couch in my mother's apartment. Whenever I saw Bill, he gave me a sheepish expression. I could not forgive him.

Although we lived in the same house, our lives became separate. I spent more time downstairs with Robin. I cleaned our apartment, but I no longer cooked for Bill. He now ate most of his meals out.

I never told my parents what the problem was. It was obvious that Bill and I were leading separate lives. I did not try to hide my coldness toward him.

My confrontation with Bill gave me courage to confront my mother over the care of Robin. I was still insecure and had doubts over my ability to take care of my child. My mother continued to denigrate me. She continually reminded me that I was unfit to be a mother and that Robin would be "back in the hospital or dead" if I took care of her. Bill's affair made me feel that I was a failure as a wife. I wanted to be a success as a mother. About a month after I found the note, I boldly announced to my mother, "I will care for the baby all by myself."

I expected my mother to explode, and she did. She said all the predictable things. "What the hell do you know about babies? If it were not for me, the baby would be dead. You do not even know what to feed the baby. There's no way in hell that you can be a mother."

When my mother cooled down, I calmly picked up Robin and carried her upstairs. My mother did not try to stop me. I thought she really wanted to give up the responsibility. After all, she was forty-five years old and a six-month-old baby might have been too much for her.

I enjoyed having my baby back. As I was carrying her upstairs, I was talking to her in baby talk. Whenever I asked her something, she would gurgle back to me. When I asked her if she was hungry, she responded with the loudest gurgle of all.

I had jars of baby food in the apartment. I put her on the couch while I heated up a jar of liver. When it was ready, I sat down with Robin. I was not used to feeding her, and it took me about ten minutes to get her positioned.

When Robin was properly positioned, I put on her bib and started to feed her. I dipped the spoon into the liver and gently put it into Robin's mouth. She quickly spit it out. I tried again, but her reaction was the same.

I kept trying. Eventually the baby started to accept the food. Rather than immediately spitting out the liver, she wrinkled up her face, then swallowed. It was slow going, but Robin finished off the small jar of baby food. She made strange faces throughout the meal. I thought this was natural.

Soon after she finished eating, Robin started to vomit and gasp for air. I felt sick and panicked! While I was trying to slap Robin on the back and wipe her off at the same time, I got sick to my stomach and started to vomit.

I did not know what to do. I stood up with Robin in my arms, still choking, and ran downstairs. My mother heard the noise and was waiting at the base of the stairs. She grabbed Robin, shouting, "*Dominic, the baby is dying again!*"

I started crying as I was running down the steps. When my mother took the baby, I ran into her bathroom and finished vomiting. My stomach settled after several minutes, and I sheepishly walked into the living room.

My parents had stabilized the situation. My father was holding Robin, while my mother was cleaning her.

"I just fed her; I don't know what happened."

"You stupid ass! This baby will surely die if you take care of her."

I became afraid of Robin. I was afraid that I would hurt her. I had thought anyone could feed a baby.

Robin remained in my mother's apartment. She would cry whenever I came near her. I became very frustrated. I felt like a double failure, as a wife and mother.

The following day, I walked into the room that my mother had set up as a nursery to see Robin. As soon as I approached the crib she started to cry. The baby made such a racket that my mother came running in.

"What the hell did you do to the baby?"

"*Nothing!* I just gave birth to her." I went storming out of the room.

My relationship with Bill was strained. We did not live like husband and wife. We only talked to each other when other people were present. We wanted to keep up appearances.

I just could not forgive him. I spent as much time as possible in my mother's apartment. I hated to go upstairs. Whatever disagreements that I had with my mother, I felt Bill's disloyalty was more personal; it hurt more.

I was used to my mother's admonitions; they were expected. I wanted a different type of relationship with my husband. I wanted respect and loyalty from my spouse.

My mother was an overbearing influence not only with me, but also with Bill. She never lost the opportunity to tell him that he rented space in her house. "A man should be able to buy a home for his family," she said.

Bill was generally a big, easygoing guy. My mother continued to degrade him. She told him that he did not make enough money to support his family. If she saw him with a beer, she called him a drunk. He had every reason to hate his mother-in-law.

By taking care of Robin, my mother was commenting on my motherhood abilities. She also refused to eat my cooking, calling it "junk" on many occasions. She would continually degrade my domestic skills.

Whenever she was in my apartment, she found something to criticize. She thought my furniture was junky; she thought I should have rugs; she hated my Priscillas. She could never say that the apartment was dirty.

I made a common mistake: I tried to cure the symptom of the problem and not the cause. I thought that if I moved into my own house, I could solve my problems with Bill and my mother.

I talked it over with Bill, and he was receptive to the idea. Although our relationship was not good, I thought that it would improve if we had our own place.

The thought of being away from my overbearing mother was another factor that made home ownership desirable. I could tell that Bill was getting very angry with my mother. At first he tried to laugh off her insults. But he had recently started to respond to her insults with insults of his own.

Neither Bill nor I had ever owned property, so we enlisted my father's help to find a place. We discussed our finances with him, and he figured how much house we could afford. For about a month the three of us went house hunting evenings and weekends.

We found a little single-family house on Salem Street in Malden that Bill and I both liked and could afford. It was a five-room, two-story house with a small attic. It was big enough for the three of us.

Bill got a GI loan. That, together with our small savings, made us home owners. About three months after we first saw the house, we were moving in.

Robin stayed with my mother while Bill and I were moving our stuff and fixing up our new home. It took a month before we had things the way that we wanted them.

Bill and I were able to buy some new furniture, and my parents gave us a living room set as a housewarming present. The house was in pretty good shape. A few of the rooms needed painting. Bill and I did that ourselves.

116

When Bill and I were settled in our new home, I went to my mother's place to pick up Robin. When I arrived, my mother had a little surprise for me. She told me that she had hired a woman to live with us and take care of Robin.

"How can you do that without telling me? Robin is still my child. Look; Bill and I don't want any strangers living with us," I told her.

"Jenny, you're being selfish. You will probably kill Robin if you are left alone with her. This is my gift to Robin. You should be grateful!"

I relented. I still felt guilty about my inability to properly deal with Robin in a crisis.

Agnes Brill moved in two days later. She was a widow with three grown children. She was in her late fifties and very skinny, with a huge mole on her left cheek.

It was hate at first sight. Agnes was very aggressive and treated me like her servant, not like her boss. In addition to taking care of Robin, she also did the cooking and the cleaning. That would have been swell, except that she considered herself the housekeeper in charge, and me a third-class maid.

Agnes was my mother's surrogate in taking care of Robin. If I picked up my daughter in the presence of Agnes, I would be immediately reported to my mother. She then would call me and tell me to leave Robin's care to Agnes.

In addition to her overbearing personality, Agnes was a wino. She always had at least one bottle of muscatel in her room. I could frequently smell it on her breath, although it never seemed to interfere with her work. She approached her responsibilities with a cold-blooded efficiency.

I was pissed off and finally told Agnes, "YOU'RE FIRED! Get the hell out of my house."

"Your mother hired me, your mother pays me, and only your mother can fire me."

I was boiling mad. I called my mother, but she was not home. I talked to my father and told him what had happened. He was very cool about it. He said that he would explain the situation to my mother.

That evening my mother came over to my house. I was out shopping. Bill was home. He and my mother had a talk about the situation. My mother convinced Bill that it would be best if Agnes stayed.

When I got home and began to explain the situation to my mother, I found myself outvoted. I told her that I wanted to fire Agnes. I gave her the reasons, telling of Agnes's affection for alcohol.

My mother was not moved. She insisted that Agnes stay, and Bill agreed with her. She reiterated my shortcomings as a mother, how Robin would not be safe alone with me. Agnes stayed.

After a while, I could not stand being in the same house with Agnes.

Dina James was now Dina Flaherty. She lived in Revere with her husband and baby son. Revere borders Malden, so she was only a ten-minute drive away. I had run across her several months ago, and we were calling each other frequently.

Dina and I had a lot of catching up to do. She told me how she had split up with Joe. She met Johnny Flaherty soon after. After a whirlwind courtship, they had married and had a son.

I told Dina my horror stories. My marriages to Victor and Bill, my adventure in New York, my experience with Agnes. I also told Dina about my current difficulties with my mother. She knew my mother and was not surprised with the latter.

Dina told me about her personal life. She also was not happily married. Her husband was an alcoholic. He spent most of his free time at the South Boston barrooms. He came home only to sleep. He gambled or drank away most of his pay. Dina frequently needed help from her family to pay the bills. She was very close to filing for divorce.

Both Dina and I had unhappy family lives. We had so much in common, we started to spend more time together. We went out to lunch and to matinees. She had a baby-sitter. I had Agnes.

One night, Dina asked me if I would like to go out for a drink. I told her that I rarely drank and that I couldn't go because I was married and it wouldn't look right.

Dina laughed. "Oh, come on, Jenny. Don't be a prude. You don't have to do anything, but it would be nice to dress up and get out of the house."

Bill was still "working late," and I was getting bored watching television. I finally agreed.

Dina had not changed. She still liked to party. We agreed to go the Gold Star Lounge, a little club near Malden Center.

It was so dark inside, I needed to light a match to see, until my eyes got acclimated to the dim lighting. Dina and I found a table near the bar. After a few minutes, my eyes adjusted and I looked around the place. I did not like what I saw.

Bill was sitting at the end of the bar, next to a brunette with hair halfway down her back. He had one hand on her back and one hand on her front. I could not see what the latter hand was doing, but it was very active.

I sat and stared at them, while I turned pale. Dina immediately saw that something was wrong. When she asked, I just pointed to Bill and his friend.

"I'd introduce you to my husband, but he is occupied at the time."

Dina grabbed my arm and pulled me out the door. "Well, Jenny, they never change. Hey, you didn't even want to go out for a drink because you felt guilty. How do you feel now? Do you still feel guilty?"

"Hell, no!"

We got a cab near the Gold Star Lounge, then went to a dance hall near Scollay Square in downtown Boston. I just wanted to get far away from Bill.

The hall was loaded with young men. I was a hit as soon as I walked through the door. Guys were coming over to me and asking for a dance even before I had a chance to sit down. I felt better.

I thought Bill's infidelities may have been as a result of my inadequacies as a wife. My self-confidence was shaken. Hearing the wolf whistles and compliments built up my confidence as a woman.

"Hey, gorgeous, want to dance?"

"Baby, you're too pretty for a place like this; let's go to a quieter place."

"Honey, I want to take you home in my seabag."

If I were to hear the same comments today, I would consider them degrading, not complimentary. Attitudes can change a lot in thirty years.

I danced with everyone. The men would not let me sit down. As soon as I finished one dance, another guy would cut in.

The music was early rock and roll, a lot of Elvis and Buddy Holly. Most of the dancing was fast. After two hours, I was very tired. I pushed aside several prospective dance partners and sat down.

I had two drinks, whiskey sours. I rarely drank, but I needed some alcohol tonight. I went dancing to punish Bill. I drank to punish Bill. I wound up punishing myself.

I could not hold my liquor. One drink was all that was required to get me drunk. After the second drink, I started seeing double. Dina and I sat and rested for about a half hour while I recuperated from the effects of my two drinks.

As we were sitting there, two marines in their dress blues walked in. They went to the bar and got their drinks. One of them stared straight ahead at the whiskey bottles in back of the bar. The other one surveyed the room. When he saw me, he stopped looking around. He fixed his stare on me.

"He likes you, Jenny," Dina whispered.

"Big deal." I turned my back to him.

He came over to the table and pulled up a chair on the other side of the table. Physically, he resembled Vito. He was tall, although he was several inches shorter than Vito. He was also handsome, with coal black hair.

119

He was drinking before he came into the hall. He reeked from alcohol.

"Well, hello, doll. Seeing you're the best-looking broad in the place, I just had to meet you."

I was still under the influence of the two whiskey sours. "Thanks, buddy. I know that I'm the best-looking girl in the place, but I'm also a married girl. It's too bad that you are not the best-looking man in the place. Now, *get lost!*"

"Look, whore, don't give me any shit!"

I reached across the table and slapped his face. He stood up and started to walk around the table. By this time we had attracted a crowd. The bartender told the marine to quiet down or leave the club.

He did not say anything; he just staggered back to the bar. When he reached it, he ordered another beer. When his drink was served, he turned around and continued to stare at me.

I tried to ignore his gaze but couldn't. I felt as though his eyes were staring right through me. I told Dina that I thought we should leave. She agreed.

Dina and I collected our things and prepared to leave. As we did, the marine staggered over to me and smiled. The closer that he got, the stronger the liquor smell became.

"Hi, we were never introduced. My name is Sergeant Rollins, Jesse Rollins. Who the hell are you? Don't you know that I can get any woman that I want? Wassa matter, honey? Do I upset you?"

"Don't let it bother you. I'm not interested in you or your troubles."

He got angry, apparently not used to being rejected by women. He staggered back to the end of the bar mumbling, "Fuckin' broad."

Dina and I had our things together and walked toward the door. As we walked past Sergeant Rollins, he took off his cap and bowed very low. We walked past him and out the door.

We talked about him as we left the hall. I told Dina that I'd never met such an obnoxious, conceited man. He thought that he was God's gift to women.

"Are you going to say anything to Bill about this?" Dina asked me.

"Of course not. Two can play this game. I'm just going to go out every night and have a ball, and if he should find out, well, then he'll know how it feels to be hurt."

Bill was home when I arrived, and he could tell that I had been drinking. He was very upset. He grabbed me by both shoulders. "Where have you been? It's after midnight."

I struggled from his grasp and walked toward Robin's room. I was still very angry at Bill. The picture of him in the Gold Star Lounge fondling another woman was burned into my memory. I knew that I could never forgive him.

Our marriage had never fully recovered from the first incident. We hadn't slept together since. We became more like roommates than husband and wife.

Robin was sound asleep. I closed the door to her room. Bill had left the living room and gone to bed. I went to sleep on the couch.

During the day, I assisted Agnes with the housework and with Robin's care. At night, I would dress up and go over to Dina's house. From there, we would go out dancing and/or drinking. We found a place in Boston that we both liked. It was a small club, the Cafe 700.

Unlike the larger dance halls, where Dina and I would be harassed, this club had a different atmosphere. We were usually left alone.

I became a regular drinker. Prior to my troubles with Bill, I rarely drank. Whenever Dina and I went out, I would have one or two adult beverages.

We would occasionally be asked to dance, but mostly Dina and I would sit and nurse our drinks. We would discuss our failing marriages and frequently cry on each other's shoulders.

One Thursday evening, we were sitting at our usual table when Dina looked up and saw a familiar face. She stared at him for a moment, then turned to me. "Hey, Jenny, an old friend of yours just walked in," she teased.

I turned around and saw Jesse Rollins in uniform, standing at the bar. He spotted me immediately and walked to our table with a big smile on his face. As he approached us, I noticed that he smelled of after-shave lotion, not alcohol. It was early in the evening, and he probably did not have time to get drunk.

"Well, now, we're in a different place, but you're still the best-looking broad. Why don't we try all over again, huh? I'm Jesse, and I'm very sober. How is that?"

He seemed a different person, friendly and charming. He also still had the dark good looks so reminiscent of Vito. I returned his smile.

"Hi, I'm Jenny. Would you like to sit down?"

He pulled up a chair and sat down. He was a much different person this time around, polite and relaxed. He told us that his job in the marines was as staff driver. He drove the senior officers from the local naval bases around the area.

He was a lot easier to get along with when he was sober. He was from Graysville, a small town in Maine, and had joined the marines when he was seventeen. He was in the marines for eight years, spending most of his time "driving the brass around."

121

I told him about my marriage to Victor. I talked about Bill and Robin and my frustrations being a wife and mother. I probably told Jesse more than I should tell a stranger, but I felt very relaxed with him.

He was very supportive of me. He told me of other unhappy Marine Corps marriages. He told me, "The Corps probably breaks up more marriages than anything else."

We spent the evening telling each other our life stories, and the evening flew by. It got late in a hurry, and at midnight I told him that I had to be going.

Dina had left about two hours earlier. Jesse and I had an intense two-way conversation. Dina had quietly excused herself and left.

When I told him that I had to be going, his face dropped. "Look, Jennifer, I know that you're married. All I know is that I have to see you again, even if we just have a quick drink. How about it?"

I agreed to meet Jesse at the same place at seven the following evening. We shook hands and I went outside and hailed a cab.

I could not get Jesse out of my mind. It was partly due to his resemblance to Vito. Although he was a little shorter, he had a strong physical resemblance to Vito. Jesse had the piercing blue eyes and coal black hair that I found so attractive.

Jesse also had a relaxed and friendly personality that could hypnotize a girl. I had forgiven him for the previous incident. I just figured that it was a temporary aberration. I thought that I saw the real Jesse this evening. I did not understand alcoholism.

The following evening was just as pleasant as the last. This time Jesse talked more about his roots, rather than about the marines. He had grown up with an adopted sister. After telling me about his sister, he told me that his mother was an alcoholic and started to laugh. "That's a hell of a sickness, huh?"

He then got to the good stuff. Jesse said that when he was seventeen, he had gotten Linda Kramer pregnant. She came from one of the richest families in town. His family was dirt poor, so there was not much chance for the couple.

Linda's parents had sent her out of town to have the baby. It was later put up for adoption. Jesse joined the marines to "get the hell out of there." He sounded very mixed up when talking about his family and his life in Maine. He was not as relaxed as when he was talking about the marines.

I could empathize with him. My family life was also mixed up. The more we talked, the closer we became. My initial physical attraction to him evolved into an emotional bond.

The more that he talked about his alcoholic mother and the

problems of growing up poor, the more attached to him I became. He showed a vulnerable and emotional side that I had not seen in too many men. I enjoyed his company. I wanted to spend more time with him.

I gave him more of the details of the relationship between me and Bill, including our nonexistent love life.

"Why don't you leave him, Jenny? Is it because of your baby?" Jesse asked me.

"It is more because of my parents. I could not disappoint them. I'm only twenty-one years old. If I were twice divorced, my parents, especially my mother, would die."

"Well, what if you fall in love, really in love, what about then?"

I laughed. "But I'm not going to."

I was lying. I knew that when I looked into his eyes I was starting to feel something. I thought that it was because his looks and easy manner reminded me of Vito. I knew that I was attracted to Jesse, but I was sure that nothing would come of it; after all, I was a married woman.

Jesse and I started to "go steady." We saw each other almost every night. We would always go to a club, dance, and have a few drinks. Unlike the evening when I first met him, his drinking was controlled. He would have one or two beers and would never appear drunk.

Jesse was always friendly, charming, and respectful. I fell deeper in love the more that we saw each other. I had not felt this way about anyone except Vito. I knew that I loved Jesse for himself. I no longer thought of him as a Vito clone.

I knew that I had a problem. I was married to Bill, even though at this point in our marriage we were going our separate ways, though we were still living together.

Jesse and I were never intimate. Although he suggested that we "spend some time alone, truly alone," we always dated where there was a crowd. My religious influence was very strong. I could not have sex with someone to whom I was not married. Adultery was totally out of the question.

I did not know how I would break the news to my family and to Bill, but I knew that I must. I knew that my feelings for Jesse were real and I must deal with them. I could not face my mother. I decided to talk to Bill first.

I stayed home and waited for Bill the following evening. We sat down and talked. I told him that we both knew that our marriage was in trouble. I told Bill that I did not love him and I was sure that the feeling was mutual. I told him that I had met someone else and I wanted a divorce.

He did not want to face reality. "I don't believe that you feel this way, Jenny. Why didn't you discuss this with me earlier? Why did you have to go looking for some other guy? There has got to be some way that we can straighten things out."

"I'm sorry, Bill, but we have to face facts. We haven't had a marriage for some time. It began falling apart when you started your skirt chasing. Did you expect me to just sit home like some nice little housewife? I started going out to get even with you. I did not expect to fall in love, but I did."

"Look, Jenny, you can't do this. I'm not going to give you a divorce. I'm going to talk to your parents. Maybe they can talk some sense into you."

"Bill, please don't tell my parents, not yet. It will just confuse things if you get them involved. Let's settle things between us now. Let's try to reach some kind of agreement before we tell my parents."

"I'm sorry. Maybe they can talk some sense into their daughter."

The following evening, Bill visited my parents. While the three of them sat in my parent's living room, Bill told them that their daughter was fooling around with another guy and wanted a divorce.

My mother, although always willing to find fault with her daughter, had trouble believing Bill. My father also could not believe it.

My mother called me on the phone and told me to come over to her house "right now." I knew what she wanted, so I left immediately. I wanted to get this over with.

"Jenny, your husband told us things that we do not believe. Is it true that you are breaking up another marriage? *I just don't believe it!*"

"Look, Ma, there's more to it than that. I did not break up the marriage; Bill did when he started to run around with other women. I just started to go out nights when I found out what Bill was doing."

"I don't care what *he* did; I care what *you* did. You're just acting like a common whore. If this marriage falls apart, it's your fault. I want you to stop seeing this other man. I want you to be a wife and a mother."

"Will you tell Bill to stop seeing *his whores?*"

"I'm not worried about his whores, I'm worried about *my whore.*"

I could not argue with my mother. She had an old-fashioned view of things. The man is right and the woman is wrong. If Bill was screwing all the women in Boston, and I just had a drink with another man, I would be the villain. That is why I did not want my mother brought into this. It would mean a conviction without a trial.

I did not try to explain things to her. She had made up her mind. It would not matter that I was in love with Jesse. It would not matter that we did not have sex. I was a married woman who had a drink with another man; I was therefore a whore.

I was disappointed in my father. He did not get involved. He just sat there and listened to my mother eviscerate me and support my husband. I know that Dad was with me in spirit; I just wish that he had the nerve to stand up for me.

CHAPTER TWELVE

I had no support. I could not explain how a married woman could go out at night without her husband. I could not explain how good Jesse made me feel after many months of a sterile marriage. Things were very black and white. Bill, being a man, could do no wrong. It did not matter how many girlfriends he courted.

I had trouble understanding how a woman could support this position. But my mother was from the old school. There was a definite double standard.

I left my parents' house very upset. Bill left about a half hour after I did. By getting my mother's support, Bill thought that he had won the argument.

"Bill, we can't continue to live here together; our marriage is over. I want you to leave."

"It's my house, too. There's no way *I'm* leaving."

"Look, Bill; this can't go on. I'm going to see a lawyer."

Bill still did not believe that I was serious. It was as though I was the only one who knew that the marriage was over.

I knew that I could not stay there with Bill. I called Dina and asked her if she had an extra room. Fortunately, she did.

I started packing the following day. When Bill came home and saw that, he knew that I was serious about moving out. He immediately called my mother.

Bill and my mother did not get along until recently. Bill was big and easygoing and tried to get along with my mother, but she never missed an opportunity to harass him. Only recently, when they both had a common opponent, did they form an alliance.

When my mother heard that I was packing, she hurried over. She said that it would be best if she took Robin until things settled down. I agreed. I was in no mood to fight with her. Dina only had one room available. It was not big enough for Robin, Agnes, and me. There would be no one to take care of Robin when I was working. My mother loved Robin and could take good care of her. I could only love her.

While living with Dina, I planned on pursuing the divorce. Bill kept trying to call me and get us back together. It got to the point where I

126

just hung up on him. I found it easy to ignore Bill. He was not part of my life.

My parents were very hurt. Their daughter had shamed them, again. They were very conscious of peer and family pressure. It was a disgrace to have a twenty-one-year-old twice-divorced daughter.

It was the woman's job to maintain the home and the family. I had done a poor job of both. A man's indiscretions could be ignored; a woman could not appear to have an indiscretion. If she did, she would be crucified.

My mother crucified me with her words. I tried to see Robin every day. Whenever I went over to my parent's house, I would meet my mother's wrath.

"This is all your fault. If you weren't such a little whore, your family would be together and I wouldn't be the object of shame. This new bum that you think you love will be no better than the others. He'll just treat you like the slut that you are, then leave you and find another slut. Then I'll be left with the shame of having a whore as a daughter."

Every night when I went to visit Robin, I was the object of a similar diatribe. Every night I tried to defend myself. "Look, Ma. I did not break up the marriage. Bill is the whoremonger. I *caught* him fondling one of his girlfriends in a bar. He was whoring around when he told me he was working late. I did not go out looking for someone. Dina and I went out to relax. I had to relieve the pressure caused by having a screwed-up husband. The marriage was over before I met Jesse. I met him, and we fell in love. We *never* had sex. I *didn't* do anything wrong.

"You're lucky, Ma. You found the right man. There are woman who are not so lucky. I love Jesse; I hope that he is the right man."

Every night my mother refused to listen. I kept trying to win her acceptance. I never succeeded.

"Jenny, you're nothing but a little slut. You should have been born *dead*! I made a mistake in not beating that little whore out of you.

"I'm not going to let you corrupt Robin. You may have given birth to her, but she *will not* be raised as your little whore. She will be raised to be a respectable woman. You can visit her, but *that's it*! I don't want your sluttiness to rub off on her. One whore in the family is enough. *Do you understand?*"

"Yes, Ma."

Even though I could not get my mother to love me, she did love her granddaughter. My parents loved Robin and took very good care of her. She was always well fed and had clean new clothes and plenty of toys. My child's welfare was my primary concern. I would put up with my mother's insults as long as I knew that Robin was properly cared for.

127

I felt like a member of the lost generation. An outsider would think my mother had a baby late in life. Robin appeared to be my mother's child. I was just a visitor.

The strain of the situation affected me physically. I was getting constant headaches. The impending divorce from Bill, the aggravation of dealing with my mother, and my separation from Robin did a job on my nerves. My doctor prescribed Valium. Valium became my crutch.

I continued to see Jesse. He was the duty driver at the Charlestown Navy Yard, so he always had a car, which he used to visit me on his evenings off.

I knew that I was right about Jesse. He was only the second man that I truly loved. I had let Vito get away. I would try to keep Jesse. I had known the pain of being with a man that I did not love. I wanted to be with Jesse as much as possible. The more time that I spent with him, the more vivid my love became.

Love is something that develops. I was not attracted to Jesse the first time that I met him. He was an obnoxious drunk. Our subsequent encounters were different. I saw his human side. He was funny and charming.

Jesse and I enjoyed each other's company. We went to movies, dining, roller-skating, the whole works. It was not the activity that was enjoyable; it was his company. He was glib and relaxed, and he made me feel relaxed. I did not need the Valium when I was with him.

Jesse only had one flaw. He had a problem with alcohol. After a while, when we went out he would frequently drink too much. I preferred to go to places that did not serve alcohol.

Alcohol changed Jesse's personality. He would turn nasty and mean and would frequently pick fights with me. The following day he would call and apologize profusely. I always forgave him. I did not want to believe that he had a serious problem.

I knew nothing about alcoholism. I did not know that it was a disease. I did not know that it was hereditary. I was a very light drinker. My limit was one drink. If I had two, I would feel a little woozy and have to stop drinking.

When Jesse and I went to a club, he would frequently down seven or eight beers before I half-finished my drink. He bragged that he could drink as much as a case of beer at one sitting. I was amazed at the resilience of his bladder. Love is truly blind. I did not want to believe that Jesse had a serious flaw. I had bragged about him to anyone who would listen. If I admitted his drinking problem, I would admit to another failure in choosing men. I therefore ignored his drunkenness as best I could. I assumed that it was a problem that I could solve. As I said,

I did not realize that it was a disease. I did not want to recognize a problem with Jesse, because I had other problems to deal with.

Bill and I owned our house jointly. Since I was not living there, I was not making payments. I was paying for my room and board at Dina's. Bill was also not making mortgage payments.

I received the foreclosure notice at about the same time that I was to go to court for the divorce. I sued for custody and child support. I also wanted to sell the house.

I called Bill and confronted him about the problem with the foreclosure. He did not want to face the issue.

"Jenny, I don't give a shit about the house or anything else around this place. You won't see me in court. You'll never see me again. I'm going home where I belong."

I went to court with my parents. True to his word, Bill was not there. I was granted custody of Robin and twenty dollars a week child support. I never received a penny of it. The bank was granted custody of the house. I was barely old enough to vote, and my second marriage had dissolved. I felt like shit!

My father was great. He knew that Bill was gone and that I needed help with Robin. He wanted Robin to live with him and my mother permanently. He did not need child support.

I was working as an electronics assembler, but I was not making enough money to live independently with Robin. I needed help, and fortunately, my father was able to provide it.

I was hoping that my life would stabilize. I was rid of Bill, and my parents were taking good care of Robin. I was able to save some money from my weekly paychecks. My relationship with Jesse was the biggest loose end in my life.

I wanted Jesse to be Mr. Right so badly that I ignored his faults. I only wanted to think about the good times and about the friendly, charming Jesse.

When I told Jesse that the divorce was granted, he was very happy. He said, "Now you can be all mine."

Jesse wanted to go out to celebrate and said that he would pick me up at eight that evening. I felt that a huge burden was lifted off my shoulders. I also wanted to celebrate.

I took extra time getting ready for our evening out. This was to be a special evening for me. I wanted it to be a watershed in my life. It was to be the end of an unhappy relationship and the beginning of a relationship with a man that I loved.

Eight o'clock arrived, but Jesse did not. Then nine o'clock, then ten o'clock, then eleven o'clock, then midnight, then 1:00 A.M., and still no

Jesse. I had tried to call him at the base several times during the night without success. Finally, at 1:00 A.M., I went to bed but could not fall asleep.

I was not angry; I was worried. I thought Jesse was hurt. I was afraid that he might have gotten into an accident. I placed a call to the police at about midnight, asking if a marine had gotten into a car accident. They said no. I felt better, but I was still worried.

I was tossing and turning in bed for about an hour when the phone rang. It was Jesse. He was drunk and incoherent. He was badly slurring his words, but I was able to understand his message.

"Hello, honey, it's me. Sorry I'm late, but I've been delayed. I'll be over in a few minutes to pick you up."

"*Go to hell!* I'm not meeting you at this hour. Go back to the base and sober up."

"*Fuck you, bitch!* I'm coming over whether you want me or not. I'll break down the fuckin' door if I have to."

"If you come over, I'll never see you again."

I had been worried that he had gotten into an accident; now I was beginning to think that this relationship was an accident. I went to bed and tried very hard to forget our exchange.

I could not sleep. It was about two-thirty in the morning when I heard an auto horn blaring and someone screaming. I looked out of the window and saw Jesse standing by the side of a gray navy auto. He had one hand through the driver's window, honking the horn, while he stood there and screamed at the top of his lungs. He was so drunk that I could not make out his words, but his diatribe sounded like a drunken cacophony of expletives.

I grabbed my robe and ran downstairs and onto the porch. Jesse had a crazy look on his face, and his uniform was torn and disheveled. When he saw me, he took his hand off the horn and stopped screaming.

"*Jesse, what the hell are you doing?*"

He ran toward me and onto the porch. He grabbed my arm and started dragging me toward the car. I tried to get away, but he slapped my face and cursed at me.

"You filthy little *whore*, who the hell were you fuckin' while you were waiting for me?"

He threw me into the front seat. Then he walked around to the driver's side and got in. I was in shock and could not move.

Fortunately, Dina had heard the noise and came running out of the house. She saw me being thrown into Jesse's car and ran toward it. She opened the passenger door and pulled me out while yelling at Jesse, "Jesse, if you don't let her go, I'm calling the police!"

130

"I don't give a fuck who you bitches call."

Moments after Dina pulled me out of the car, Jesse sped off, nearly hitting several cars as he swerved all over the road. Dina helped me into the house.

"You poor kid. You never have any luck with men. This guy is just another drunken asshole. Please stay away from him. He's crazy enough to kill you."

"Please, Dina, leave me alone. I'm going to bed."

I stayed awake for the remainder of the night. I called in sick at six-thirty, went back to bed, and finally fell asleep about an hour later.

The following evening Jesse called. He behaved as if nothing had happened.

"Hi, honey, sorry I couldn't make it last night, but I had a few too many beers."

"Jesse, what the hell is wrong with you? Don't you remember what happened last night?"

"No. I only remember having a few beers too many and hitting the rack."

I proceeded to tell Jesse in vivid detail our encounter of the previous evening. I could not jog his memory. He proceeded to apologize profusely for any improper actions.

"Jenny, please meet me tonight, just for an hour. I promise that I won't drink. I just have to see you. I'm sorry if I did anything wrong last night. I just drank too much and don't remember."

I was softhearted and softheaded. I still loved him. "Okay, Jesse, I'll see you. *But no drinking!*"

He said that he would see me in two hours. He was right on time. He was driving the same official navy car that he had the previous evening.

I was standing on the porch waiting for him as he pulled up in front of the house. He jumped out of the car and ran to the porch. He put his arms around me, lifted me up, and kissed me. He was sober. He acted as if the activities of last night never occurred. After he held me and kissed me, I also forgot about last night.

It was nine o'clock on a pleasant spring evening when he arrived. We sat on the porch and talked and kissed and talked. It was a very enjoyable evening. We spent most of the evening holding hands and necking. Jesse wanted to go some place more private to consummate our relationship.

I told him that I wanted to be more than his mistress. He became indignant and told me to grow up. The "bad Jesse" started to show, and

131

the evening lost some of its magic. He sulked like a little boy who did not get what he wanted.

"Look, Jenny. You're no virgin and you shouldn't act like one. We've known each other for months. I think it's about time that we got together. Your little 'hard to get' act is a little much for a woman with your past."

"What do you mean, 'a woman with my past'? Just because I'm divorced, that doesn't mean that I'm trash."

I saw both Jesses on that evening. At first I saw the friendly, affectionate Jesse. When I refused his sexual advances, I saw the frustrated, horny Jesse. I blamed all of Jesse's problems on liquor. I thought if he were sober, everything would be okay. Then I saw that there was an unpleasant side of him that was not liquor-induced. The evening ended soon after Jesse realized that he would not get his sexual satisfaction.

We made a date for Friday evening, which was two days hence. I spent those two days wondering which Jesse would show up. I felt that I was losing control of the situation. I loved him and wanted to help him. I just did not know how.

On Friday evening, Jesse showed up on time at eight o'clock. We decided to go to the Cafe 700. The club was crowded and there was barely enough room to dance. Jesse was sober when he picked me up, but he started to chug the beers soon after we entered the club.

We would dance; then he would have a few beers; then another dance. I sat at our table sipping ginger ale while he drank his beer. By the time we had our fourth or fifth dance, Jesse was drunk and I was angry. I told him that I wanted to leave.

"Sit down and be quiet. We ain't goin' to leave until I'm finished."

He turned around toward the bar and continued his drinking. I picked up my jacket and walked out the front door. I walked down the street toward the subway station, which was about three blocks away.

I was about one block away from the Cafe 700 when Jesse's car pulled alongside me. He leaned over and opened the passenger door.

"Get in the fuckin' car!"

I did not want to create a scene in downtown Boston, so I got in. He was very drunk and the car was weaving all over the road.

"Jesse, what's the matter with you? Why don't you try acting like a civilized human being? I can't take any more of this crap. Take me home *immediately*!"

He did not respond to me. He drove past the Charles Street "T" station, and over the bridge. Instead of going to Malden, he headed for his base in Charlestown.

132

"Jesse, where are we going? I said that I wanted to go *home!*"

"Shut up, bitch!"

He knew the marines who were on duty at the gate, so he was not stopped as he drove past them. He just slowed down, and when they saw who it was, they waved him through. He was weaving all over the road, and I thought he might hit one of the guards. They must have been accustomed to his drunken escapades, because they gave him plenty of room as he went through the gate.

Jesse drove to a part of the base that was under construction. There were cement foundations for three buildings. The area was very dark and isolated. The nearest light was several hundred feet away. He stopped the car and turned out the lights. I was frightened.

"Jesse, what the hell are we doing here? I told you to take me home."

"Come on, Jenny. It's that time. Stop pretending that you're a virgin. You know the scoop."

He then grabbed my arm and pulled me toward him. He picked me up off the front seat and threw me onto the backseat and jumped on top of me. I screamed, but he pressed his mouth on mine to suppress my outcry.

He had his arms around me, keeping me pinned against the seat while he kept his lips pressed against mine. I thought that I would choke; the stench of alcohol almost made me throw up. I tried to scream; I tried to move. I could do neither.

He finally lifted his head, and I was able to scream, *"Jesseeee, Jesseeee, get off!"* The car windows were up, and I knew my shouts were in vain.

He kept me pinned down with one hand. With the other, he lifted my dress and tore off my panties, lacerating my hip in the process. He then started to fumble with his own clothes. Within moments, his pants were around his ankles.

My screams turned to whimpers. I was breathing heavy and crying. Jesse had a crazed look on his face but said nothing. He took his left hand and lifted my right leg. He moved his hips against mine and penetrated me.

I took both hands and covered my eyes, while he grunted, groaned, and took his pleasure. It seemed like he spent years inside of me. In reality, it could not have been more than a minute.

When he finished, he let out the biggest groan of all and froze for several seconds. Then he rolled off me. I had been called a whore my whole life. This was the first time that I felt like one.

I felt wet and dirty as I pulled my dress down. He also adjusted his clothes. I wanted to open the car door and run, run anywhere, but I stayed in the car. There was nothing more that he could do to me.

When he adjusted his clothes, he moved closer to me and started kissing me and telling me how much he loved me. "Jenny, I love you so much. I'm sorry that it had to be this way, but I just couldn't help myself."

I was humiliated. I could not respond to him. All I could do was cry. When Jesse's sweet words did not have their desired effect, he got angry. I was supposed to enjoy getting raped.

"Well, it could not have been that bad. What the hell is wrong is you. After all, you're not a baby, you know."

"You're right, Jesse; I'm not a baby. Not anymore, thanks to you. Take me home."

He responded with a smug smile. "Sure, baby. I'll take you home so that you can dream about me. It's past your bedtime anyway."

Jesse climbed over the seat and got behind the wheel. I stayed scrunched in the corner of the backseat. I picked my purse up off the floor and took out a mirror. I was a different woman. I wanted to see what I looked like.

We drove back through the main gate. The sentries saluted with smiles on their faces. I'm sure they knew what had happened.

Jesse kept up a drunken soliloquy all the way to Dina's house. I was no more a part of his conversation than I was a part of the sex act. I was an object of verbal and sexual abuse.

As soon as we pulled up in front of Dina's house, I jumped out of the car and ran into the house. Dina was sitting in the living room as I came through the door. She got up and ran toward me and saw my disheveled appearance.

"Well, it happened, huh? It wasn't all that romantic, was it? He's a mad dog, and someone should kill him. You should call the police or at least report him to his commanding officer."

I did not answer her. I continued to cry and ran up the stairs and into the bathroom. I filled up the tub and undressed. I wanted to soak forever. I felt that I would never be clean again.

I never thought about reporting him. I did not consider it Jesse's crime. I carried much of the burden of guilt. This was not our first date. I knew about his alcoholic outbursts. I should not have been surprised if his anger and violence were directed at me.

I sat in the tub and thought about Jesse. I knew that he needed more help than I could give him. I still loved him, but I could never cope with him. I gave up any thought that we could have a future together. But I did not understand my feelings. How could I still love him?

I told Dina that I did not want to speak to Jesse. I was sure that he would want to speak to me. When he sobered up, he would be a different person. I could not deal with his Jekyll and Hyde personality.

I was right. Jesse called many times the following day. Dina kept making up excuses. Finally he told her that if I didn't speak to him, he would come to the house. The next time that he called I spoke to him, even though Dina warned against it.

The "other" Jesse was on the line. This time, he was crying.

"I, I'm sorry, Jenny. I had to speak to you. I don't know what happened. I could not control myself. I love you so much that I just went crazy. Please forgive me. I just can't lose you. You mean too much to me. You're the only good thing that ever happened to me."

"Jesse, how could you call me after what happened last night? Do you know what you did?"

"I know; I know. I'm sorry, but I just couldn't help it. You mean so much to me. I just could not control my feelings. Let me make it up to you. We could start over. Jenny, I have the weekend off. Would you like to go to Maine and visit my parents? It's about a three-hour drive."

This was the first time that Jesse ever mentioned my meeting his parents. I had ambivalent feelings. I knew that I still loved him. I agreed to go with him if he promised not to drink. He agreed and said that he would be at my place by eight Saturday morning.

Jesse was sober when he picked me up. It was a long trip, but the miles flew by. Jesse was as gregarious as he ever was. It was as though he had completely forgotten the events of several days ago. After several hours of listening to the "good Jesse," I also began to forget them.

Jesse and I made a quick stop for breakfast in Coontoocook, New Hampshire, and were back on the road. I asked him if he had told his mother that he was bringing me home.

He laughed. "Hell, no. It's my home, too. Why should I?" He then looked at me with his boyish grin and winked, and I knew why I always forgave him. He pulled me close to him and put his arm around my shoulders. We rode the final hour snuggled together.

As we neared his hometown, he told me not to close my eyes or I would miss it.

"Oh, come on; it can't be that small."

He laughed. "Want to bet?"

Graysville *was* a small town, but not that small. The place was very clean. The houses were mostly single families, on about two acres of land each.

Jesse gave me a tour of the town. It took about ten minutes. There were not many tourist attractions in Graysville. He took great pleasure in pointing out the home of Linda Kramer, the girl that he had impregnated. He seemed very proud of his accomplishment.

He pulled into the driveway of a large green house with a big porch. Before we got out of the car, I saw a tall, thin woman with glasses run toward us. When Jesse got out of the car, she ran over toward him and gave him a big hug and a kiss.

When they separated, Jesse introduced me to his mother. "Jenny, this is my mother, Dorothy Rollins."

"Pleased to meet you, Mrs. Rollins."

She just nodded at me. Either she was a very quiet woman or she did not like me.

Jesse broke the ice. "Mom, why don't we show Jenny the house?"

They showed me the house. Their home was kept very clean, but the newest piece of furniture must have been at least twenty years old. They had things that I had never seen before, like a triple-decker table and a cuckoo clock with four cuckoos.

Jesse maintained his affectionate ways. We walked through the house with his arm around my waist. Sometimes he used the other arm to muss my hair. I felt embarrassed and was glad when the tour was over.

We went into the kitchen, and Jesse and I sat at the table. Dorothy walked toward the refrigerator and asked, "Jenny, do you want a beer?"

"No, thank you."

"Well, Son, do you want one?"

I gave him a look that would melt stone. "No thanks, Mom. Could I have a cup of coffee instead?"

Dorothy boiled the water for instant coffee. When she brought the coffee to Jesse, she turned to me and asked where I was from. I told her, "Boston." There was no follow-up question. That was all that she wanted to know about me.

After she put the coffee in front of Jesse, she went to the refrigerator to get a beer for herself. She and Jesse talked about life in Graysville. Jesse had not been home in months and wanted to catch up on the local gossip. They acted as though I were not there, I was not brought into the conversation. Dorothy drank like Jesse, very quickly. After five minutes she was on her second beer.

After about a half hour, Dorothy was feeling no pain. She suggested that Jesse visit Cecile, the next-door neighbor. She had been asking about Jesse, and Dorothy thought it would be a nice gesture if we went over to see her.

We went next door to Cecile's house. Cecile was a large middle-aged woman with gray hair and an outgoing personality.

"Dottie, how are you? You been your old ornery self? I see you finally brought Jesse over."

"Yeah, I brought everyone over to see you. Why don't you bring us some beers?"

Cecile and Dorothy went through a six-pack in no time. Jesse and I watched them drink. I understood why he had a drinking problem. The whole damn town was alcoholics.

When we went back to Dorothy's house, Jesse's father and adopted sister were waiting for us. His father was about six feet tall, with a heavy build and salt-and-pepper hair.

Jesse's sister was something else! She was almost as large as Jesse and his father and looked very masculine. She had a ruddy complexion and facial hair. If Jesse didn't tell me he had a sister, I would have thought he had a brother.

Jesse's father was very nice to me. He talked candidly to me about the family's drinking problem. He had no choice; Dorothy was staggering around and muttering incoherently. He did not drink and was obviously disturbed by his wife's addiction.

Leona, Jesse's sister, excused herself, and when she returned she was wearing nothing but her bra and panties. I stared at her, but to her family this was her normal attire. She looked more masculine undressed, with hairy legs and unshaven underarms. I went over to the couch and sat next to Jesse. He told me about the "facts of life" in Graysville.

"Look, Jenny. Things are different out here in the country. All people do is drink and go to bed with each other's wives. Most of the women in the town are drunks. Running around in your underwear is no big deal."

Dorothy wanted us to stay for the night. "I've got a few cases of beer in the cellar. We would have a high old time tonight," she said.

Jesse indicated that he would like to stay. There was no way that I wanted to stay in this madhouse.

"I'm sorry, but I have to be home tonight," I said politely.

I took Jesse's hand and led him to the door. His father gave us a cordial good-bye. Dorothy gave me a cold, blank stare. I pushed Jesse out the door.

Jesse was subdued on the return trip. He would have liked to stay and drink. If I were not with him, I'm sure he would have joined his mother in her state of inebriation. He pulled me close to him and let me know how he felt about my stifling his drinking. "You may be little, but you're rotten. You kept me from doin' a little partying."

I did not answer him. We snuggled all the way home. I loved him, and I thought that I could stifle his drinking permanently. I now knew where he got the problem, and I thought that I could solve it. All he needed was love and understanding.

CHAPTER THIRTEEN

That evening, Jesse dropped me off at my parents' house. I wanted to see Robin. My mother was surprised to see me, but she asked me if I'd like a little supper. I said, "No thank you," and went straight to Robin's room. My mother followed me.

Robin was now eighteen months old. She was growing into a pretty little lady. She had blue eyes and long curly black hair. I reached over the crib to pick her up. When I picked her up she started to cry and reached over to her grandmother. I just held her tighter, but the crying got louder.

My mother became upset. "Put the baby down so that she'll stop crying. She's not used to you."

"Look, Ma. She's going to have to get used to me. I *am* her mother. Let her cry. She'll stop pretty soon."

"Some mother you are. You broke up your home. You found another bum to go out with; you're happy. You don't give a damn for your daughter."

"That's not true, Ma. Jesse is not a bum. You never even met him. I wish you would. Please, just see him once. I really love him. You know, Ma, that if I could take care of Robin I would. I love her more than *anything!*"

"I'll never meet that bum. He will never bring you happiness, Jennifer. Mark my words. You have seen nothing but tears with him, and if that's how things start, that's how they must end."

My stomach tightened. "You're wrong, Ma. You'll see. We will eventually get married, and everything will work itself out. You're wrong this time, and I'm going to prove it to you. We will have a good life, and Robin will, too."

When I said "Robin" my mother flew into a rage. "You wouldn't take this child and make her live with you and that bum!"

"Ma, she's my child."

"But I raised her, *not you!* Look, Jennifer, if you love your father and me, you won't take Robin. You should leave her with us until your life straightens out. Why make her suffer? For God's sake, consider the

139

welfare of your baby. If you take her, you will be punished your whole life. NEVER FORGET THAT!"

Robin continued to whimper while my mother and I exchanged opinions. I put the baby back in her crib and before leaving tried to get in the last word with my mother.

"Ma, I'm not close to getting married again. I just hope that our relationship can develop into marriage."

"Good-bye, Jennifer. Think about what I said."

When I got back to Dina's house, the phone rang. It was Jesse. We discussed the trip to Maine. He asked me if I would like to go back. I changed the subject.

"Jesse, what do you think about us taking Robin out tomorrow? We could take her for ice cream or something."

"Yeah, Jenny, that's a good idea. I think it's about time that I finally met Robin. I'll be over about eleven tomorrow morning."

When I hung up with Jesse, Dina and I sat and talked over a cup of coffee. I told her about my trip to Maine and about my encounter with Jesse's family and neighbor.

"Girl, you're *nuts*! You know this guy is *trouble*. It seems that his family is nuttier than he is. If you were smart, you would give up on him and find a decent guy."

It seems that everyone had the same opinion about Jesse. I thought that they did not understand him. I had seen his dark side, but I had also seen his good side. I loved him and thought that with the proper guidance, I could change him.

I did not understand alcoholism. I thought it was brought on by his being in the marines. Through Bill, I had known other marines, and most of them were drunks. I thought that it was an occupational hazard; alcohol went along with the uniform.

I was confused after my meeting with Jesse's mother. He had told me that his mother was an alcoholic, but I had to see it to believe it. What I had blamed on his being a marine had genetic roots. My romantic view denied the reality of the situation. I was stubborn. I was looking for a happy ending.

I picked up Robin early on Sunday morning and took her back to Dina's house to await Jesse. He arrived right on time. It seemed as though Robin liked Jesse as much as everyone else did. I put her in a big easy chair. Whenever he got close to her, she started to cry.

"Jenny, your daughter is spoiled; it doesn't look as though we can get along."

"Don't worry, Jesse. She just has to get used to you. She sometimes acts that way with me."

140

Jesse sat on the arm of the chair and tried to talk to her the way that he talked to an adult. He did not feel comfortable in the world of baby talk. His efforts were futile. I suggested that we go out for ice cream. Jesse quickly agreed.

Jesse was wearing his dress blue uniform. He usually wore a green or khaki uniform. Dress blues were usually reserved for important ceremonial occasions. I was glad that he thought meeting Robin was important enough to wear this uniform.

We went to a drive-in. Jesse walked up to the counter and came back with three vanilla ice cream cones. He gave one to Robin and one to me. He got back behind the wheel and started to eat his own ice cream.

I had dressed Robin up like a little lady, with a little pocketbook, gloves, and a hat. She was standing up on the front seat between us licking her ice cream. Jesse wore a contented look. He had finally made friends with Robin!

I returned to my ice cream. When I looked back toward Jesse and Robin, I saw that she was standing close to him near the back of the seat. She was happily absorbed with her ice cream and did not seem to notice or care that it was dripping on the back of the car seat and on Jesse's uniform.

I did not want to disturb this peaceful scene, so I said nothing. Jesse continued to make friends with Robin. Every time he would say something to her she would pucker her lips and crinkle her eyes as if to cry.

Robin continued to lick on her cone, oblivious to the mess that she was making. The ice cream had melted enough that it was now dripping all over her, too.

"Give Mommy the ice cream, honey, so that I can clean up."

Robin refused to relinquish the cone. I made the mistake of trying to forcibly remove it from her. When I grabbed her hand, the cone flew from her grasp and into Jesse's lap. Robin immediately started to cry.

"What the fuck is going on? You just ruined the trousers of my best uniform."

I didn't tell Jesse that the jacket was ruined about five minutes ago.

"Please, Jesse, I think that we should go home. Could you drive us to my parents' house?"

When we got to my parents' house, I went in with Robin, while Jesse waited in the car. We had only been gone about a half hour. My mother startled me when she answered the door.

"What's the matter? He didn't love having the baby along?"

"Oh, it's not that. Robin spilled ice cream all over his dress uniform."

"So what! All babies make a mess."

"Yeah, I know, Ma. It was the first time that they'd seen each other. It will be better next time."

"No, it won't! It will be exactly the same the next time. He is *not* for you!"

My mother took Robin's hand, and I turned toward the car. "Look, Ma; I have to go. I'll talk to you later."

When I got back to the car, Jesse was using his handkerchief to wipe the ice cream off of his uniform.

"Jesse, Robin will get used to you. It's just a matter of time."

"Yeah, but will *I* get used to her? That's what I would like to know. Let's go back to Charlestown. I have to get a fresh uniform. Look, Jenny, I love you, but the kid, well, hell, I'm a marine and I'm going to stay in the service. I can't have a kid change my career."

"I know, Jesse, but she's my child and I love her."

"Okay, okay, Jenny. Let's drop it."

Jesse drove to the base and changed while I waited in the car. While I was waiting, a couple of Jesse's friends came out of the barracks and recognized me. I had met Jack and Ronnie before when we ran into them in the downtown Boston clubs.

Jack was a lifer like Jesse, but Ronnie just wanted to do his time and get out. Ronnie's last name was Donetelli, so we had a common heritage. Ronnie and I had exchanged stories about our Italian parents. The guys leaned against the car talking while Jesse changed.

When Jesse returned, the three of us were laughing and talking. His jealousy started to show. "Hey, guys, I'm in a hurry. Jenny and I have to get going."

"Yeah, I'll bet. Hey, listen," Ronnie said. "We're off-duty. How about if all of us go for a few drinks and a few dances? We'll go and raise a little hell."

When Jesse heard the word "drinks" his attitude changed. He was more accommodating. I cringed when I heard that word.

Jack and Ronnie climbed in the backseat, and we headed to a place called the French Club. It was late Sunday afternoon, and the club was nearly empty. Jack and Ronnie kept pumping change into the jukebox, and I took turns dancing with them.

Jesse sat at a table by himself and drank. He did not dance. He just sat there and stewed. He kept downing beers and watching us dance. His frown became a scowl.

I got tired and had to sit down. Jack and Ronnie came with me to the table and ordered beer. I had a ginger ale. When our drinks came, Jesse stood up and grabbed my arm.

"You fuckin' tramp. Are you going to screw everyone in the place?"

Jack pulled us apart. "Jesse, what the fuck is wrong with you?"

"There is nothing wrong with me; it's that fuckin' whore Jenny. She's no damn good."

Jesse was still holding me with one hand when he slapped me across the face with the other. I was knocked off the chair and onto the floor. Jack stood between me and Jesse, while Ronnie helped me back up into the chair. Jesse wanted to hit me again, but he was too drunk to get past Jack. He just slumped back into his seat.

Half of my face was still stinging, plus I got terrible stomach pains. I felt nauseous.

"Jenny," Ronnie asked, "is there anything that I can do?"

"Ronnie, I feel sick. I think that I should see a doctor."

Ronnie helped me to the car, while Jack dragged Jesse outside. Jack poured Jesse into the backseat and got in after him. Ronnie drove, and I sat next to him. He took me to the emergency room of Massachusetts General Hospital. Jesse passed out on the way to the hospital.

I told the emergency room physician that I had fallen down and banged my head. He looked askance at me but did not challenge me. He told me to go into an examining room. A nurse followed me in and told me to undress. They took X rays and blood tests and asked me many questions.

When the examination was over, the doctor came back into the examining room holding several sheets of paper. "Jennifer, do you have any *other* children?"

"What do you mean, *other* children? I have one child."

The doctor smiled. "Well, my dear, you're about to have another."

"Doctor, are you *sure*? You can't be mistaken, can you?"

"No, Jennifer, the test is conclusive. You are going to be a mother . . . again."

I put my head back on the examining table and stared at the ceiling. I couldn't be pregnant, not like this. My mother had called me a whore my whole life. I guess she was right. There was only one right thing to do: I had to get married.

The nurse applied some salve to my black eye, and I got dressed. I was talking to myself and shaking when I left the examining room. Jack and Ronnie came up to me and asked if I was all right. I cried and told them, "I'm pregnant." They tried to reassure me that Jesse would "do the right thing."

When we returned to the car, Jesse was still in the backseat, smoking a cigarette. He was still drunk but was coherent. "Well? What did the doctor say? Did I kill you?"

I didn't answer, so he started to yell. "*I asked you a question!*"

143

"Jesse, the doctor said that you are going to be a father."

Jesse sobered up in a hurry. He took a long drag on his cigarette. I wanted him to tell me that everything would be all right, that he would marry me. That was not what I heard.

"Look, Jenny; you could go to a home for unwed mothers, put the kid up for adoption. We could still see each other. Nobody has to know what happened."

I put both hands on my stomach and silently wept for the life that I was carrying. Its own father didn't want it. Who else would? I knew that I could never do as Jesse recommended. "Jesse, you're going to marry me whether you like it or not!"

He did not answer.

Ronnie drove me home. I ran through the front door, past Dina, who was sitting in the living room, and upstairs. I went right to bed but couldn't sleep. The abdominal pain and nausea would not go away. In the days that followed, I could not eat or sleep. I had told no one else about my pregnancy.

My mother knew that I was not feeling well and recommended that I see a doctor at St. Elizabeth's Hospital. I knew that I needed prenatal care, and I followed my mother's advice and made an appointment with Dr. Fortunato.

As soon as I walked into the examining room, I told Dr. Fortunato that I was pregnant. He told me to get undressed and sit on the examining table. After he examined me, he told me that I had a bad nerve condition and that was no good for me or the child.

He asked if he could talk to my husband. I told him I was not married. He sat and looked at me for a few moments, then asked, "Does your family know about the situation?"

"No, and I don't want them to know."

"Well, then, who is taking care of you?"

"I need no one. I'm taking care of myself."

Dr. Fortunato told me that he wanted to admit me to the hospital for my nerve condition. He said that I was run-down and should be under observation for a while. I insisted that I could not stay in the hospital.

He was adamant. "Jenny, I'm a friend of your family. I have known your mother for many years. It's my duty to inform them of your condition.

"Knowing your mother, I'm sure that you have been brought up right. I'm sorry for you and for the disgrace that this illegitimate child will bring to your family."

"Dr. Fortunato, I'm not happy over what happened, but I don't think that it's your place to judge me."

"Young lady, I'm going to call the admissions office; then I will talk to your family. Just stay here and a nurse will take you upstairs."

The nurse came by five minutes later, and we took the elevator to the sixth floor. She took out some keys and opened a door that led to a large hallway that was lined with semiprivate rooms.

I was ushered into one of the semiprivate rooms at the far end of the hall and given a hospital gown. As I was changing, a woman came out of the bathroom. She was a skinny woman about fifty years old with a little blue bonnet on her head.

"Hi, I'm Sister Marie, your new roommate."

"Hello, I'm Jennifer. Why are you here? You don't look very sick to me."

"Jennifer, I'm not sick. I'm here because they have no place else to put me. Why are you here?"

"I'm here for a rest."

Sister Marie laughed. "Well, dear. You won't get any rest here."

I did not understand what she meant then, but I was soon to find out. Moments later, I heard a bone-chilling scream out in the hall. I ran out of the room and into the hall. I did not see anyone. I went to the nurses' station in the middle of the hallway. "What was that noise? Who was screaming?" I asked.

The nurse scowled as she said, "What are you doing here! You should not be out of your room."

"I just want to make a phone call; they took my money when they took my clothes. Could I use the phone at the nurses' station?"

The nurse did not say anything. She just looked at me as if I had asked her for her last nickel. I knew that I had to get out of this place.

"Well, I am going for a walk; then maybe I won't be so jumpy." I left the nurses' station and walked to the end of the hall. The door was locked. I swiftly walked back to the nurses' station. "The door is locked. Let me out of this place."

The nurse was not helpful. "Now, Jennifer, calm down. Everything will be all right. Just go to your room and rest."

"*Rest! Rest!* I don't want rest. I want to get out of this damn place. Where are my clothes? Get my clothes! Let me out. Get my doctor. I don't belong here. I'm going to have a baby. I shouldn't be here. This is all a mistake."

As I was yelling at the nurse, I was grabbing things at the nurses' station. The nurse held my hands and called for help. A big man in a white coat ran down the hall and took me back to my room and closed the door.

He threw me on the bed. "Be quiet, young lady, or we will have to

145

use force to keep you still." I rolled over on the bed, away from my keeper. I lay with my eyes closed for a few seconds. When I heard him leave, I opened my eyes and saw Sister Marie sitting on the bed next to mine.

"Well, Jennifer. How do you like your new home?"

"It *sucks!*"

My stomach started to churn. I was in prison. I had committed no crime except getting pregnant, and that was done without my consent. I had to contact Jesse. I had to see my parents. Somebody had to get me out of here.

A different nurse came into my room, carrying a clipboard with a pen dangling from it. The clipboard had a form attached. "Jennifer, you have to sign this form."

I took the clipboard and read the form. It was an authorization for shock treatments. I flung the clipboard to the far corner of the room. Sister Marie and the nurse jumped.

"I'll never sign anything like that. If I don't see the doctor, I'll sue the whole bunch of you," I said.

The nurse picked up the clipboard and left.

Sister Marie got up from her bed and sat next to me and asked, "Are you afraid of me?"

I did not want to look her in the eye. "Of course not."

"Jennifer, do you like Bible stories?"

"Yes, very much."

Sister Marie stood up, went to the cabinet, and took out a well-worn Bible. She came back to my bed and said, "Lie down, Jennifer, and I'll read to you."

I was not listening; I was thinking about my baby and my imprisonment and Jesse and my parents, and how I got into this mess and how the hell could I get out of it.

My first night was horrible. Women were screaming all night. I could not sleep at all. I was glad that the door was locked. Sister Marie was sleeping like a baby, with a contented smile on her face.

The following morning, I had visitors. My parents came with Aunt Theresa. I was ecstatic. I thought they were there to spring me. When I saw my mother's expression, I knew otherwise.

"I'm sorry, Jennifer, but you're going to have to stay in the hospital. We spoke to Dr. Fortunato. He told up that you have a bad nerve condition. You could have a nervous breakdown if you came home."

"Ma, *please*! I will have a nervous breakdown if I stay here. This is a *madhouse*! You have to get me out of here."

"Look, Jennifer, you are not going anyplace. You got that bum Jesse to blame for all your problems. I'm trying to help you. You are just an ungrateful little bitch."

I was sobbing. "Ma, you don't know what you are talking about. *Please! Please!* Get me out of here."

My mother stood there stone-faced. I ran over and hugged my father. "Please, Dad. Take me home," I begged. He was softer than my mother but his message was the same.

"Don't worry, Jennifer. You need the rest. You will be home in about a week. Dr. Fortunato said so. You will be a new woman."

"Yeah, Dad, but did he tell you what kind of woman I'd be? *Look!* If I stay here, I will really go nuts! You don't know what kinds of things go on in a place like this."

"Honey, please do as I ask and stay here. The doctor knows what is best for you. Spending a week here won't hurt you. It should do you a lot of good."

"But, Dad, this is a damn madhouse!"

"Please, Jennifer. I'll visit you every day."

"Okay, Dad."

I knew that my confinement hurt my father almost as much as it hurt me. He was just going along with my mother's wishes. I wished that he would tell my mother to go to hell and lead me out of this madhouse.

My mother changed the subject. My brother, Sal, had recently joined the army. She told me how proud she was. I felt sorry for the army!

"Jennifer, you are so selfish. You never ask about your brother, Salvatore. He's a man, Jennifer. He just joined the army to defend our country. We're having a farewell party for him on Friday night. It's too bad that you got yourself into this mess, or you could come, too.

"I'm going to miss your brother. The house will be empty with him away in the army. You brother has never given me any grief, unlike his sister, who has given me *nothing but grief*. I wish it was you who was going to be away for two years, not him."

My brother did go into the army, but not for long. He was assigned to Fort Jackson, South Carolina, for boot camp. He was only there a couple of weeks. It seems like the cooking, the weather, or the 5:00 A.M. reveille did not agree with him, because he wound up with a discharge and one of the shortest military careers on record. My mother had many influential friends high up in the Massachusetts political hierarchy. Many were judges. When my brother informed my mother that army life was not for him, she pulled a few strings, and voilà, he was a civilian again.

My mother thought nothing of manipulating the system to spare

147

my brother the agony of army life, but she would not pick up a pen or utter a word to spare her daughter the hell of living in a madhouse.

Sister Marie broke the ice. "Mrs. Vicci, I'm Sister Marie, Jennifer's roommate. She doesn't really belong here; she's real upset. I had to read to her last night to calm her down."

My mother looked at Sister Marie like she was a pariah but said nothing.

I addressed my mother. "Ma, I want you to promise me that if Jesse calls, you will tell him where I am."

"Jennifer, what's the matter with you? You're here because of that bum! Do you want him to hurt you more than he has already? I won't let that piece of trash near you!"

I thought that Dr. Fortunato might have told my mother about my pregnancy. My baby's welfare was a major concern. I was about three months pregnant. "Ma, I have to make plans; that's why I have to talk to Jesse. Will *you* stay with me until the baby is born?"

"*What baby!*" my mother screamed. "You mean that dirty bum has gotten you pregnant? Will he at least marry you? Probably not! He soiled his little whore, and he thinks he will dump his problems on *me*. Well, he's wrong."

My mother was turning red. Aunt Theresa had her arms around my mother, trying to calm her down.

I put my hands over my eyes and started crying. "Please, Ma. I'm going to have a baby. I need help."

"*Help! You need help?* I'm the one who needs help. Do you have any idea of the shame that you bring on me and your family? You're a dirty little tramp who has done nothing but disgrace us. I . . . would . . . be . . . *ecstatic* if you and that little bastard that you are carrying died. I'm going to go to court to have Robin taken from you, permanently. You're an unfit mother."

I got up and ran out of the room and down the hall. I was stopped by the locked door at the end of the hallway. I was banging on the door, crying. A couple of nurses ran up to me and brought me back to my room. One of the nurses told my visitors that they should leave, because I was so upset. After they left, I was brought a sedative and quickly fell asleep.

When I awoke, the room was empty. The same nurse who had brought the authorization for shock treatments was back with the same paper on the same clipboard. I refused to sign it, again, and requested that I see Dr. Fortunato.

The nurse was pissed off. "The doctor will see you when he is ready," she said and stormed off without my signature.

She left the door to the room open. I wanted to take a walk. It was a long corridor, and I walked slowly. The ward was quiet. There were about a dozen people sitting on a bench outside one of the rooms. They looked "normal" sitting on the bench. As they came out of the "treatment room," they looked like zombies. They just stared into the distance, oblivious to what was going on. I stood there for several minutes observing.

A nurse saw me and asked me what I was doing.

"Looking," I replied. "What do they do in there?"

She explained, "That is where we give shock treatments."

I ran back to my room. That was what they wanted to do to me. That would probably kill my baby. I had to get in touch with Jesse. Somebody had to help me get out of here.

I was sitting on my bed catching my breath when Sister Marie walked into the room, sat down, and retrieved a book from under her pillow and began to read aloud. Just then, a woman ran into the room screaming. She grabbed everything on a nightstand and flung the items to the ground. I screamed to Sister Marie to "get the hell out of here."

She sat there as if this were a common occurrence and told me to "sit still while I finish the story." The other woman was running around the bed grabbing sheets and throwing them in all directions.

I yelled at Sister Marie, "The hell with your story! Get out of here!" I tried to pull her off the bed and out of the room. She seemed to be glued to the bed.

Nurses heard the commotion and came running into our room, grabbed our visitor, and dragged her away. I sat on the bed and shook.

That afternoon, my parents came to visit me. I was more determined than ever to get out of here as soon as possible. I knew my mother was heartless, but there was a chance that my father would help me.

When my parents entered my room, my father put his arms around me and kissed me. My mother gave me a halfhearted, "Hello, Jenny."

"Dad, please take me home. I'll do anything that you ask."

He looked at my mother. She gave him a cold stare. "Well, angel, the week isn't up yet."

"Please, Dad, what's a few more days? It can't make that much difference. I'm okay. This place is for crazy people. I never belonged here in the first place. I could get hurt if I stay here much longer. Ple-e-e-e-e-ease, Dad, I'll be all right if I go home."

I was able to get through to my father. "Okay, Jenny, I'll speak to the nurse. We'll get in touch with the doctor and arrange your release," he finally said.

I was ecstatic, but my mother was not. "Jennifer, if you come home, you must never see that bum again. We will find a place for you to go and have your baby and put it up for adoption. We must hide this shame as best we can," she told me.

This happened about fifteen years before *Roe versus Wade*. My options were limited. It was either my mother's option or marriage. I would have preferred marriage. But I would have agreed to anything to get out of this madhouse. "Sure, Ma, I'll do whatever you say."

Although I promised my mother one thing, I had every intention of doing the other. I was going to get Jesse to marry me, whether he wanted to or not!

My father did not have an easy time getting me out of that place. The nurse had trouble getting in touch with Dr. Fortunato. Then he did not want to release me. Both parents had to talk to him. We had to wait for him to come to the hospital to talk to my parents. He was finally convinced that the city would be safe with me walking the streets.

I walked out of the hospital at nine that evening. I had a new appreciation of freedom.

CHAPTER FOURTEEN

My mother was busy planning my life as we drove home. "Jennifer, we have to find a place for you to go and have that little bastard before you start to show. We can't let anyone know that my *unmarried* whore of a daughter is going to have a bum's child. We must hide this shame. I will lose all the respect of my friends if anyone finds out. We can worry about finding someone to take the little bastard later."

My father drove without saying a word, while my mother rambled on about the shame that I brought on the family. I sat in the backseat and gritted my teeth, while I listened to my mother's diatribe.

I was going to marry Jesse and keep my baby. Whatever doubt that I had was erased by my mother's harangue. I grew angry as I sat and listened. As soon as my father pulled into his driveway, I threw open the door and ran out of the car. I did not stop running until I got to Dina's house.

When she saw me, she hugged me and asked what had happened. I told her the whole story over a cup of coffee. She said that my room was waiting for me. It was the closest thing to home that I had.

After I told her about my adventure in the madhouse, Dina told me that Jesse had been calling continuously. She had his number at the base and she agreed to call him and tell him what happened and that I was okay. It was late, and he said that he would come over the following evening.

I wanted to collect my thoughts before I spoke to him. He came to Dina's at seven the following evening. "Jenny, how are you? I missed you. Dina told me that you were in the hospital. What happened?"

I told him the whole gruesome story; then I wanted to get down to business. "Jesse, *marry me*. I'm pregnant with your child. We could have a good life together. We need each other."

He was not as enthused as I was. "Jennifer, we should think this over. Just because you're pregnant, that doesn't mean that we have to get married. You could have the kid and put it up for adoption. I might even ask around and see if I could find someone who can take care of it. See, Jenny, there are lots of things that you can do."

"Jesse, I made up my mind. I want to get married."

151

"*Look, Jenny; you* should think this over."

"I did think it over. If you don't see it my way, I'm going to go to the base commander and tell him my story. Well, Jesse?"

After a short pause, Jesse responded stoically, "Okay, Jennifer, we'll get married."

One week later, we were married by a justice of the peace. The wedding party consisted of Jesse, me, Dina, and her husband, along with Jack and Ronnie. Jesse started celebrating before the wedding. It was a noon ceremony, and he showed up drunk. Jack and Ronnie managed to restrain him, but he had a little trouble with his "I do's."

I was just starting to show and was glad to get this over with. After the wedding, I called my parents to tell them that I was married. My mother answered the phone and was less than happy to hear from me.

"Hello, Ma. I just called to tell you and Dad that Jesse and I just got married," I said apprehensively.

"So you and that bum *did* get married. Your parents want no part of *your family*. As far as I am concerned, I have no daughter. You will never be welcome in *my* house!"

My mother was still taking care of Robin. I wanted to have my family back together. When I got settled, I wanted Robin.

Jesse and I rented a run-down flat in Sullivan Square, not far from the Charlestown Navy Yard. I had quit my job and was spending my days cleaning the place and preparing for the baby, but my biggest job was Jesse.

Jesse and I never had a honeymoon. As soon as we decided to get married we went shopping for an apartment. After the wedding, we went out to eat, and when we got home, Jesse passed out drunk on the couch. That was how our marriage began. That was also an indication of our future.

Jesse rarely came home after his tour of duty was finished at the base. I would frequently not see him for days. When he did come he was usually drunk. When he did drink he was violent. He would come home drunk, beat me, and then pass out.

I was afraid, and I was fearful for my baby. When he came home drunk, I would cover my stomach with my arms so that he would not hurt the baby.

This pregnancy gave me problems at about six months. I became sicker than I had been with Robin. I had not seen a doctor yet, and this seemed like a good time to start. I went to the Chelsea Naval Hospital for a checkup.

I was a wreck. I was run-down and in poor health. My bruises were also quite apparent. I had a long talk with the doctor. He told me that I needed lots of care and rest. He asked me about Jesse, and I told him about the beatings. He wanted me to report Jesse to his commanding officer. I told him that I would consider it.

When I got home, I told Jesse about the doctor's appointment. I said that he had prescribed some medicine along with lots of rest. I did not tell Jesse that the doctor thought that I should turn him in. I did not want to make a bad situation worse.

For a while Jesse took pity on me and the beatings stopped. It may have been my being in the third trimester. He cut down on the drinking and started to come straight home when he finished his work. He frequently brought Ronnie home with him. He was proud of my cooking and how nicely I had fixed up the apartment. I thought that there was a chance that we could have a marriage. He even tried to be affectionate.

"Hey, do you know something? I love you, Jenny! I don't ever tell you because it might go to your head, and we can't have that, can we?"

I would call my mother frequently. I wanted to see how Robin was doing. She always told me that Robin was well. I was reassured knowing that Robin was taken care of. Occasionally I would hint that Jesse and I should come over to visit her. My mother would never allow it.

"What, you two come over here to visit that little girl! I'm bringing her up properly, to be a little lady. I don't want her to get any bad ideas."

"Please, Ma. Let me come over alone during the day?"

"Look, Jennifer; I don't want you to come over here. I don't want anyone to see you in that condition. I'll never be able to hold my head up again."

I got very depressed and just moped around the house. I felt that I had lost Robin. I was also fearful for the child inside me, but for different reasons. Jesse was very unpredictable. Sometimes he would not come home at all. Sometimes he would come home drunk and in a violent mood. I was more concerned for my unborn child's welfare than I was for my own.

Life with Jesse was schizoid. For all the unpleasant incidents, there were tender moments that gave me hope that he could reform.

One day he received a call from his mother at the base. She was drunk and wanted Jesse to come home and live with her. He tried to explain that his job and his family were in Massachusetts, not Maine. She was not rational, and this call upset him a great deal.

He had a few drinks on the way home. When he came into the apartment he just plopped himself on the couch and stared at the ceiling. I went up to him and asked, "What's the matter, Jesse?"

He stood up, put his arms around me, and said, "Honey, please give me strength. I feel very weak."

We stood there for minutes and held each other. At moments like this, I was optimistic that things could change and we could have a "normal" marriage. I savored the tender moments and tried to forget the bad incidents.

Jesse was behaving himself as I came close to term, and I was keeping my fingers crossed that it would last. I was about a week overdue when Jesse came home in an exceptionally good mood.

"Hey, Jenny. One of my buddies from the base just bought a house in Norwood, and he invited us over. It would be a good opportunity for you to get out of the house."

"Jesse, I'd like to go, but I'm already overdue, and Norwood is quite a way from the naval hospital."

Jesse mussed my hair and said, "Hell, Jenny, you would be ornery enough to go and have that kid tonight just to mess up my night. Well, we won't go. We'll stay here and wait for the baby."

He made me feel guilty. "Okay, Jesse. We'll go." I got dressed, and we left for Norwood.

As soon as we arrived, I knew that I had made a mistake. The house was full of drunken marines. Many had spilled onto the front lawn. Inside the house was a big table loaded with beer coolers and whiskey bottles. The only food I saw was a few cans of peanuts.

Jesse introduced me to all his friends, one of whom suggested that Jesse join them in a card game while the women talked. There was a small group of women sitting in the dining room. I joined them, while Jesse played cards.

As we sat and talked, Jesse would come into the room and kiss me on the cheek, as if to say, "There. I had a few drinks, and I'm okay. Don't worry." I was worried! He was drinking heavily.

As the night wore on, I got a horrible back pain. It would last a few moments and then disappear, only to reappear a short time later. I did not say anything to the other girls. Finally I got one pain so bad that I had to double over. I yelled, "*Jesse-e-e, Jesse-e-e!*" He did not answer; he kept playing cards.

The girls gathered around me. One of them said that I was in labor and should get to the hospital right away. I continued to call for Jesse. Still no answer. Several of the girls grabbed the marines that they were with and told them the situation. They then found Jesse and pulled him from the card game and brought him to me. He was dead drunk as he came into the dining room.

"All right. What's the matter? You just hate to see me have a good time, is *that* it? You're afraid that I might have a drink, so you have to find a reason to make me leave, is that it?"

"*Jesse,* I'm having the baby; I'm in severe pain. We have to leave for the hospital *now!*"

"What a horrible fuckin' time to have a baby, just as I'm startin' to have some fun."

He grabbed my arm and dragged me out to the car, cursing all the way. He threw me into the front seat, then staggered to the driver's side and got in.

The drive from Norwood to Charlestown took close to an hour. Jesse was all over the road. I was sure that he would get into an accident. I yelled at him to slow down and be careful. He pulled the car off to the side of the road, dragged me out of the car, and repeatedly slapped me across the face. I was crying uncontrollably.

"If you don't stop whining, I'm going to give you a reason to cry."

I tried to muffle my sobs as best I could. We got to Charlestown without getting into an accident, but I noticed that we were heading home, not to the hospital. I pointed this out to Jesse.

"We're going home," he replied. "I know that you were faking that shit just to get me to leave the party. Well, you ruined my evening. Are you happy? I'm going home and hit the rack."

When we got back into our apartment, Jesse undressed and went to sleep. My labor pains had been growing stronger; they were stronger than they had been with Robin. I climbed in to bed to see if the pains would let up. As soon as my head hit the pillow, my water broke.

I jumped out of bed and tried to wake Jesse. He did not budge. Panic-stricken, I called my mother to tell her that the baby was coming. I did not give her time to respond. I hung up and called the police.

Minutes later, they arrived. I was screaming as they took me to the police car. I told them I wanted to go to the naval hospital. They turned on the sirens; one of the policemen stayed with me in the backseat as we streaked to the hospital.

I was scared and in great pain as I was helped into a wheelchair at the hospital's emergency entrance. I was greeted by a young sailor eating an apple. He wheeled me into the emergency room, where I was greeted by a doctor. He helped me onto the table, where he examined me, then told me that the baby was coming and there was no time to prep me. I had never experienced such pain in my life.

I delivered by natural childbirth. When it was over, the nurse gave me a beautiful baby boy wrapped in a blanket. I held my son for a few minutes, then handed him back to the nurse. The doctor came in and asked, "Where is your husband? I think that he should be notified that he is a father."

I turned my head and began to cry. I did not answer the doctor at first. When he asked again, I told him where to get in touch with Jesse. I did not tell him that Jesse was passed out drunk at home. I gave him the number to Jesse's unit at the base.

I was lying there staring at the ceiling, feeling sorry for myself, when I saw two boys walk into the room. It was my brother, Sal, and his friend Ernie. Sal walked over to the bed and kissed me on the forehead.

It seems that my mother had a fit after I called her. Her screaming woke up Sal. He thought that I should have company, so he called Ernie and they came over. It was great to have company, any company.

Sal told me that he had seen his nephew and that he was "very cute," then told me about Robin. She was getting big and sassy. I felt better after Sal left. At least someone cared. I fell asleep soon after he left.

The following morning Jesse came to see me. He stumbled in, very hung over. He was ill at ease and at a loss for words. When he bent down to kiss me, he still reeked of booze. I turned my head away from him.

"I've just been to see the baby, and he's very cute. He's got hair all over his body, and his head is a little pointed."

I got very excited. Jesse was describing an ape. I thought that there was something wrong with the baby that the doctor or my brother did not want to tell me. I had just seen the baby for a few moments and did not examine him that closely. I yelled so loudly that a doctor and several nurses ran in.

I told them what Jesse had said, they started to laugh, and when they got a whiff of Jesse they told him to leave. The doctor said, "He must have stumbled down to the lab and looked at one of the animals. I'll bring you your son to put my mind at ease."

My son looked so tiny and helpless. I put him beside me in the bed and looked at him. He was worth every pain that I had gone through. He was squirming around. I put my finger into his hand. He held it and did not want to let go. I kissed him on the head and made him a promise. "As long as I can breathe, I will always love you. You will never do without, no matter what I have to do."

I named him Jesse Jr. Jesse Sr. insisted, and anyway, I did not have a name picked out. I thought it natural for a father to want a son named after him. I took Jesse Jr. home several days later. I took care of him all by myself. He was a wonderful little boy. He was a happy baby and did not give me any trouble.

Although Jesse acted like a doting father, I did not trust him to be alone with the baby. I was afraid that he would hurt his son when he was drinking.

My parents did not see too much of their new grandson. They avoided him, never bought him any presents, and seemed to want to believe that he did not exist. I would speak to my father on the phone, and he would talk about the baby. My mother treated him as though he were the son of the devil. Our conversations about my son were short and terse. She never forgave me or him that he was conceived out of wedlock.

Soon after my son was born, Jesse's mother would visit us regularly. She became a nuisance. She would show up on Friday nights, and she and Jesse would drink away the weekend. I was afraid for the baby.

"Hello, little Jesse. I'm your grandma, Dorothy . . . wassa matter? You look hungry; isn't your mama feedin' youse?"

"*Dorothy,* get away from the baby."

An angry, inebriated Jesse would join in, "That's my mother you're talking to. She has every right to talk to her grandson."

"I DON'T CARE WHO SHE IS! I don't want any drunks near my baby."

Dorothy and Jesse would usually back off and go back to their drinking.

After a while, my mother softened up a little and allowed me to visit Robin. I was allowed into her house, but I was not treated like a daughter and Jesse Jr. was not treated like a grandson.

Once when Jesse Jr. was about six months old, I bundled him up and took the bus to my mother's house. When she opened the door, she immediately made me feel unwelcome.

"Jennifer, I don't want you to take that little monster anywhere near Robin."

"Look, Ma; he's Robin's brother, whether you like it or not. I should take Robin and raise both children together. They are brother and sister. They should be together."

She became enraged. "You husband is an animal. I will never let my granddaughter be raised by an animal."

"Ma, what about Jesse Jr.?"

"What that animal does with his own bastard is his concern. That little monster will grow up to be just like its father. It's in the blood. I don't want that mad dog going anywhere near Robin. That's all there is to it."

I tried, but as usual, I could not get through to my mother. I picked up Jesse Jr. and went home. One month later, Jesse received transfer orders. He was going to Camp Lejeune, North Carolina.

I had mixed feelings when he told me. North Carolina was not within commuting distance of Maine, so I could look forward to weekends without Jesse's mother. On the other hand, I would miss my friends and family. But at least I had been there before, so the area was not unfamiliar.

I had to make a decision about Robin. Although my mother was taking good care of her, I wanted her with me. Even though she did not live with me in Massachusetts, I could visit her regularly and be somewhat of a mother to her. Living in North Carolina, I would rarely see her. Jesse and I would have to move within a month, so I had to make a decision quickly. I decided to talk to my mother again and try to get Robin back.

I called my mother and said that I wanted to come over. I went alone, expecting another vicious argument. After she told me to sit, I explained the situation. "Ma, Jesse just got his orders. He's being transferred to Camp Lejeune, North Carolina. We'll be leaving in a few weeks."

My mother broke out into an unexpected smile. "Jenny, that's wonderful. This move should be good for you. This will give you a new start. You and your husband can start a new life."

"Okay, Ma. Since we are leaving shortly, when would be the best time to pick up Robin?"

I expected all hell to break loose, but my mother was calm. She did not scream. All she did was turn white.

"Look, Jennifer, I think that you should reconsider taking Robin. Your husband is a drunk. He has hurt you; he might hurt Robin. After all, Robin is not his daughter; he may be resentful of that. Living down south with two babies would be very hard on you. Robin is comfortable here. She loves your father and me. She is well fed and clothed and lives in a comfortable home. You could not take care of her this well. It is not fair for you to come in here and uproot her.

"Jennifer, just once, use your head. If you listen to me, I promise you that I will take the baby down south to visit you. When you are settled in, you can have Robin permanently."

I got the battle that I was expecting, but instead of a verbal battle, it was a rational one. My mother's argument made sense. I agreed to her terms.

In the weeks prior to the departure, my mother was very good to me. She did things that she had never done before. She baby-sat with Jesse Jr.; she helped me pack; she cooked for me. She was acting totally different.

About a week before we were to leave, my mother invited me over to her house. I dressed my son and we went to visit Grandma. My mother greeted me warmly and had coffee waiting as I entered her house.

When we sat down she asked, "Jennifer, would you do a favor for your father? We want to cover Robin under your father's hospitalization.

If we got a separate plan for Robin it would be much more expensive. We need you to sign some forms. Could you please do it for us?"

"I don't know, Ma. She should be covered by Jesse's military hospitalization."

"I know, but you and your family will be down south. It will be much easier for us this way. Robin will get better care if we can take her to the hospital of our choice."

"Okay, Ma. You win!"

"That's great, Jenny. We'll have everything ready for your father when he comes home."

My mother made a phone call and returned to me. "Jennifer, we can go right over to the offices of a friend of mine and sign the papers."

We went to the offices of Mario Crocci, attorney-at-law. When we arrived, the papers were waiting. My mother hustled me into a chair next to his desk. Mr. Crocci put the papers in front of me, and I signed them without reading them. After I did, he said, "It's a good thing that you signed custody of Robin over to your mother. It would be messy and expensive if your mother had to go to court to get it."

I closed my eyes and clenched my fists. I was disgusted and shocked that my mother could be this deceitful. I had screwed up again and was afraid that my actions might harm Robin.

My mother could see what I was thinking. "Don't worry, Jenny. I won't use this authority unless there is an emergency. I just did it because I love Robin and I want to be able to take care of her," she said.

My mother drove Jesse Jr. and me home. We did not speak during the trip. I was embarrassed. I could not tell Jesse what I had done. He had berated me for much smaller things.

Jesse bought a beat-up old Chrysler with a trailer hitch. On departure day we loaded up the trailer with our stuff. We got a car seat for Jesse Jr. and he had the backseat all to himself. We stopped by my parents' house before we headed south.

My mother came out with Robin, and I kissed both good-bye. I was able to choke back tears as I kissed Robin. I went over to my father and put my arms around him, and the tears started. He then walked over to Jesse, shook hands with him, and wished us luck. We got into the car and drove away.

We had twenty-four hours to report to Camp Lejeune. Jesse reassured me that it was plenty of time. He also reassured me that it would be a pleasant trip. It was a horrible trip. The car ran horribly and Jesse had to stop several times to fix it. We did not have much money, so we slept in the car instead of a motel. Jesse did not know the roads, so we got lost several times. It was a very long trip.

We finally arrived at Camp Lejeune at about nine in the morning. Jesse reported to his unit and checked in, while the baby and I waited in the car. When Jesse reported in, he inquired about housing. There was no military housing available, and we would be put on a waiting list. The marines in the reception area told him about available housing about ten miles from the base.

There was an old two-family house, owned by an old woman. She was renting out the first-floor apartment. We had to find a place quickly, so we jumped at this opportunity. As soon as Jesse finished checking in, we went looking for this place.

It took us about two hours to find the place. It was out in the country, and the nearest neighbor must have been at least a mile away. The place for rent was in a small white house with a big porch that wrapped itself around the front of the house. Sitting in the car, all I could see was woods, grasslands, and chickens. I had a case of déjà vu. I was reminded of my experience with Bill in North Carolina several years earlier.

I did not mind the woods and grasslands, but I was afraid of birds. I was a city girl, but I knew chickens were birds. I refused to get out of the car with the army of chickens pecking around the car. Jesse asked me why I did not get out of the car. I told him, "I'm afraid of chickens."

He scratched his head. "Hell, if this isn't a pisser. I'm dead tired, I'm hungry, we need a place to live, and you won't get out of the damn car because of some chickens. Come on, honey; get out. I'll chase away the chickens."

"Okay, Jesse, as long as you make sure there aren't any birds around. I'm awfully afraid of birds."

Jesse chased away the chickens. When they were gone, we walked to the front door. The old woman answered the bell and confirmed that she had an apartment available. She showed it to us. It had a bedroom, kitchen, and living room. We would have to share the bathroom with the old woman.

The toilet had no water. We would have to fill the tank with a bucket from a well outside. The place was dirty, smelled of mildew, and was infested with insects. Jesse said that he would take it. I was angry with his decision. When the old lady left, I let him know of my dissatisfaction.

"Jesse, are you crazy? This is a rathole. I *won't* stay here with the baby."

"Jennifer, *we have no choice.* We need someplace to live until military housing comes through. We might not have to wait too long. Look, Jenny; you're good at fixing up places. If you work at it, you can make it look real cute."

"Sure, but I've never built a house before, and this place is going to have to be rebuilt to make it look halfway decent."

I did not change his mind. Jesse and I unpacked the trailer and started to set up housekeeping in this horrible place. I thought to myself, *Thank God my little girl is not here. At least Jesse Jr. can stay in the crib.*

Jesse Sr. did not help me clean up the place. After we unloaded our stuff, I started cleaning, while Jesse collapsed on the couch. I could deal with dirt, it was the insects that gave me trouble. This house must have had some of the biggest ones in the world. When I started cleaning, I disturbed quite a few large bugs. When I saw one, I would scream and run away. This would disturb Jesse, and he would get off the couch in an angry mood.

"Jenny, stop being such a baby. You have to toughen up. These are just bugs. You should be like me. Not afraid of *anything*!"

I tried, but I could not suppress my fear of bugs. When I was opening a drawer, something big and hairy lunged at me. I slammed it shut and started screaming. Whatever was lunging at me was caught in the drawer, and one of its legs was squirming.

Jesse heard me screaming and strode into the bedroom. "Okay, Jenny, I give up. What've you got now?"

"Something jumped out of the drawer at me."

I did not tell him that it was caught in the drawer. He walked up to the dresser and opened the drawer. When he did, the biggest spider that I had ever seen jumped out and onto the floor. It looked as big as a cat. Its body was covered with fur. Jesse turned white. He couldn't kill it by stepping on it. He ran to get a weapon. I took Jesse Jr. and ran outside.

The outside was just as dangerous as the inside. I was surrounded by chickens, so I sought refuge in the car. I sat in the car with Jesse Jr. and awaited rescue from the wild kingdom. After a few minutes Jesse came out of the house. "How long do you expect to hide in the car? If you like, I could get your things and you can live in there."

He chased away the chickens and laughed. I was angry. "*Jesse, I want to go home!*" I knew that it was impossible, but I felt good when I said it. I was awake most of the night watching for little pests.

The next morning Jesse got up to report for his first day on the job. I had nothing to do but clean the house and take care of the baby. There was no telephone, no television, and no modern kitchen appliances. There was an old icebox and a gasoline stove.

The heat was oppressive. I spent much of the day on the porch trying to escape it. I stayed there until the chickens started to gather; then I would retreat inside and do my housework, while trying to avoid the bugs. I found a corner of the porch where I was safe from the poultry and the pests. It was my retreat. I either held Jesse Jr. in my arms or put him in the crib. They were the only places that he was safe.

We were miles from the nearest store. Jesse did not leave me any money, so I could not have bought anything even if there were a store next door. My first day back in North Carolina was very unpleasant!

Jesse came home very late, close to midnight. He had stopped for happy hour at the NCO club and was feeling no pain.

"Jesse, you can't keep this up down here. You have to think of the baby. If anything happens, we're stranded," I told him.

He staggered over to me, mussed my hair, and said, "Don't be such a big baby. Everything will be all right." He went to the crib and started playing with his son.

Jesse and I had different lives. I was confined to a small apartment; he had the whole base to roam around on. Whenever Jesse had some time off, I took him shopping. I wanted to make sure that we had enough food and formula for the baby. Jesse was so unreliable that I could not rely on him to go shopping by himself. He thought the only necessity was beer, and it was the only thing that he would buy if he went by himself.

Camp Lejeune was a huge base, with many NCO clubs and many happy hours. I don't think that Jesse missed any of them. He would leave for work about six in the morning and not return before midnight. He paid no attention to me or the baby. He couldn't have cared if we starved.

On weekends, I would drag him to the PX, the Laundromat, and the Piggly Wiggly. During the week, I was imprisoned, with no money, no transportation.

I was not well. I had had asthma as a child, but it had not bothered me for many years. It came back, and I would be up most of the night wheezing and coughing. I started to lose weight rapidly. Jesse took me to the base hospital.

After the examination, the doctor gave me a shot and told us that I should move out of the area, to help my condition. The climate was aggravating my condition. Jesse assured the doctor that he would put in for a humanitarian transfer. I was skeptical. Upon leaving the hospital, I asked him, "Jesse are you really going to request a transfer?"

"Of course not! There is nothing wrong with you. You just have to get used to the place. You'll be okay."

On the way home I wanted to pick up some baby food and other things. Jesse also wanted to make a stop. He needed a few cases of Budweiser. When I told him that baby food was more important, he just laughed. "If Jesse Jr. runs out of baby food, I'll share my beer with him.

That will make a man out of him," he said. Jesse always thought of himself first. His wife and child always came second.

I was still having asthma attacks and was sick most of the time. Jesse Jr. was about eight months old and starting to toddle around. Taking care of him was almost a full-time job. I was starting to get disgusted. I was getting no help from Jesse Sr. Our home was just a place for him to pass out drunk. He provided no financial support. I had to get a part-time job as a carhop at a fast-food restaurant to feed the baby.

I threatened Jesse that if he didn't sober up and support us, I was going to take the baby and leave him. He ignored me. He did not want to be a husband and a father. He wanted to be a marine and a drunk.

One night, when Jesse did not show up at all, I was thinking how fortunate Robin was that my mother was taking care of her. She was not subjected to this horror. That was a night when I had a bad asthma attack and Jesse Jr. spent most of the evening coughing. I was praying that we did not need any emergency attention, as we were so isolated and Jesse was out drinking.

CHAPTER FIFTEEN

Jesse did not come home until eleven the next morning. He reeked of alcohol, and he had lipstick on his face and on his uniform. He did not even try to hide it. I had been sick the whole night. I felt worse when I saw Jesse.

"Jesse, you no-good alcoholic whoremonger. Your son and I spent a horrible night while you were out partying. You don't give a damn about your family! *Get out of here!* Go back to your whore and your booze!"

He lunged for me and grabbed the top of my dress with his left hand. With his right hand he struck me repeatedly on the top on my head, knocking me to the floor. "You little bitch, you can't talk to me that way! I'll teach you respect, if I have to beat it into you."

He went over to the crib, where Jesse Jr. had started crying, looked at the baby, and said, "Shut the fuck up; you're worse than the bitch that gave birth to you." He then shoved the crib across the floor, so that it knocked against the wall.

My head was pounding, but seeing what Jesse did to my son enraged me. I lunged at him, kicking him in the shin and pounding on his chest with one hand and scratching his face with the other. He started to flail at me with both hands, until he knocked me to the floor. While I was down, he kicked me in the stomach until I felt that I had no breath left. When he was sure that he had done enough damage, he left the house and drove away. It was about an hour before I was able to pick myself off the floor.

I needed help. There was no one here that could help me, so I swallowed my pride and decided to ask my family for help. There was a pay phone in a store over a mile away. I rummaged through the house until I found enough change, picked up the baby, and started walking toward the store. I had no baby carriage, and the heat was oppressive.

After about an hour I arrived at the store, which was next to a trailer park. I was tired, sweating, and barely able to make the last few steps. I asked a lady at the general store to show me to the pay phone. She pointed to the corner of the store. I called my parent's number and found out that I did not have enough change, but fortunately my mother accepted the charges.

"Jenny, hello. Hello, Jenny." It was so good to hear her voice. I was choked up and could not say anything. I stood by the phone and cried. I tried to talk, but the tears muffled my voice. "Jenny, is that you? Hello? Why can't you talk? What's the matter?"

After a few moments, I settled down. "Hello, Ma, I'm okay; I'm just tired. I'm calling from a pay phone in a store. Sorry I haven't called before, but it's difficult to get to a phone. Ma, look; things are very bad here. I've been very sick. My asthma has been terrible. But that's not all. It's Jesse; he's like a madman. We just had a terrible fight. He hit me and almost hurt the baby. The drinking is out of control. I just can't take it any longer. I have to get me and the baby out of here!"

"Jennifer, I told you that man was not human, but you didn't listen. If you want, I can help you get out. What is the name of that airport that you are near?"

"New Bern, Ma, New Bern, North Carolina."

"Okay. I'll have your father arrange to have tickets available there tomorrow. You be there with the baby, and we'll get you back to Boston."

"Okay, Ma, I'll be there."

I needed a ride to the airport. It was doubtful that Jesse would take me. Before walking home, I decided to make one more call. I called Jesse's commanding officer. I did not know his number, but I called Camp Lejeune Information to get the number for the commanding officer of the Nineteenth Transportation Battalion, Jesse's unit.

I got the battalion headquarters and asked to speak to the CO. They told me he was not there, but the executive officer, Major McDonnell, was available. I told him about my problems with Jesse. I cried as I related today's incident, about how Jesse had abused me and the baby, and asked the major if he could provide a ride to the airport.

McDonnell was not sympathetic. He told me, "If the marines wanted Sergeant Rollins to have a wife, they would have issued him one." He did tell me that I would have a ride to the airport at eight in the morning. I told him where I lived, said good-bye, picked up the baby, and started walking. I was hoping that Jesse would not be home tonight, as I was afraid of how he would react.

The walk back seemed twice as long as the walk to the phone. Jesse Jr. felt like he had gained ten pounds. It seemed like it was over one hundred degrees. I could barely breathe by the time I got home. I put the baby in the crib and collapsed on the bed.

When I got up, I packed my stuff and the baby's stuff in four suitcases. I made sure Jesse Jr. had enough to eat on the ride. I put the suitcases by the door and went back to bed. Jesse did not come home that night.

We were waiting for our ride to the airport at eight in the morning when I saw Jesse pull into the driveway. He sprang out of the car and slammed the door. He stormed into the house, grabbed two of the suitcases, ran out to the car, came back, grabbed the other two, and took them out to the car. I picked up the baby and followed him out of the house. Thanks to the major's sick sense of humor, Jesse was my ride to the airport.

Jesse did not speak during the hour-and-a-half ride to the airport. He took out his anger by driving like a madman. I was holding the baby tightly in my lap.

When we got to the airport, Jesse opened the trunk and threw our suitcases on the side of the road, outside the terminal. When I asked him to please take them inside, he responded, "Do it yourself, you fuckin' whore." It took me three trips to take the bags and the baby into the terminal.

Piedmont Airlines did not fly directly from New Bern, North Carolina, to Boston. It made stops in Washington, D.C., and New York City. In New York we had to deplane and catch another airline to Boston. In New York, I was in the Piedmont terminal with four suitcases and Jesse Jr. when I saw a familiar face. It was my mother. She was there to assist me on the last leg of my trip. I needed help, since I had an asthma attack on the plane.

I was very ill by the time Jesse Jr. and I arrived in Boston. My asthma, along with the events of the last two days, had weakened me. We took a cab to my parents' house. I hugged my father and ran into Robin's room, where she was napping.

I went back into the living room, where I collapsed into an armchair. My mother recommended that I see her doctor. I said, *"No, thank you,"* after my other experience with my mother's medical referral. I decided to go the Chelsea Naval Hospital for an examination.

The following morning, I left the baby with my father and went to the hospital with my mother. I waited about an hour to see the doctor. He gave me a complete examination. I had to run around the hospital to get blood tests and X rays. When it was over, he gave me a shot for the asthma. He told me that I was undernourished and I should improve my diet. He also told me that I was pregnant. I screamed, *"Ooooh, noooo!"*

I wanted to run screaming down the hall. I threw my hands up and walked around the examination room yelling, *"No, no, no!"* I was hoping things would begin to settle down for me. I was going to have another child, and Jesse was running around scot-free. He was free to drink and chase women. I knew what I had to do. I had to get a job so that I could support my growing family.

When I composed myself, I went to the reception area, where my mother was waiting for me. I told her, "The doctor gave me a shot for the asthma and told me that I should eat better, but other than that, I'll be okay."

When we arrived home, Robin was playing with Jesse Jr. Robin was treating him as if he were her doll. I ran over to Robin, picked her up, and hugged her. I don't think she recognized me, because she struggled and screamed.

When I put Robin down, my mother took me into one of the bedrooms and showed me a crib that she had bought for Jesse Jr. My father picked him up and put him in it. I was thrilled and thanked my parents.

We went back out to the living room. I told my parents, "I'm sure that I did the right thing leaving Jesse. Life with him was just unbearable."

My mother agreed. "You're lucky that you left when you did. That bum could have ruined your life."

"Look, Ma; I just don't want to talk about him."

"Jennifer, you're fortunate that you came home. You were probably living like an animal down there. I can see that you have lost weight. Wasn't that slob feeding you? Well, anyway, you're better off here than being barefoot and pregnant down there." I almost choked when she said the word "pregnant."

I was content at my parents' house. The next few weeks passed quickly. The asthma attacks stopped and I was putting on some weight. I was not yet two months pregnant and had not started to show yet. I did not tell my parents and was worried how I would deal with it in the coming months.

I was upset that I had not heard from Jesse. Even if he were angry with me, he should feel some concern for his son. I would try not to spend too much time thinking of Jesse Sr. The pain was too fresh in my mind.

When I was home about a month, I received a call from Jesse. I asked him what he wanted.

"Jenny, I want you and Jesse back. I had about a month to think about things, and I realize that I was wrong. I want the chance to make things right."

"I've had plenty of time to think, too. I don't think that I want to spend the rest of my life with a violent drunk."

"But, Jenny, things will be different. I've changed. I won't drink anymore; I'll stay at home nights and take care of you and the baby. I swear I've changed."

"Look, Jesse, you've had many chances and you've blown them all."

"Well, if you don't believe me, *fuck you!*" He hung up.

When I told my parents that Jesse had called, my mother became incensed. I had not spoken about him since my first day back home. My mother's anger was released.

"Why the hell is that bum calling you? Didn't he do enough damage? After all, we paid for your plane ticket, not him. I wish that we never heard of him. That worthless creep is only good for one thing, making babies."

My heart sank when she said that. I had kept my secret, but I knew that I could not keep it much longer.

Later in the day, I received another unpleasant phone call. It was from Jesse's mother. I had not heard from her since I left for Camp Lejeune. She had not changed. She was drunk and slurring her words.

"Jennifer, why didn't you call me? You could of least let me know how my grandson was doing. Y'know, you upset Jesse somethin' awful when you left. Jesse Jr. is his son, too. Why did you do a dumb thing like that?"

"Look, Dorothy; I just got rid of one drunk! I don't want another one." I hung up the phone.

I could not rid myself of the Rollins family. Jesse called the next night. He was stubborn, insisting, "Jenny, you have to come back home. I miss you very much." He was also contentious. "I hope that you don't have a boyfriend up there. If I caught you with someone else, I'd kill the both of you."

Jesse started to call every night. Our conversations were short and unpleasant. I was always upset when our conversations ended. It was as though he was aggravating me on purpose. This was also a difficult pregnancy, and Jesse only caused more anxiety.

I could eat very little without vomiting. I spent many days sick in bed. My mother suspected something and wanted me to see a doctor. She never guessed that I was pregnant again. I knew that I had to keep my secret as long as possible.

I was up against a wall, again. I would be showing very soon, but I could not tolerate the verbal abuse that I would get from my mother.

Jesse was still calling regularly, promising to change if I went back to him. I did not believe him, but I had to make a decision soon. I chose what I perceived to be the lesser of two evils. I decided to go back to Jesse, after making him promise to quit drinking, stay at home at night, and be a good father. He also had to send me the money for the trip.

I was skeptical of Jesse's promises, but I knew that I could not live with my parents any longer. With another child on the way, I could not live independently. The third alternative was returning to Jesse.

Hours after I agreed to go back to Jesse, I received a call from his mother. It seemed like he had called his mother asking for the money to pay for my passage to North Carolina. "Jennifer, why can't your parents pay for your trip? Why does my son have to pay for it?" she asked.

I considered it an easy enough question. "*Your son* has to pay for it because it is *his responsibility.* I left because of him. I don't care how he gets the money."

"I don't see why you need plane fare. Why don't you take the bus? The Greyhounds are very comfortable. They even have toilets."

"I said *plane fare* and I meant *plane fare!*"

Dorothy became very angry. "Look, you spoiled little Wop; if I'd have my way, you'd walk." She hung up.

As usual, Dorothy was drunk. I was hoping that she would see the light when she sobered up. Jesse would usually drink away his pay and apparently had had to rely on his mother's assistance in supplying my passage. About two hours later, Dorothy called back. She had not sobered up.

"Okay, Jennifer, we'll do it your way. I'll mail you a check to cover the fare to Camp Lejeune. Just tell me how much it is and where you're livin' now."

I gave her that information. After I did, she began to give me a lecture on the responsibilities of a wife.

That evening at dinner, I announced my plans to return to Jesse. I was not surprised at my mother's reaction.

"How can you go back to that animal after the way that he treated you and the baby? Beating you! Starving you! I think that you're crazy; that's what I think. I hate that man, and I'll never forgive him for what he did. *Never!*"

"Ma, it's not fair that you and Dad have to support me. It's Jesse's responsibility, and he has to face up to it. Jesse's family is paying the fare back to North Carolina. I'm going back because I have to, and that's all there is to it."

"Jennifer, you are making another *big* mistake. Jesse and his goddamn family are just a bunch of no-good drunks. He doesn't give a *damn* for you or your child!"

"Ma, I'll be leaving in a few days, as soon as his mother sends the money."

"Please, this may be your last chance to change your mind. That

169

animal could kill you and the baby. Do something intelligent, for once in your life. Stay here! Don't commit suicide!"

"I'm sorry, Ma. It's something that I have to do." I stood up and went to my room.

Two days later, I received $150 from Jesse's mother. As soon as I did, I made reservations, and called Jesse and told him my flight number and arrival time. He promised to meet me at the airport.

I spent the following morning running around gathering my things and the baby's things. I did not want to leave, but I could not bear my mother's reaction to my pregnancy. I was willing to risk life with Jesse rather than face my mother's scorn. I wanted to do the right thing. I wanted a family life. I had that chance with Jesse. I would risk a lot to have it, including my life.

At eleven I left for the airport. My father hugged me and wished me luck. My mother and Aunt Theresa drove me and Jesse Jr. to the airport. Our luggage barely fit into the trunk. We just made our flight. After checking the luggage, I carried the baby through the terminal and onto the crowded plane.

The first available seat was next to a tall brunette who looked as though she had stepped off the cover of a fashion magazine. I plopped myself into the aisle seat, with Jesse Jr. on my lap. A baby is an excellent icebreaker. The brunette and I began talking immediately. Her name was Sandy Webster, but her maiden name was DiGiovanni. She was from New York but was visiting relatives in Boston. Her husband was also in the marines. We had so much in common and spent the whole trip chatting. We were both city girls living the vagabond military life. The time went quickly.

Sandy didn't like the military life either. But her husband was not a lifer, like Jesse. When his enlistment was up, he was getting out. They lived in a trailer park outside Camp Lejeune and did not have any children. She played with Jesse Jr. the entire trip.

When we landed in New Bern, we exchanged addresses. She gave me her phone number; I wished that I had a phone number to give her. Her husband, David, was talking to Jesse at the gate. When they saw us, they rushed toward us and hugged their respective wives. Jesse took his son and held him close. Jesse and I made plans to get together with Sandy and David. We got in our cars and went home.

Jesse told me that the government housing came through. We would soon be living in a nice development, Midway Park, near the main gate of Camp Lejeunc. Our new home would be available in about a month. Until then we would be living in the same old dump.

Jesse was sober. So far he was keeping his promise. He was very affectionate during the drive home. Even though I had Jesse Jr. on my lap, his father was kissing and snuggling with me. I did not tell him that I was pregnant.

I felt sick when we arrived at our house. It was worse than I remembered. Jesse was not much of a housekeeper. I don't think the place was cleaned since I left. I had tried to make it at least livable, but due to Jesse's neglect, it had reverted to a pigpen. I proceeded to make it presentable for the remainder of our stay there.

Housing was not my major concern; Jesse was. He was very sweet and affectionate, but he could change very quickly. I wanted to believe his reassurances. Just after we walked into the house, he took the baby from my arms and put him in the crib. Jesse put his arms around me, kissed me, and said, "Everything will be okay from now on. You just wait and see, honey. I love you, and I learned a lesson. Honest, I have. I won't ever hurt you again." I desperately wanted to believe him.

Things went smoothly for the next month. Jesse stayed away from the booze, and I was hopeful that things really would change. I was busy preparing for our move to Midway Park. Jesse took me over there and showed me our new house, a small tract house with two bedrooms and a little yard. It was in a development with hundreds of similar houses and seemed like a palace compared to where we lived now.

I bought three rooms of furniture on credit, together with curtains, dishes, and the other stuff needed to begin life in a new house. When we did move in, one of the first things I did was have a phone installed.

Jesse Jr. was just starting to walk. He was getting fat and could not go too far. He would take one step and fall, get up, and try again. He was a joy to watch. He had deep blue eyes and hair white as snow. He was very attached to me. He would scream whenever I left him. I had done everything to spoil him, but I didn't care.

I told Jesse that I was pregnant just before we moved. He was very nonchalant, saying, "That's great, Jenny. Jesse Jr. will have a little playmate and will not get spoiled. You'll have to divide your attention between two babies."

I laughed. "I'll love my next child three times as much, because it will be my third."

Jesse pulled me into his arms. "Jenny, you know, I wish that I met you before I messed up my life. I want you to know that whatever I did, I love you."

Jesse and I became very close to Sandy and David. We spent a lot of times at each other's homes. Sandy would baby-sit for Jesse Jr. Sandy's mother even sent little gifts for him.

Things were going well until we received a letter from Jesse's

171

mother. In the letter Dorothy said she missed Jesse very much and would be coming down to visit. I did not want her and expressed my feelings to Jesse. He was angry for the first time since I came back.

"She's my mother and she is welcome in *my* house. You have *no* say in the matter."

"But, Jesse, she's an alcoholic. If the two of you get together again, there will be trouble. I don't want you drinking. She will only bring out the worst in you. Think of Jesse Jr. Think about the baby on the way. Think of *me*!"

"I don't give a shit. She is my mother and she is welcome here!"

The following day, I took the baby to Sandy's house and talked to her about my problems with Jesse's mother. We drank coffee and talked. I told her all about Dorothy's alcoholism and how I believed that she was a bad influence on Jesse. Sandy sympathized with me and promised to visit me every day as long as Dorothy stayed. Sandy did not drink. Maybe we could overwhelm Dorothy with our sobriety.

Dorothy arrived about a week later, by train. Jesse picked her up at the depot. The first thing that she did when she walked through the door was ask for a beer.

"I'm sorry, Dorothy, but we don't have any in the house. I don't like alcohol here," I replied.

"I don't care what you like here. *Jesse,* go out and get a few cases."

I did not say anything; I just gave him a dirty look. He avoided my eyes and went out the door.

I was so angry, I did not talk to Dorothy while Jesse was gone. I went into the baby's room, leaving her alone in the living room. Jesse came back about a half hour later with two cases of beer. I remained in the bedroom while mother and son opened a case of Budweiser.

I stayed out of the living room while the two drunks did their thing. While I was in the kitchen, I heard Dorothy go into Jesse Jr.'s bedroom. He was standing on the floor, and Dorothy was trying to get him to walk toward her. She was sitting on a footstool with her legs open, and a can of beer in her hand. Jesse walked into the room at the same time I did.

I walked over to where the baby was standing, picked him up, and started to walk out of the room. Dorothy turned to her son and asked, "Jesse, are you afraid to have me near your son?"

"Of course not, Mom!"

Jesse walked over to me and tried to take the baby away from me. The baby screamed as he became the object of the tug-of-war. I was able to shove him out of the way, but he stumbled toward me. I turned to Dorothy.

"I don't care what Jesse said! I don't want my son near a couple of drunks. If you don't like it, you can get the hell out and go back to Maine."

I ran out of the room with the baby in my arms. Jesse stumbled after me cursing. "That's no fuckin' way to talk to my mother. I want you to get back here and apologize. If you don't, I'll beat the shit out of you!"

Just then the bell rang. Sandy and David were at the front door. I was embarrassed at the scene that confronted my guests. The living room was littered with beer cans, the place reeked from alcohol, and I was being pursued by two drunks.

After I opened the door and greeted them, Sandy addressed Jesse. "I'm surprised to see you drinking. I thought that you had given it up."

Jesse smiled and replied, "You know how it is. Hey, Sandy, I want you to meet my mother. She's visitin' us from Graysville, Maine."

"Hi, Sandy. I'm glad to meet ya. I'm glad to meet any friends of the family. Ya know, Jesse ain't the only marine in the family; I got a brother that retired—"

I let Dorothy bore Sandy and David with her family history while I put Jesse Jr. to bed.

When I returned to the living room, Dorothy was continuing with her family history and Sandy and David were listening politely. Dorothy and Jesse were the only ones drinking and were halfway through the second case of beer by the time Sandy and David left, about two hours later.

I walked them to the car. Sandy shook her head as she said, "Jenny, I really feel sorry for you. You have a couple of real winners. You are going to have some serious trouble. If you like, I can keep little Jesse at our place for a while. He'd be safe there, and it would be no trouble for me."

"Thanks a lot, Sandy, but I should be able to keep things under control. If I can't, I'll call you. Bye."

They got into their car and drove off as I returned to the house. I was greeted by Dorothy's complaint: "Jenny, you know, your friends were pretty cold to me. They hardly spoke and they didn't drink nuttin'."

"You're just upset because they're not alcoholics like you and your son. If they were drunks, you would've loved them."

Dorothy was too drunk to respond; in fact, she and Jesse were too drunk to move. I went to bed and left them to finish off what was left of their second case of beer.

In the middle of the night I was awakened by a dull thud in the living room. When I went out to investigate, I found Jesse passed out on the floor, surrounded by beer cans. He had urinated all over himself. I tried to wake him but couldn't. The combined urine/beer stench was more than I could handle.

I found Dorothy in the bathroom, passed out in a pool of vomit. I began to gag as I tried to wake her. She couldn't move. I let her lie there as I ran back to the bedroom. I was not able to fall asleep that night.

In the morning, I dressed, fed Jesse Jr., and drove him to Sandy's house. I told Sandy about what had happened last night and asked her to keep Jesse Jr. for the day. She readily agreed.

When I arrived home, Jesse and Dorothy were both awake and sitting in the living room. Just as I closed the door behind me, Jesse ran up to me and slapped my face. "Where the hell have you been?"

I shoved him away and said, "Get out of my house, the both of you! If you don't leave, I'll call the police. Jesse, everything was going along okay until that alcoholic mother of yours showed up. I can't take it anymore! Both of you, *out!*"

Jesse ran toward me with fire in his eyes. "Jennifer, I don't give a shit what you think. Get your ass into the bathroom, and *clean* the motherfucker."

"Clean the motherfucker yourself!"

Jesse hit me on the side of the head, knocking me to the floor. While I was down he kicked me repeatedly. I passed out from the pain.

I later learned that Sandy came to my house soon after I passed out and found me on the floor. Both Jesse and his mother were gone. Sandy called the ambulance, which took me to the naval hospital at Camp Lejeune.

When I came to, I was being attended to by a very stern-looking commander, who introduced himself as Dr. Wilson. He appeared to be in his midfifties, with gray hair. He sat on the stool beside me and asked how I was feeling. I told him about my abdominal pain. He told me that the X rays had revealed a fractured pelvis and I was in danger of losing the baby.

When he asked me the cause of my injuries, I turned my head away from him. I was sure that he knew, but talking about my life with Jesse would only add to the pain. Instead, I asked the doctor if someone could check on my son. He said that Mrs. Webster was taking care of the baby and he was fine.

"Mrs. Rollins, I know that your husband did this to you. I know why you don't want to talk about it. I'm going to call your husband's commanding officer and report this."

Just then, Jesse walked into the room. "Jenny, are you okay?"

Dr. Wilson stood up. "Are you this woman's husband?"

Jesse replied, "Yes, sir."

"Sergeant Rollins, I know that you have done this to your wife, and I'm reporting this to your commanding officer. If you so much as pat her on the head, I'm going to guarantee you a court-martial. Do you understand, Sergeant?"

Jesse glanced at me as he answered, "Yes, sir."

Dr. Wilson left the room, leaving me alone with Jesse. There was no remorse in him. "What the fuck did you tell the doctor? You don't look to be in such bad shape. Y'know, your big mouth could get me court-martialed."

I wanted to beat him as badly as he beat me. "Jesse, I don't want you near the baby. He is safe with Sandy. If you go near him, I *will* have you court-martialed."

"Don't worry; I won't go near the little pussy."

"*Jesse,* I also want that mother of yours to be gone *immediately.* I never want to see her again."

"Why should she go? She just got here!"

"She had better be gone by the time that I get out of here! She can get a room or return to Maine or *go to hell* for all I care. As long as she is *out!*"

He scowled at me and left. I stayed in the hospital for a week, and he never visited me.

It took about a week before I was able to walk with crutches or a cane. I did not lose the baby but had continuous abdominal pain. Sandy visited me every day in the hospital. She became very attached to the baby and thought he was a "little doll." When I was discharged, Sandy drove me home.

When I went back to my house, I did not know what to expect. The house was empty. I didn't know if Dorothy had left or if she and Jesse were out partying. The doctor told me that I needed bedrest, so Sandy offered to keep Jesse Jr. until I felt better. She would bring the baby over every day to visit. I was very grateful to Sandy. I don't know what I would do without her.

I did not see Jesse until the next evening. He staggered into the bedroom. "Hey, Jenny! What are you doing in bed? You should have a hot meal ready for me and not be goofing off. Where the hell is my son? Did you *give* him to that stupid Italian girlfriend of yours? You fuckin' Wops stick together."

I did not answer Jesse. It does not take much to provoke him when he is drunk. I could not take any more beatings!

"Well, Jenny. You got your wish. My mother is gone. But I'm going to get even with you for this one."

CHAPTER SIXTEEN

I was not due to have the baby for at least another month, but I went into labor early. I had not seen Jesse for two days, so I called Sandy. She and David took me to the hospital. I was at the hospital for about twelve hours, and it was a difficult birth. It was worth it when I saw my son. He was beautiful, with dark eyes and dark hair. I was grateful for my wonderful children.

I finally saw Jesse, a day after I gave birth. "I'm sorry that I wasn't here, but I got tied up. Hey, it seems that you got a thing for boys. What are you going to call him?" he asked.

"I thought that I'd call him Todd."

Jesse smiled and said, "Well, that's a good name." Jesse talked as if nothing had happened. I was just glad that he was sober.

Sandy came in minutes later. She kissed me on the cheek and said, "Jenny, I've got a big surprise for you. Just close your eyes." I did. Seconds later she said, "Okay, you can open them now."

My parents were standing at the foot of the bed. My mother walked over, leaned over the edge of the bed, and hugged me. I started to cry. "Ma, Dad, when did you get here? Did you know that I was going to have a baby? How did you find Sandy?"

"We were worried about you. We came for a surprise visit. We met Sandy when we went to your house. She told us everything. Why didn't you tell us that you were pregnant? We just saw your new son, and we think that he is handsome."

"I should be going home soon. Then we can be together."

"Don't worry about a thing. We're staying with Sandy and David. Jenny, can you get out of bed? There is something that I want to show you."

I struggled out of bed and walked over to the window with my mother. Robin and Jesse Jr. were playing on the grass with David. I waved to them and started crying again. When Jesse Jr. saw me, he started bouncing about and waving to me. Robin stood up and waved with both hands.

I walked back to bed and climbed in. Jesse had been quiet since my other visitors arrived. I'm sure that he was afraid that my parents would want me to go back with them, so he was trying to be on his best behavior. "Mrs. Vicci, why don't you and Mr. Vicci stay at our place? We'll have the whole family together."

"That's okay, Jesse; we'll stay at Sandy's place."

Everyone but Jesse wished me well, kissed me good-bye, and left. When they were gone, Jesse asked, "Jennifer, are you going to tell anyone what happened?"

I was very tired when I responded, "Jesse . . . no, Jesse, if you can just behave yourself, I won't tell anyone."

He grunted, "Okay," and left.

I was lying in the hospital bed reflecting on the mess that I was in and the problems that lay ahead. I knew Jesse's promise would be as short-lived as his other promises. The only thing that was certain was that "the other Jesse," the mean alcoholic, would surface soon and I would be faced with another confrontation.

Jesse was a coward. When he was drunk, he would beat me. During his alcoholic binges, he did not start fights with other men, let alone other marines. He saved his violence for me. I was no threat to him. I was a woman who was a foot shorter and a hundred pounds lighter than he was. I was a perfect opponent for a big coward.

I was not just fearful for myself. I was afraid for my two sons. I was afraid that Jesse would direct his violence against them. They were more defenseless than I was. Before Todd was taken back to the maternity ward, I looked into his eyes and tears came into mine. I thought that he was so vulnerable, so small and helpless, living in the same house as Jesse.

I wanted to run, run to safety with my sons, but I had no place to go. I probably could go back to my parents, but I faced another type of cruelty with my mother. She was not an alcoholic, but she also had two very different personalities. In her own way she could be as cruel as Jesse.

Dr. Wilson came to see me. I immediately asked when I would be discharged. "You're scheduled to be released tomorrow, but with that Neanderthal that you got for a husband, I'd keep you here a lot longer. Do you have anyone other than him to help you at home?"

"My parents are visiting from Massachusetts, plus I've got a very good friend who can help me."

When Dr. Wilson left, I went to the pay phone in the hall and called Jesse. I told him that I would be going home tomorrow and gave him a list of things to get. The following morning, Jesse showed up at eight and took Todd and me home.

I did not tell my parents that I was coming home, but they were at my home when we arrived. They looked surprised to see me. Jesse Jr. was especially happy to see me. As soon as I walked through the door he started yelling, *"Mommy, Mommy!"* He then toddled over to me, while still yelling, wrapped his arms around my legs, and *bit me*! I guess he was upset that I had left him and he was showing some of his father's violent tendencies. It was not a reassuring thought.

I handed Todd to my mother, while I walked over to Robin, who was sitting on the couch. I sat next to her and put my arms around her and hugged and kissed her. She looked like a little doll in a black and white sailor suit.

Just then, Todd began to cry. I walked over to my mother and took him in my arms and cradled him until he stopped. Jesse Jr. was curious, so I knelt and said, "Jesse, look at what I brought you; a little baby brother." He did not seem too impressed. After he looked at Todd for several seconds, I stood up and put Todd in his new crib.

After I tucked the baby in, I turned around and saw Jesse Jr. turn blue and faint. My mother ran over to him, screaming incoherently. My father saw the pandemonium, walked over to where Jesse Jr. lay and picked him up. Dad patted the baby on the back as he walked around the room. Slowly Jesse Jr. came out of it and began to cry. I was also in tears as I took him from my father's arms.

Before anyone could say anything, I told Jesse, "Hurry up; we have to take the baby to the hospital immediately." He ran out to the car. I followed right behind holding Jesse Jr.

We sped off toward the naval hospital. About ten minutes later, we were taking the baby into the emergency room. We told the physician on-duty what had happened. He took the baby into an examining room. I was very anxious as I waited outside.

After what seemed like hours, the doctor came out. "Mrs. Rollins, it doesn't appear serious. He had a temper tantrum. He just held his breath until he passed out. He is probably jealous of the new baby. Just reassure him that you still love him and he does not have to feel threatened by his new brother."

I was relieved. While Jesse drove us home, I held the baby extra tight and snuggled with him all the way home.

My house was mass confusion. Three small children were a handful. I still had problems getting around due to my fractured pelvis. Sandy and my parents tried to help, but I considered the children my responsibility.

As usual, Jesse was no help. The only difference this time was that there were others who witnessed his apathy toward his family. Evenings and weekends he watched television, usually sports. He did nothing to help with the children or the housework. My parents noticed his attitude and questioned me about it. I only shrugged. I did not consider his apathy that bad, and I did not want them to know about the abuse.

My parents stayed about two weeks. I tried to get closer to Robin. She was my daughter, but she considered her grandparents to be her parents. She felt alienated from me. When Sandy and I took Robin shopping, she turned down the clothes that we offered to buy her. She said, "Keep the dress; I want Mommy and Daddy." I was insulted, but I understood.

Jesse was relieved when my parents left. He had stayed sober the entire two weeks, and the strain was starting to show. After he drove my parents and Robin to the airport, he stormed back into the house and said, "Well, Jenny, I behaved myself for your parents. It's time that I did a little livin'. I earn my pay, I'm goin to spend it on me. If you need money to feed your little brats, get a job!"

Jesse reverted to his old ways. What little support he had provided disappeared. He showed no interest in his sons. I don't think that I could have gotten by without Sandy and David. They came by almost every night, bringing groceries and other stuff that I needed to care for my children.

I knew that I had to get a job. I could not depend on charity. Sandy tried to talk me out of it, saying that she and David could continue to help. But supporting my children was my responsibility.

I applied for a job as a carhop at the same restaurant that I had worked at previously. I would work split shifts and be paid thirteen dollars for forty hours, plus tips, which was not much, even in 1963. But it was enough so that I could feed and take care of my babies. Jesse never came home, so there was no reason to tell him about the job. Sandy would baby-sit while I worked, and David would drive me to work and pick me up at night.

The drive-in had a loud rock and roll band. The marines would drive in by the carload to have a beer and listen to the music. Sandy came to visit me at the end of my first night. I had made about twenty dollars in tips. I felt like a millionaire!

My happiness ended when I got home that night. Jesse was eating at the kitchen table. There were about a half-dozen empty beer cans on the table.

"Jennifer, where the fuck have you been?"

"Working!"

"*Working!* Working where?"

"I got a job carhopping at the drive-in."

I could feel the anger building. "Why the fuck do you have to get a

179

job serving a bunch of horny, drunk marines? You're just a fuckin' little pig, running around in your skivvies with your ass hanging out. Your job is *here*! Quit that fuckin' job and stay home."

"Jesse, you can rant and rave as much as you want. As long as you don't support your kids, someone has to." I was tired and went to bed. Jesse stayed in the kitchen, drinking and cursing.

The following morning, I found getting out of bed very difficult. My fractured pelvis had not completely healed, plus my stomach pains had resumed. Both children were crying and hungry. Jesse Jr. had climbed out of the crib and while playing with a container of baby powder spilled it on the floor. When he was bored with the powder, he found some liquid shoe polish, which he also spilled. He then walked through it, leaving footprints throughout the place.

I gave both boys baths, then fed them. While Jesse Jr. was eating and Todd had his bottle, I cleaned the house and made Jesse's dinner in case he came home that evening. By the time six o'clock rolled around and I had to go to work, I was pooped. I was dead on my feet when my shift began, and the drive-in was so busy that I did not have a chance to sit down.

That was my daily routine. The strain took its toll. When I went to the doctor for my checkup, he told me that I was run-down and in no shape to maintain that schedule. He wanted me to quit my job. I would have liked to quit my job at the drive-in and stay home with the kids. Many military wives could, but their husbands did not drink away their paychecks.

Jesse was a staff sergeant. Although he did not make big money, it was enough to support a family in government housing, with PX privileges.

I could not deal with Jesse. He wanted a family, but he did not want the responsibilities. He wanted a home, and he wanted his freedom. He put a terrible strain on me, and there was nothing that I could do about it. The only options were staying with Jesse or going back to my parents. I chose the lesser of two evils.

I was always dealing with two Jesses. There was the drunk, sometimes cruel, sometimes apathetic Jesse. There was also the "good Jesse." When he was sober, he sometimes acted like an affectionate, concerned husband. I probably saw enough of this "Jesse" to keep me with him.

Just when I saw enough of the "bad Jesse" and I would want to leave, I would get a dose of the "good Jesse." It was like a drug, a ray of hope, a dream. I wanted to believe that the "bad Jesse" would someday disappear and I could build a life with his alter ego. Jesse was crazy. I was young, innocent, and a dreamer.

180

Occasionally Jesse would surprise me. He did one night when I arrived home from work. He was sitting on the couch sober and watching television. That itself was a surprise. "Jenny, I changed and fed the kids. They are both sleeping."

I did not want to know what he was up to, so I went into the kitchen and made coffee. He followed me, sat beside me, and said, "Look, honey; I want you to quit that job. I'm not going to hit you. I've been doing a lot of thinking. Maybe if you weren't working we could try to be a family, go hunting and do things like that together."

I lit a cigarette and looked at him. "Well, Jesse, if you want to be a family there's plenty that you can do. I won't quit working. I can't depend on you for food or money for the boys. You're going to have to prove yourself to me."

He walked over and put his arms around me. "Jenny, you know that I love you. I'm a messed-up guy, and I need your help."

I repressed a smile. I wanted to believe him but couldn't. "Look, Jesse, if you want to prove yourself, you can come home nights and take care of the kids. You can also drive me to and from work. I think that we have imposed enough on Sandy and Dave."

"Okay, Jenny, I'll do everything that you ask, if you'll go hunting with me."

"Jesse, you're nuts. That's a crazy bargain. Anyway, you should know that I'm too squeamish to kill anything."

"Oh, come on. You'll enjoy it. It will be a weekend in the fresh air. Just you and me together."

I did not know what was going through Jesse's mind. He might want to shoot me and claim that it was an accident. I was afraid of Jesse and suspicious. But I was also hopeful. "Okay, Jesse, I'll give it a try. I'll arrange for Sandy to watch the kids this weekend."

For the remainder of the week, Jesse kept his word. He was home every night. He drove me to and from work, and he took care of the kids when I worked. I made sure Todd had enough formula for the weekend and prepared for my big adventure with Jesse.

Jesse got me out of bed very early Saturday morning. He dressed me in red so nobody would shoot me by mistake. Sandy picked up the kids Friday night, so I was already to go.

We drove about a half hour into a heavily wooded area. Jesse took two guns out of the backseat, and I followed him down a small trail. After walking five minutes, Jesse stopped and told me to "stay here" while he scouted around. The spot he picked was behind a clump of trees, overlooking the dirt trail.

He left me one of the rifles. I knew nothing about guns. Jesse gave me a ten-second lesson: "Look, all you do is look through the sights and pull the trigger. There is nothing to it."

I was terrified and regretted my decision to come. I whistled to take my mind off the situation. When I did, Jesse came running back like a madman, screaming, "What the fuck are you doing? Are you a dummy or somethin'?"

"What are you talking about? I'm not doing anything."

"Honey, were you whistling or not?"

"Yes, I was whistling."

"Well, don't, okay?" He shrugged and went off into the woods again.

As I was sitting on the ground, I spotted four eyes in the distance. It looked like two hunters. I thought that I should warn Jesse, so that he did not shoot them by mistake. I could not see him, so I shouted, *"Jesse-e-e!"* The two men heard me and ran like crazy in the other direction.

Jesse also heard me. He was fuming as he ran to where I was sitting. "What the hell are you doing? I had one of those deer in my sights. Why did you shout? You scared them away!"

"Jesse, I thought that they were two men. I did not want you to make a mistake and shoot people."

"Oh, shit."

Jesse went back into position to shoot more deer or men or whatever it was that he was hunting. I stayed hidden, hoping that Jesse would find whatever he was looking for and we could go home.

After I was in the woods for a couple of hours, nature called. Being a city girl, I assumed that there were toilet facilities in the woods for hunters. After all, the Boston Common had a toilet! I thought that Jesse would know where these facilities were, so I called out to him, *"Jesse-e-e!"*

Jesse was angry as he approached me. "Okay, honey, I give up. What is it now?" he asked.

"Jesse, I have to go to the bathroom; where is the ladies' rest room?"

"What ladies' rest room?"

"You know, the one that the state builds in the forest for hunters."

He took me by the hand, saying, "Why, sure, Jenny, come with me." He took me up a hill, behind a big tree. "Your bathroom, my lady."

"What bathroom?"

"Look, dummy; there are no bathrooms in the woods. You have to go behind a tree."

"No way, Jesse. I want to go to a gas station."

"Either do it here or hold it in; I don't give a shit. I'm going to get in some hunting if it kills me." He returned to his spot and left me alone.

I returned to my spot, sat, and waited for Jesse to get finished with his hunting so we could go home.

I was afraid of birds, even domesticated ones. I reacted badly to chickens, and I reacted even worse to a bird that landed near me. It was a small bird with dark coloring that landed on the ground within ten feet of me. I looked at it, and it stared back at me. I picked up the gun, pointed it toward the bird, and pulled the trigger. The blast knocked me to the ground, but the bird flew off. I no longer had to go to the bathroom. I had urinated in my pants.

Jesse came running over toward me, took one look, threw his hat to the ground, and said, "I don't even want to know what happened this time." He pulled me to my feet and said, "I've had enough for one day; let's go." He walked very quickly toward our car. I tried to explain about the bird, but Jesse wouldn't listen. I was glad that I was getting a chance to change my clothes.

On the ride home, Jesse took his hat off, swatted me with it and said, "You're a dumb broad, but I love you." I was glad that he was not angry.

I went home and changed; we then went to Sandy's to pick up the kids. Jesse Jr. ran toward me. I picked him up and twirled him around. While I was greeting my kids, David asked Jesse what he had brought back. Jesse laughed. "Dave, never take your wife hunting. These city girls just can't hack it." While we were sitting and drinking coffee, Jesse gave a full account of our adventures. David and Jesse laughed; Sandy and I didn't.

I had agreed to spend another day with Jesse in the great outdoors. He decided to go fishing. He said, "I'll make you a marine wife if it kills you."

He invited Sandy and David along. Sandy responded like any normal city girl: "I can't swim and I don't like fish."

I did not want to go either, but Jesse convinced me. "Look, Jenny; what can happen just going fishing? Any dummy can fish!"

The following morning, as we were getting ready to leave, I again tried to talk Jesse out of taking me along. "Jesse, I'm afraid of boats and I can't swim; why don't you go alone?"

"Don't worry; I'll be there and I *can* swim."

He drove us to a place along the coast that rented out rowboats, bought a box of worms, and picked out a boat. I looked at it and froze. It was an old, dilapidated little thing that had several inches of water in it. Jesse told me, "All rowboats have water in them. You are supposed to bail them out." I did not feel any better.

Jesse was intent on making me a Marine Corps wife. I had flunked hunting and did not think my grades at fishing would be any better. Jesse rowed us out to sea until land was barely visible. He anchored the boat and baited my hook and gave me a short lesson on the use of a rod and reel, and I was on my own. I sat in the boat holding the rod. It was a nice, clear day, and things were peaceful.

I was almost enjoying myself until I saw what I thought were whales. I had never seen anything like them before. I started to panic as three of them approached the boat. *"Jesse, Jesse,* they're too close; they'll turn the boat over!"

He was reassuring. "Don't worry; they're only porpoises. They're harmless."

Just then, I felt a tug on the line. *"Jesse,* I got something. Help me. Help me pull it in."

He was no help. *"Do it yourself!"*

I had a tug-of-war with the fish when all of a sudden it jumped out of the water. It was huge; I thought that I had snagged one of the porpoises. Whatever it was, I was standing up in the boat pulling on the line. *"Jenny, sit down!* I'll help you!"

I gave up the battle and threw down the rod just as Jesse was moving from his seat to where I was sitting. He tripped over the pole and fell into the water. He was surrounded by porpoises. He grabbed the side of the boat and climbed in, then got back to his seat, grabbed the oars, and started rowing back to shore. He did not say a word, and neither did I until the boat was docked.

He got out of the boat, found a bench, and took off his shoes. He smiled as he told me, "Jennifer, you flunk out as a fisherman, *too.*" He sat on the bench for about five minutes; then we got in the car, drove to Sandy's, and picked up the kids.

That night, Jesse told me that he had transfer orders to the naval base at Lakehurst, New Jersey. "We'll be leaving in three weeks. You'll like it there. It's closer to Boston." Jesse Jr. was playing on the floor. "I guess I haven't been a father to him, have I?"

"No, you haven't, but it's never too late to start."

I quit my job and told Sandy about our transfer. I would miss her. We had become like sisters. We promised to write and call each other often. I had a lot to do. First, I had to take the boys and me to the doctor for a checkup.

I went to see Dr. Wilson; I felt comfortable with him. He gave the boys their examination. I was glad when he told me that everything was okay. He then called me into the room for my examination. He was irritated when he said, "Jennifer, you're pregnant. You're very fragile. You should not have any more children!"

I never practiced birth control. I was not aware of birth control techniques. Such things were not discussed in the convent. My mother never gave me a lesson in the "facts of life." The subject never came up in conversations with my friends. I never discussed it with my husbands. In the 1950s and early 1960s, there was minimal media exposure of the subject. As a good Catholic girl, I was supposed to get married and have babies. It was as simple as that.

My children were a great pleasure to me. I was not fearful, as the doctor was. I enjoyed my children. But I was fearful of Jesse's reaction. I decided to tell him right away. I did not want him to return to his "old" ways. I needed him to be a stable, reliable father.

When I got home I told Jesse the news. He was not surprised. "That's great, Jenny. Just make sure that it is a girl this time."

Sandy came over every day to help me get ready for the move. When moving day came, we both cried. I would miss her a lot. She was probably the best friend that I ever had.

We drove straight through to New Jersey without stopping. It was about a ten-hour trip. Jesse Jr. couldn't sit still and Todd was cranky during the whole trip.

When we reached Lakehurst, we stopped at a drive-in for coffee, bought a newspaper, and searched for a place to rent. We found a small furnished three-bedroom house with a yard for the boys on the outskirts of the town. The house was unoccupied and we were able to move in immediately.

Jesse immediately checked in at the base while I got the house ready. With all the moving that I had done, I think that I could get a house fixed up in record time. It was difficult to do the house while taking care of two little kids. After about a week, I had the house cleaned, the curtains hung, and an adequate stock of groceries.

While I was busy with the house and the kids, Jesse was also busy. He started to return to his old ways. During that first week, he would go out nights with his new friends from the base and stay out all night. Things got worse in the ensuing weeks. He would come home drunk and violent and break the furniture and fixtures.

Jesse then came after me and the kids. He would frequently hit me and go after Jesse Jr. I would stand in front of him to protect him, and I would get beaten again. I begged Jesse to get help for his drinking problem. He wouldn't do it. He did not consider it a problem. "What do you mean, *get help*? I don't need help. I don't have a problem. I enjoy having a beer. I can quit whenever I want to!"

Jesse would usually knock me down with one blow and stagger on to another target. One evening, he was drunker and angrier than usual.

He stormed through the front door and attacked me as if he were fighting a man. He punched me and knocked me against a wall. He continued to flail away. When I fell to the ground, he kicked me repeatedly. He left me lying on the floor while he staggered to the couch and collapsed.

Jesse Jr. was screaming while he ran toward me. I was covered with blood as I grabbed my son and struggled to my feet. I was yelling for help as I limped into the bedroom and broke a window with a brush. I lost consciousness and collapsed holding my son.

The woman who lived next door heard my screaming and called for help. I awoke in the hospital. I was very weak and dizzy, as a doctor was leaning over the bed telling me that I had lost the baby. I had also lost a lot of blood and would need surgery to stop internal bleeding. He told me that my children were fine and were being taken care of by the next-door neighbor. He then administered the anesthetic.

When I awoke following the surgery, a frightened Jesse was by my bedside. He put his head down on the bed and started to cry. "Jenny, I'm sorry. I didn't mean to hurt you. I just lost control. I just don't know what is wrong with me."

I was sick and very weak. I had no pity for him and I was only thinking about the child that I had lost.

He kept crying and holding my hand. "Please, Jenny. Don't tell anyone what happened. I know that you lost the child. Don't tell the doctor that it was my fault. Please, Jenny."

I couldn't bear to look at him. I turned away from him and stared at the wall. I hated him for what he had done. He was not a man. He was an animal. I had made a mistake staying with him. My mistake had cost the life of my unborn child.

The doctor returned while Jesse was at my side. "Mrs. Rollins, you're lucky to be alive. We were able to stop the bleeding, but you're going to need a lot of rest. I suggest that you do not have any more children."

He then turned to Jesse. "Mr. Rollins, your wife came here in very bad shape. She had bruises and lacerations all over her body. What happened!"

Jesse was a very skillful liar. "I have no idea, Doctor. She is very accident-prone, taking care of two kids and all that. I'll get her to be more careful."

The doctor looked askance at him. "Well, whatever happened, Mrs. Rollins will have to stay in the hospital for a week."

I interrupted him. "Doctor, I can't stay. I have two children to take care of."

The doctor looked at Jesse. "Well, young lady, you do have a husband to help."

I panicked. "No, Doctor. I have to take care of my children; I can't leave them with anyone else. I can't leave them with my husband." I was afraid of what Jesse would do if he had the boys.

The doctor understood the situation. "Look, Mr. Rollins; the police should have been called this time. If Mrs. Rollins or her children are harmed, they *will be* notified." He then left me alone with Jesse.

After the doctor left, Jesse tried to apologize. "Jenny, the boys will be fine with me. I'll take good care of them. You can rest knowing that everything is okay. I'll take emergency leave so that I can be home all day and night. That way you won't need a baby-sitter. I'll do it any way you want. Just tell me."

"Please, Jesse. Leave; just leave! I don't care what you do. Just leave me and my sons alone!"

"Okay, Jennifer, okay!" He sulked out of the room. After he left, I cried my eyes out.

The police had never been notified. The woman who heard my screams had run over to my house after I broke the window. *She* had called the hospital for an ambulance. My unborn child was killed and I was beaten to within an ounce of my life. Domestic violence at that time was not considered a crime. I was afraid of what would happen if I swore out a complaint against him. I was also afraid of what life would be like with him. Jesse was capable of anything.

Jesse visited me daily during my ten days in the hospital. He was trying to be good, but it was too late. I was just putting up with him.

He picked me up on the day of my discharge. I couldn't wait to get home and see the boys. There was a teenage baby-sitter watching the children. Jesse Jr. was sleeping when I went into his room. I kissed him, and he awoke and cried, "Mommy! Bad Mommy. You went away and left me."

Tears streamed down my face as I hugged him. "Yes, honey, but I'm home with you now, and I won't leave you again."

I lifted him out of bed, set him on the floor, and held his hand as we walked over to Todd's crib. We both watched as he lay sleeping peacefully. My children were my whole life.

CHAPTER SEVENTEEN

Jesse realized that he had killed his unborn child and almost killed me, so he was very supportive as I recuperated at home. He followed a predictable pattern. He would beat me senseless and then be kind as I healed. Once I was back on my feet, I would be a target.

The Italians have a saying: "everything comes in threes." This is the sign of the cross. This was my third marriage. Jesse was my cross to bear, and I had to bear it. I understood that. I did not want my children to suffer because of it. That night I prayed to Saint Anthony to help me find a way. I could not find it on my own.

We lived in New Jersey for six months when Jesse received orders to Parris Island, South Carolina. I felt like a gypsy. We were always moving.

Jesse had a ten-day leave before reporting to Parris Island. I went home to Massachusetts with the boys, while he went to visit his family in Maine. I was to go to Maine to meet him, and we would then go to South Carolina.

When I met him in Maine, his drinking was out of control. He was drunk the three days that we were together. He was united with his favorite drinking buddy, his mother. We were constantly arguing. I was embarrassed because Jesse Jr. was seeing him drunk all the time. I could not wait to leave Maine.

After Jesse nearly beat me to death in New Jersey, his drinking tapered off. But when he hit Parris Island, he was drinking as much as ever. Lakehurst was a fairly small naval base. Parris Island was the Marine Corps Recruit Depot. It was loaded with marines that Jesse could drink with, and drink he did. I would ask him to get some milk or other groceries, and he would stagger in two or three days later. I had difficulty supporting the boys on the meager allowance that Jesse gave me. It was like old times: His beer came first. On paydays, he never came home. He would go to Beaufort and visit all the joints where he would spend his pay on booze and broads. He would return home in a stupor and beat me. At various times, he gave me a broken nose, a broken jaw, black eyes, and fractured ribs.

I was frustrated, angry, and lonely and depressed. One night I called my mother and asked her if I could come home. However repressive things would be at home, life with my parents just *had* to be better than this. Unfortunately, when I explained to my mother that I would like to move back to Massachusetts, I received an unwelcome yet predictable response.

"Jennifer, you know that you always have a home here. I just *do not* want that animal's children. If you come back, you do it *alone.*"

"Ma, it's bad here; I don't think that I can take it anymore. I've taken some bad beatings; I'm afraid for the boys. I'm afraid for me."

"I told you that you have a home here, but it's *my* home, and you must abide by *my* rules. If you want to come back, fine. But that animal's children must stay with him or his family. *Do you understand?*"

"Yes, Ma. I understand."

I could not accept my mother's terms. I could not leave my children. I was stuck. I was not the only one in this predicament. There were a lot of other marine wives in the same situation as me. They were trapped with no place to go and no money.

The weather in South Carolina was not good for my health. My asthma returned and I became ill with colitis. My sons were growing and taking care of them became a bigger chore. Even with my frail health, I kept a tidy house and always made sure that the boys had clean clothes and enough to eat. It seemed that the only time that I got an opportunity to sleep was when they were sleeping.

Just when I thought that things could not get worse, they did. Dorothy came south for a three-week visit. Jesse would come home every night when his mother visited. I had four people to pick up after, two children and two drunks. Dorothy never lifted a finger to help; instead she would hang around the house in a shortie nightgown and panties. She always had a beer in her hand.

The woman had no shame. We lived in close-quartered military housing, but that would not stop her from going outside in her underwear. She would run around the neighborhood with a beer in her hand and her ass hanging out. I was hoping that the MPs would throw her in jail.

When she and Jesse were loaded to the gills, they would leave little presents for me: Dorothy would vomit and Jesse would urinate all over the place. When he was drunk he had difficulty differentiating a toilet bowl from a punch bowl. After cleaning up after these degenerates, cleaning the boys was a pleasure. I was fearful that the children would catch something living in this environment. When the three weeks were up, I prayed to every saint I knew that Dorothy would not return.

My energy was drained by the time Dorothy left. I made an appointment with a doctor at the nearby Beaufort Naval Hospital. After an initial examination, he recommended a battery of tests. He suspected ovarian cancer. I would have to stay in the hospital for about a week while the tests were conducted.

I was dazed when I returned home. There was no one that I could talk to. My two sons were with the baby-sitter. After I sent her home, I sat and cried my heart out. My sons saw me crying and ran toward me. Although they were very young, they knew that I was in distress.

Jesse Jr. was barely three years old, and Todd was almost two. They both came running toward me. I picked up Jesse Jr. and sat him in my lap. He put his arms around me and patted my head. "Don't cry, Mummy; I love you."

I picked up Todd, and I had both boys in my lap. I held both of them very tight. They were my life. They were the only ones who cared. I worried about them. If anything were to happen to me, who would take care of them? I was worried only about my children.

When Jesse came home I told him about my visit to the doctor and he was quick to offer his comments. "Why the fuck do you want to go for those silly tests? That crap is all in your mind. The doctors don't know *shit*. You should stay home and take care of your family." I did not debate him. You cannot argue with a jackass.

I arranged to get a baby-sitter while I was in the hospital. Before the week was up, the doctors had a diagnosis. I did have ovarian cancer. I was also pregnant. The doctors decided to wait until I delivered before giving me a hysterectomy. They would do a cauterization immediately, and then I could go home.

I was very depressed when I went home. I knew that I had to stay out of Jesse's way. I could not take any more beatings, not in my condition. He was not providing the support for his family. He was back to spending his entire pay on beer. At any given time, the house had five to ten cases of beer, while the refrigerator was nearly empty. He could easily.consume a case in one sitting.

I was afraid of his violent reaction to alcohol. When he was drunk, he could go after me or the children. I was always fearful of what he would do to the kids. I felt relieved when he finally passed out drunk, although he usually did considerable damage.

When drunk, Jesse would break, rearrange, and soil the furniture. Alcohol frequently left him in a state of incontinence. He would use any part of the house as a toilet. He stood on my coffee table and urinated while he pivoted in a circle, soiling the couch, the rug, and anything else in his line of fire.

I would tolerate this behavior as long as he did not assault the children or me. I considered my primary job to be protecting my children from their father.

As I approached my ninth month, I was convinced that things could not get any worse. I was wrong. Jesse received orders to Vietnam. In thirty days he was to report to the USS *Boxer,* for transport to Southeast Asia.

This was early 1965. America was building up its troop strength in South Vietnam. Most marines were eagerly awaiting their opportunity to serve their country in war. That is, most marines, but not Jesse. He was brave when it came to fighting with his wife or intimidating his children. He was not so brave when faced with the prospect of facing men . . . with guns.

Jesse joined the marines in 1950, just before the Korean War began. He never got to Korea. He spent that war driving some general around Japan. It did not appear that Jesse would be so lucky this time. He was headed into a combat zone and did not like it.

When he received his orders, he acted like I had never seen him act before. He received a thirty-day leave before he had to report to the *Boxer.* He spent the first week drinking and crying.

"I don't want to go there, anyplace but there. I could get *killed*! I'm a driver; they don't need me there. Let them send the dumb fuckin' grunts."

Jesse was very depressed. I tried to stay away from him as much as possible. There was a very important issue to deal with, other than his cowardice. That was what to do with me and the kids.

"I don't give a *fuck* what you and your little babies do. They're sending me overseas to get my ass blown away by a bunch of fuckin' gooks!"

Jesse was constantly on the phone to his mother. He decided to spend the remainder of his leave with her in Maine. I would take the kids and go to my mother in Massachusetts. I tried to explain that my mother probably would not take the boys. She would not take two more kids, with a third on the way. She was already taking care of Robin. Three more would be too much.

"Fuck your mother! I'm going home to Maine. I don't care what you do!" Jesse told me.

We packed quickly and loaded up our U-Haul. It was a very uncomfortable trip for me. Several times I thought I might give birth in the car. The boys were restless and jumping most of the trip. Jesse drove straight through from Parris Island to Massachusetts, stopping only for gasoline and coffee. I did not tell my parents that we were coming.

My mother had one hell of a surprise when we pulled into her driveway. Jesse stayed in the car, while the boys and I went into the house. My mother was shocked, not only to see me, but to see me nine months pregnant.

She invited me into the house and put on a pot of coffee. The boys followed me in. As I plopped myself onto the couch, they began to roam around the house. They had been penned up in the car for so long, they acted as though they had just been released from a cage. My mother was getting nervous with them running around the house. "*Jennifer,* I don't want your kids messing up my home. Get them to sit still."

My mother poured two cups of coffee and brought them into the living room, where she joined me on the sofa. I had told her that Jesse had orders for Vietnam and would be gone for thirteen months. She did not know my plans. Neither did I!

"Jenny, what are you going to do while Jesse is away? You are not planning on staying here, are you?"

"Yes, Ma. I'd like to."

"There is *no way* that you and that tribe of yours are going to stay here. Take them to Maine! Let that animal's family take care of you and your little monsters. He thinks that he can dump his garbage here; well, he's wrong," she told me. "I've been raising Robin since she was born. I am making a little lady out of her. I don't want her corrupted by your little animals. They have been raised by a no-good drunk. They have the bad blood of their father. To make things worse, there is another little animal on the way. I *don't* want them here!"

My mother got up, took Robin by the hand, and brought her back to the sofa. She lifted Robin on her lap and hugged her. She did not want Robin to be poisoned by contact with her brothers.

I was not surprised by Mother's reaction. But I just wanted a home for me and my family. I had nowhere else to turn.

After a while Jesse came into the house and said that he was leaving for Maine. I asked if we could change our plans and I would accompany him to Maine.

"Look, Jenny; you are lucky that you made it to Massachusetts without dropping the kid. I think that you should stay here."

"Please, Jesse. I want to keep the family together. I can make it to Maine with no problem."

"*Fuck, no!* Keep your pregnant ass here with your precious babies. I'm leaving for Maine. *Now!*"

He went back to the car and in about thirty seconds unloaded my mine and the boys' things on my parents' porch. He got back into the car and took off.

My mother had been listening to my discourse with Jesse. She did not like what she heard. "Jennifer, I'm ashamed of you. You live like a pig because you are married to a pig, and your children are nothing but little pigs. That animal can't take care of his family, and he wants to use my home as a dumping ground. *No . . . way!* I'm sick of solving the problems caused by that worthless thing that you married."

"Look, Ma; I got no place to go. You have an empty furnished apartment upstairs, right? Well . . . just let me use it for a few weeks. That's all, Ma. I'll keep the kids out of your apartment. I have no money. I just need a little time to get on my feet."

"Okay, but for just *two weeks*. Then you must get the hell out!"

"Thanks, Ma."

I was uncomfortable at my mother's house. She hated my sons and would use any excuse to chastise them. If they ate a cookie on the porch, she would accuse them of bringing ants into the house. If they were playing with a toy, she would take it away from them, saying they would hurt someone with it. It they tried to go into her apartment, she would attach ropes around their waists and tie the other end to the porch railing. She literally treated them like animals.

I hated the way that she treated my boys, but I could not do anything about it. "Ma, I wish that you would treat my kids like children, not like animals."

"I'll treat *your kids* any way that I want. If you don't like it, you can get the hell out of here with your *little animals.*"

I tried to call Jesse. I was desperate. I had no one to turn to. I was not surprised when he answered the phone in a drunken stupor. After my "Hello, Jesse," greeting, he mumbled something incoherent. I hung up.

I figured my first priority was finding a doctor. I was nine months pregnant and not getting any prenatal care. I contacted about a half-dozen ob-gyns; none would take me as a patient, because they did not want the responsibility of treating me this far into pregnancy.

I finally found a doctor who would treat me. I made an appointment to see him in two days. I was praying that the baby would arrive late. I had to find a place to live and had only two weeks to do it.

I called Dina and told her my predicament. I had not seen her in years, but we had remained in contact through our letters. She was working for a real estate agent in Malden and was able to help me find an apartment that was available immediately. My father secretly gave me the money for the first month's rent.

One week after I moved into my parents' apartment, I moved out. Dina helped me move out of my parents' apartment and into my new one. Actually, she did most of the work. In my condition, I found walking very difficult.

Before I moved, I called Jesse again to tell him my new address and to inquire when he would be returning from Maine. I expected him to see us before going overseas.

He was drunk, but this time I could understand him. "I'm not coming to Massachusetts. I'm going straight to Morehead City. I guess I won't be seeing you for a while. That fuckin' bitch mother of yours can take care of you and your babies."

"*Jesse, you're no damn good.* You don't give a shit for your family!"

Jesse's mother took the phone from her son. Predictably, she too was drunk and slurring her speech. "Hi, Jenny. Nice to hear from you. How are the kids? Say, we're givin' Jess a goin'-away party this Saturday night. Too bad youse can't make it."

I yelled at her. "Jesse is a father, and he is going to be a father *again* very soon! He belongs with his family!"

She laughed, hiccuped, and hung up. I felt very lonely.

I entered the Chelsea Naval Hospital the day after I moved. Dr. Feigenbaum recommended that I enter the hospital the day that I saw him, but I had to put it off for a few days. Before I went into the hospital, I had two things to do. I had to move, and I had to get someone to care for the children.

After I saw the doctor, I talked to my mother about my predicament. I would probably be in the hospital for a while, and I needed child care.

My mother was not sympathetic. "No, dear. You can give those animals away. I'm not cleaning up after those little pigs."

I started to cry. "Ma, why the hell are you like that? I'm going to call some of the family. Maybe I can get help from them."

My father's only sibling, Connie, was in the Fernald School. My mother had twelve siblings; I thought one of my aunts or cousins would help. I was wrong. I called about a dozen people, trying to get a temporary home for my kids, with no luck. They all said that they were glad that I was home, but they had their hands full with their own families. I could not ask Dina. She had a full-time job.

When my mother found out that I had sought help from her family, she was furious. "You got a lot of nerve, expecting *my* family to take care of your little animals. Send them to an orphanage. I'll make the call and deliver them *myself.* Just to make sure that they get there."

"Okay, Ma. I guess I don't have any choice."

Hours before I checked into the hospital, my mother came by to take my kids to an orphanage. She made arrangements at the Home for Italian Children in Boston's north end. I kissed the boys good-bye, telling them that they had to have someplace to stay while I was in the hospital. I promised to pick them up as soon as I could.

As I watched my mother drive off with them, I started to sob. I felt that my sons were paying for my stupidity. I was always putting myself into a corner, and my loved ones were suffering because of it. It seemed as though I never had choices; other people were controlling my life. I felt powerless to change things.

My new apartment felt empty without the boys. My mother returned to my place in about an hour, explaining that she had dropped the kids off and everything was okay. I was very hurt by what my mother had forced me to do.

"Ma, I just don't understand why things have to be done this way. Why couldn't you take care of the kids? It would have been for just a short time."

"Look, Jennifer; you are always getting into trouble. You married an animal who gives you nothing but babies. You give me nothing but heartache. I owe you *nothing!*"

"But, Ma, I'm just thinking of my boys."

"I don't care. You and your family have given me nothing but grief! Your brother, Sal, on the other hand, has given me nothing but pleasure. He has not given me one ounce of trouble. If I help anyone, it will be him. He will be getting married soon. I'm helping with the arrangements, and I'll help him and his new bride get started. He is marrying a *nice* Italian girl, not some slut. He won't disgrace me like you have. *Good-bye,* Jennifer." She left and I slammed the door behind her.

Dina came over shortly thereafter. We straightened up the apartment. Then she drove me to the hospital. I was beginning to experience back pains similar to what I had felt with the other pregnancies. As I was riding with Dina, they were coming every few minutes.

The pain was becoming unbearable. The doctor saw me immediately. When he saw that I was about to deliver, he gave me an injection that knocked me out.

Soon after I awoke, a nurse came over to me and told me that I had a son. Three boys—I couldn't believe it! I asked if he was all right. I told the nurse that I wanted to see him. The nurse laughed and told me that the baby would steal my heart when I saw him. She told me to rest and promised that she would bring the baby in later to see me.

The nurse was right: he stole my heart. He was a tiny thing with a mass of blond hair and blue eyes, and he looked perfect in every way.

I said a silent prayer to Saint Anthony, thanking him for the little baby to whom I had just given birth. I decided to name the baby Gregory. I placed him on the bed and kissed him.

I had a semiprivate room. My roommate, Lauren, was married to a navy boatswain, and she had given birth just hours before me. She asked me if Greg was my firstborn. I told her that I had three other children. She laughed and told me that I was acting like a first-time mother.

I envied Lauren. She had many visitors. Her husband brought her gifts and flowers. I never received a gift or a flower when I had any of my children. Lauren's husband would sit next to her bed and hold her hand while they talked about their new daughter. I thought that this was how it should be. That was a normal family. After a while, I would leave the room whenever Lauren had visitors. I was jealous and feeling very sorry for myself.

My mother was my only visitor, and she was not happy to be there. I asked her if she would send a wire to Jesse's ship telling him that he had a son.

"I won't have anything to do with that no-good bum!" she shouted.

"Please, Ma. Keep it down. I have a roommate," I whispered.

My mother continued at the same decibel level, "I won't shut up! I will not inform that drunken bum that he just produced another little animal!"

"Mother! Just shut up and get out!"

She stormed out of the room.

Lauren had been listening to our argument and tried to give me support. "You know, Jenny, if my mother ever spoke to me like that, I would never speak to her again."

"Well, Lauren, my mother is different. Very different." I did not want to try to explain my family to anyone. No one would believe it!

A navy doctor who was examining me wanted to know if my husband knew that he had just become a father. When I told him, "No," he volunteered to take the information and let Jesse know the good news.

Soon after the baby was born, the doctors addressed the ovarian cancer. They decided on radiation treatments, which began a week after I delivered.

My mother continued to be a frequent visitor. She continued to harp on the same subject: Jesse and the children. "Jennifer, I don't see how you stay married to that bum. Your husband, not me, should be here with you at a time like this. I have other things to do, like care for your Robin. She is turning out to be a proper little lady. If your little animals ever come out of the orphanage, I don't want them near her. They have bad blood."

Every time my mother visited, it was like a shock treatment. She did not come to comfort me. She ignored Greg. He was just another little animal to her, but she did not call him that, yet.

She came to threaten me. She wanted no part of my family and wanted to make sure that I understood her point of view. My father worked long hours, so I did not see him during the week. He visited me on weekends. He always came with my mother, and he never said much.

I stayed in the hospital several weeks. I could not wait to get home. I wanted to pick up my sons and have my family together. My mother thought that I should leave the kids in the orphanage while I got back on my feet and accustomed to my new child. But I was going to do this my way!

My mother finally relented. She offered to drive me to the orphanage to pick up the boys. After my discharge from the hospital, I carried Greg to my mother's car and we headed for the north end.

I stayed in the car with Greg while my mother went inside and got my sons. When I saw my mother come out with my sons, I put Greg in a baby restraint while I got out to greet my sons. They ran to me. I began to cry as I scooped them up in my arms to hug them.

Jesse Jr. spoke first. "You're a bad mommy to leave us."

As I kissed him I said, "Don't worry, honey; this is the last time that it will happen. I'll never leave you again."

They climbed into the backseat. I sat in the front seat with Greg, while my mother drove. Just after the car started, Greg began to cry.

Jesse Jr. asked, "What's that, Mommy?"

"I have a new baby brother for you to play with."

Jesse Jr. and Todd leaned over the seat and stared at the baby.

"Well, boys, what do you think about your new brother?"

"I think that you should send him back to the hospital," said Jesse Jr.

I loved my family and was glad to have the kids all back together again. My mother looked at me as if I were crazy. "Jennifer, I don't see why you do it. I would never clean shit from a bunch of kids. You have shamed me by having so many. So many kids that you cannot support."

"Ma, don't say such things in front of the kids. Give me your opinion in private, not in front of the boys."

"I'll say whatever I want, whenever I want to say it."

We did not speak to each other for the remainder of the trip. She dropped me and the boys off at my new apartment. Neither of us said good-bye.

I did not hear too much from Jesse. He wrote a couple of times a week, telling me how unhappy he was. After fifteen years in the service, he had just realized that military life did not agree with him. He did not relish the idea of going to war. The USS *Boxer* was going to Vietnam via a circuitous route, but it was going there.

Jesse wrote asking if there was any way that I could get him out of the marines on a hardship discharge. He was telling me that the sailors on the *Boxer* were picking on him. He was panicking! The closer that the ship got to Vietnam, the more panicky his letters became.

My new apartment was not far from my parents'. It was about a fifteen-minute walk away. If I could get a baby-sitter for Greg, I would take the boys for a walk so that I could see Robin. I wanted my mother to accept my family, and I still hoped that in time she would. Whenever she would see the boys, her reaction would be the same. She would get the shakes and hurl the insults our way.

Robin was also my child, even though she was being raised by my mother. I wished that I could raise her together with my boys. I wanted to be a mother to her in whatever small way I could. My mother was very protective of Robin. I was a disruptive and evil influence. Whenever I wanted to take Robin out, I would get an argument from my mother.

My mother had Robin brainwashed. Whenever I got near Robin, she would become upset and act very nervous with me. She would then go to her grandmother and ask permission to talk to her mother. Robin could not relax with me until Grandma approved.

One hot and muggy night, I had just put the boys to bed when the phone rang. It was Jesse, calling collect from Hawaii. I was surprised to hear his voice.

"Jenny, I miss you and the boys very much. I can't wait to see little Greg. Look, I want to come home. I don't belong here. Did you do anything about getting me a hardship discharge?" he asked.

"Jesse, I don't know where to begin."

"Don't worry; I checked into it. I'll tell you everything that you have to do." He started crying. "Jenny, I'll change if you do this one thing for me. It's the service life that turned me into a drinker. If I am out, I'll be different." Through his tears he gave me a set of instructions on how to get a hardship discharge.

I was hoping that the Marine Corps life *was* the cause of my problems with Jesse. If he lived a "normal" civilian life, things might be different. I wanted to believe that.

I ran around as best I could, considering that I had three kids to take care of, getting the stuff necessary to get Jesse out of the marines. I got a written assurance from a local trucking company that he had a job waiting. I went to the Red Cross, telling them that with my poor health and three children I needed my husband at home. I contacted my congressman and state representative and requested assistance. I went to the church, I went everywhere, to get the necessary documentation to support a hardship discharge. When I had everything together, I presented it to the military liaison in downtown Boston.

Within a month, Jesse was discharged. He had barely set foot in South Vietnam when he was notified that his discharge had come through.

Jesse was drunk when he arrived home. He claimed that he was celebrating getting out of the marines. Jesse Jr. and Todd hid behind me when Jesse entered the house. He pulled them from behind me and asked if they were happy to see him. They both began to cry.

"What the hell did you do, make them queers while I was gone? It's a good thing I'm home to make men out of them."

Jesse went into the nursery to look at Greg. He had no comment other than that he would "make men out of my sons." He reeked from alcohol as he came over to me and tried to kiss me. I shoved him aside. He staggered away from me and out the door.

Women dream and lie to themselves. In their minds, they can take an ugly duckling and change him into a beautiful swan. Our problem is confusing the fantasy with the reality.

CHAPTER EIGHTEEN

The next day Jesse went to see about the truck-drivers job that I had procured for him. His starting wage was $245 per week. He came home bragging about how much he would be earning. He never thanked me at all but acted as though he got the job on his own.

I asked him if he would like to celebrate his new job by taking his family out to dinner.

"Hell, no. I'd rather stay home with a six-pack. You guys are spoiled; you've got it too good.

"By the way, I'm going to call my mother and tell her about everything. I didn't get a chance to talk to her. We have a lot to catch up on."

"Make sure that you tell your mother that she is *not* welcome here. I'm not feeling well, and with three kids, I just cannot put up with that drunk."

"I'll do whatever the fuck I want to do!"

He called his mother and told her about the new baby and about his discharge. She did not mention Greg, but she had plenty to say about the marines. "Jesse, you're crazy to give up the marines. You are gonna be tied down now, and things will be tougher for you."

"I know, but I just had enough of the service life. It's time for a change. By the way, when are you coming to see me?"

His mother said she would visit this weekend. I was furious when he told me.

"Your mother will not visit this weekend or any weekend. I just can't deal with two drunks. Things are different when you get together with your mother. I would be embarrassed to death if my parents were to come over and see that scene," I told him.

"Tough shit! She is coming and that is all there is to it."

Dorothy arrived at noon Saturday. She was drinking in the car on her way down, so she was well lubricated when we met. Jesse hugged her and welcomed her in. I put Greg in a stroller, gathered the toddlers, and went for a walk to the park. I had a lot to think about.

My family did not know the extent of Jesse's cruelty. Now I was living near my folks. They would learn about everything, even Dorothy.

As it was, my mother did not respect me. What would things be like when she found out about Jesse and his mother? I cringed when I thought of the mess that would be waiting for me.

My boys were having fun in the park. I hated to take them home to Jesse and his mother. But I knew that we could not stay there forever. I had to face the music.

Things were not as bad as they could have been. Jesse and his mother were sitting on the couch surrounded by beer cans. No furniture was broken, and there was no sight or smell of excrement in the living room.

Jesse was bragging and his mother was encouraging him. He was telling his mother how tough he was and how he put the whole navy "in its place." I couldn't take any more of this crap.

"Hey, Jesse. How come if you're so tough, you called me crying, saying that the big bad sailors were picking on you?"

He exploded off the couch and shoved me against the wall and started to scream, *"You whore! You talk when I tell you to and not until I tell you to!"* He was screaming so loud that he frightened the boys, who started to cry.

"Put your fuckin' little queers to bed."

I stood up, grabbed Jesse Jr. and Todd, and took them to their bedroom.

While I was in there putting them to bed, I heard Jesse yell, "Hey, Jenny! My mother and I are hungry. Get us something to eat."

I would have liked to poison them both. I heated up some roast chicken and gave them sandwiches, hoping the food would shut them up. I did not want them keeping my kids awake all night. I went to sleep, hoping Jesse and his mother would pass out before they damaged anything.

The next morning, the living room looked and smelled like a zoo. The two animals had passed out, Jesse on the chair, Dorothy on the couch. There was a pile of vomit in the middle of the floor. If it were not for my children, I think I might have left it there, for the two pigs to wallow in. I had to clean it up before the boys awoke. I did not want them getting sick.

Jesse and Dorothy were awakening as I was washing clothes and making breakfast. They walked into the kitchen, and Jesse said, "Jenny, you got any coffee ready for us?" I pointed to the stove where a coffeepot was percolating. Jesse poured two cups of coffee and said, "You know, Ma, the Wops make good little housekeepers, don't they?"

I took my hands out of the dishwater and screamed at him, *"I want your mother out of this house, now!"* Dorothy started shaking as she turned away from me. I continued, "This little *Wop* is going to wop you right in the head if you two don't get out of my kitchen."

Dorothy left the kitchen immediately. Jesse followed her. I heard them talking for a few moments in the living room. Shortly after, the front door opened and closed. I looked out the window and saw Dorothy in her car, with Jesse leaning against the door. She started the motor and was on her way back to Maine.

Jesse slowly walked back to the house, sat on the couch, and turned on the television. Jesse Jr. and Todd were playing on the living room floor. Jesse Jr. walked over to his father and said, "You're a very bad daddy."

Jesse raised his hand to hit his son, but I stepped between them "Jesse, if you hit that boy, I'm going to crown you with the heaviest thing I can find."

Jesse settled down, but we did not speak for the rest of the day.

That evening, my parents came over to visit. I made coffee and tried to make them feel comfortable, but they felt the tension in the air. We were in the kitchen when Jesse Jr. came in. My father walked over to him and picked him up. Jesse Jr. was a little chatterbox. He told my father everything that had happened that day between myself, Jesse, and Dorothy. He even told about the times that Jesse hit me. My mother sat at the kitchen table with her eyes bulging, listening to my son tell his story.

Finally my mother had heard enough. She got up from the kitchen table, stormed into the living room, and confronted Jesse. "You big, worthless drunk, you've got a lot of nerve hurting my daughter and her children. Why the hell don't you go back to where you came from and leave my family alone? You and your mother can wallow in mud like the pigs that you are."

My father and I tried to calm my mother down, without success.

Before she was finished, Jesse responded, "You fuckin' old bag, why don't you mind your own business? This is my family, and I'll do whatever the hell I want. Why don't you get the fuck out of my house?" My mother stomped out of the house. My father followed her.

Jesse's drinking problem was not caused by the military. He was the same in civilian life as he had been in the marines. He rarely came home at night, but he always wanted his meals ready in case he did. He would spend his paychecks carousing. All his new friends were drinking buddies. Again, I had trouble paying the bills. I had to get credit from the local grocery store to feed the boys. I did my best to keep the children fed and clothed. I tried to insulate them from the hard realities of life with Jesse.

When Greg was four months old, I returned to Dr. Feigenbaum. The radiation treatments had not been very effective, and he recommended a hysterectomy. I could not go in for surgery now. Between Jesse and the kids, I was a total wreck. The doctor insisted that it had to be done immediately. He asked his nurse to make the arrangements and set up an appointment with a surgeon.

When Jesse came home, I explained the situation to him and asked him to take some time off from work so that he could care for the children. I knew that he was a cold and heartless person, but his response shocked me.

"Fuck, no. I have no intention of taking care of your little queers. Taking care of kids is your job. I don't give a shit about your operation. Take the kids to the hospital with you."

In a way, I was glad that Jesse refused. He probably would have hurt my sons while I was away. He could barely take care of himself.

I needed someone to care for the boys. It was déjà vu. I called my mother out of desperation. Her response was not a surprise. "Jennifer, you know that I will not baby-sit for your little animals. I don't know why you ask. Why the hell are you going in for that operation? You and the doctor are both crazy!"

I called friends and relatives, with no luck. I gave up and called the Home for Italian Children. Even they told me that they had no room. Fortunately, they had a referral. There was a Sisters of Charity order nearby that would accept my sons. I called them and made an appointment the following day.

I saw a nun/social worker, Sister Patricia. When I told her my story she said, "Jennifer, you have not married a *man*. No man would treat his wife that way when she was facing surgery. No man would shun his children as your husband has. Don't worry; we'll take the boys while you are in the hospital. If you want, we'll take them a week early so that you can get some rest before your operation."

I nodded. "That sounds good to me."

"Well then, we can send a police car to pick up the kids so they will be safe. They do not have to bring anything. We can provide all that they will need."

I started to cry. "I don't know how to thank you," I told her.

"Don't worry about thanking us; just get back on your feet. That will be enough thanks for us." Her words should have made me feel better, but they didn't.

The following day, as I was preparing the boys for their trip, I tried to explain why they had to leave again. I just told them that they had to stay there while Mommy was away at the hospital.

As I was dressing them, I thought, *What would happen if I did not survive the operation? Who would care for the boys?* I knew the answer. Nobody, not their father, not my family. They would have to spend their childhood in an orphanage. I sat down and cried. The children ran to me, put their arms around me and told me, not to cry. I wanted to cry more but instead dried my tears, because I did not want to upset them. I told them that I would pick them up as soon as I left the hospital.

The police car arrived shortly thereafter. Jesse was not home. I had not told him that I was sending our children to an orphanage, even though I didn't think that he would care. I walked with the boys to the car, kissed them, and waved good-bye. I felt as if someone were tearing my heart out as I watched the car drive away with my sons.

Jesse came home late that evening. I told him that I had sent the boys to the Sisters of Charity. He did not seem to hear me. He smelled of alcohol, and he had lipstick all over his shirt. When I asked him about the lipstick, he taunted me.

"Why do you care about lipstick? Usually you're only concerned about your little queers. Ha, if you die, in that hospital, I'm taking off and leaving them in the orphanage. I don't give a fuck about them!"

I ran into the bedroom to escape him. He ran after me, grabbed me by the shoulders, and shook me.

"If you give me any more shit, I'm going to give you the beating of you life, but I won't leave any marks on your body for any doctor to see."

He released my shoulders. I turned toward him and said, "God will make you suffer for what you have done."

He sneered and said, "You Wops with your God and your saints. You don't see them helping you now, do you?"

In the morning I asked Jesse to drive me to the hospital. He laughed and said, "Find your own fuckin' transportation."

"Look, Jesse; you have to assume some responsibility. If something happens to me, you will have an awful lot to live with."

"I have the freedom to do what I want, when I want. *No one* will take that away from me."

I called a cab and went to the hospital alone. I went to the admitting office and gave them all the necessary information. A nurse escorted me to my room. Shortly thereafter, I was given preliminary tests.

The operation was scheduled for the next morning. I called my parents to tell them that the surgery would be the next day. I also wanted to make one more attempt to get them to take care of my sons, if something happened to me.

I was very frail and I feared death. If I were to die, no one would care for my boys. I wanted my parents to promise me that in the event of my death, they would care for my sons.

My mother had not changed her mind. She said, "Look, Jennifer—you made your bed; now you have to lie in it. You and that animal produced those boys; it's your responsibility to take care of them, *not mine!*" I hung up and returned to my room.

Later that evening my mother visited me. I wished that she had stayed home. "Jenny, you know that you are making a mistake having this operation. If you do, you will surely die. If you were not having the operation, you would not need baby-sitters." I thought that my mother's tongue would kill me long before any operation would.

The following morning a nurse came to give me an anesthetic. I was in such a nervous state that it was only partly effective. When they arrived to take me to the operating room, I began to cry. "Oh, God, please, don't let me die. My children need me so much."

One of the nurses who was escorting me told the orderlies to stop. She bent over and asked my name. When I replied, she kissed me and said, "Well, Jenny, you're not going to die. I'll be here when you come down. I'm an old hand at this." She picked up my hand and pressed it in hers. It was the first act of kindness that I had been shown for a long time.

I was in a state of semiconsciousness for four days. I was in terrible pain. When I finally awoke, there was three people in the room: the nurse, Jesse, and my mother. Jesse did not say a word to me. He sat there looking out the window. My mother told me that the boys were fine and there was nothing to worry about. I asked the nurse to give me something for the pain. She gave me a shot, and I fell asleep.

Dr. Feigenbaum came to visit me two or three times a day. He was an older man with gray hair and an excellent bedside manner. He was very encouraging and told me that everything would be okay. Even though I had had the operation a week ago, I still had trouble getting out of the bed and walking.

While I was doing my exercises, a nurse came into the room and told me that I had a phone call at the nurses' station. I had great difficulty walking to the phone. Every step was agony. When I got to the phone and said hello, I was stunned. It was Dorothy. At first I thought that she had called to see how I was.

"Hello, Jennifer. I just called to tell you that I cannot find Jesse. If you see him, tell him that I want to talk to him. I want him to come back home to Graysville. I'll take care of him. I'll feed him. After all, you are in the hospital; he needs someone to look after him."

She never asked how I was or how her grandsons were doing. I did not answer her; I just hung up. When the nurse asked "What's wrong?" I told her that I did want any more phone calls. She helped me back to bed.

I was discharged about a week later. Dina picked me up and took me home. As soon as I got home, I changed into my nightgown and climbed into bed. Dina went into the kitchen to find something to cook for me. She found nothing in the refrigerator but beer and condiments. She returned to the bedroom and said, "Well, your husband has the house well stocked . . . with beer."

She had to leave to take care of her family. She asked, "Can I bring you over something from my place?" "That's okay, Dina. I'll be okay."

Soon after Dina left, I received a call from the mother superior at the home. Jesse was at the home, and he wanted to take the children home. He was very difficult to deal with. He came into the home and demanded his children. The mother superior did not want to release them without speaking to me. I did not want to cause any problems for the home, so I told her to release the boys to Jesse.

She was concerned about my health. She thought that having three small boys around the house would aggravate my condition, so she volunteered to keep the boys an extra week. She did not feel comfortable turning the boys over to Jesse. I told her that if she released the boys to Jesse, everything would be okay. I also thanked her for all she had done.

"God bless you, child. You need it," she replied before she hung up.

I had been home for about two weeks when Jesse came home drunk one night with lipstick smeared all over him.

"Jesse, where have you been?"

"It's none of your fuckin' business. You little bitch, you can't question me. I'll do whatever the fuck I want!" He walked over to me and shoved me to the floor.

Jesse picked me off the floor with one hand, and with the other hand he repeatedly hit me in the head and chest. I screamed like a wounded animal. I screamed until I had no voice left. When he was through, he threw me to the floor and left.

I crawled to the phone and called Dina. I told her what had happened and that I needed help immediately. Her mother was visiting her, and both of them rushed to my house. They were shocked to see me. "Jenny, what kind of animal would do this? I'll stay with the kids; my mother can drive you to the doctor," Dina said.

I got Dr. Feigenbaum's number for Dina. She called his office and told him that I would be right there. The doctor's reaction was similar to Dina's. "I heard of animals like the one that you married, but I have not seen cases like this. I can't see how a man can do something like this!"

He continued to examine me. The whole right side of my face was bruised. I had open cuts on my forehead, around my eye, and at the corner of my mouth. The stitches from my hysterectomy were removed recently, and he was concerned about rupturing.

He continued the monologue as he attended to my wounds. "Jennifer, you should act like a woman and throw him out of the house. Drinkers never change; they only get worse. If you don't do something, he will kill you!"

On the way home, I thought about what the doctor had said. I had no backbone. I put up with this crap for too many years. How much worse could things be without Jesse? Things were terrible with him.

When I got home, I discussed with Dina and her mother what the doctor said. I was seriously considering leaving Jesse.

Later, that evening, Dorothy called saying that she would be coming over with Leona this weekend. Things just kept getting worse. This was the last straw. I knew that I could not throw Jesse out of the house. He would have to leave of his own accord.

Dorothy and her daughter arrived Saturday morning. Jesse was passed out in the bedroom. I got the boys up and dressed before they arrived. I told Dorothy that Jesse was sleeping and to make herself at home. I took the boys and left.

I went directly to my mother's house. I was planning a trap and hoped that it would work. When I got to my parents' house, Sal was there with his bride. My mother was not happy to see me. Well, what else was new? I guess she was afraid that my sons would pollute her son and daughter-in-law.

An hour later, the telephone rang. I told my mother, "I'll answer it," since it probably was Jesse.

He was out of his mind with anger. "Don't you realize that my mother and sister are over here? What the fuck are you doing? Get your ass over here right away."

"I know that they are there; I opened the door for them."

"Well," he said, "why the fuck aren't you here cooking for them."

"*Never, Jesse, never again!*"

"Jenny, are you crazy or something?"

"No, I'm not crazy. I'm just not going home until you and your whole family clear out." I hung up.

I had to stay at my parents' house until I heard a response from Jesse. Since my mother was entertaining her daughter-in-law, she would behave and not make a scene. It was a difficult wait. I was still weak from the operation . . . and the beating. The baby insisted on being held. Time dragged on.

After four hours the phone finally rang. I got up to answer it. Jesse was on the other line. "You can shove your fuckin' house; I'm going back to Maine with my mother and sister."

"Jesse, before you go, leave the keys to the apartment on the kitchen table."

"*Fuck you!* he said, and hung up.

My mother knew something was wrong. I did not want to discuss this with her now, since we were not alone. I told my mother that I would explain it to her later. I allowed Jesse enough time to pack his things and leave. I then went back to the apartment with the boys.

After leaving, Jesse did nothing to support his sons, which was not surprising, since he barely supported his family when he lived with them. He even filed for bankruptcy to cancel any of his outstanding obligations.

I had no one to support me. The stores refused to give me credit. I was not able to feed my sons or pay the rent. I applied for mothers' aid but was turned down because my husband earned too much money. I had to sue Jesse for child support.

I called Graysville to try to work something out with Jesse. I got Dorothy on the phone. She was no help. She asked, "Well, how are you enjoying not having Jesse? That's what you wanted, isn't it?"

I felt like a beggar. My parents and other relatives gave me enough food to feed my boys. The rent was another problem. The landlord told me that I would have to give him one month's rent, $105, by the end of the week or I would be evicted.

He might as well have asked for a million dollars. I had to find a place to live, fast. My mother had an apartment available. I begged her to allow me and my boys to move in there temporarily. She said that I could move in, without the children. Even though I had been through this before with my mother, I became hysterical. "*What am I supposed to do with my children, kill them?*"

My mother calmly said, "Jenny, I think that you should give them away or put them in a state home."

"*Ma, I hate you!*" I hung up.

I sold my furniture in order to pay a lawyer to sue Jesse for support. I explained to the lawyer that I did not want a divorce, just a separation, because I was not planning to remarry.

With the money from the sale of the furniture I was able to pay the lawyer and pay the first month's rent on a crummy apartment in a run-down building in nearby Revere. The rent was only fifty dollars a month, and it was not even worth that. Dina was able to get me some broken-down secondhand furniture. It was better than nothing.

The judge ordered Jesse to pay sixty dollars a week for child support. He was bitter that he had to pay anything. He had moved out of his mother's house, and into a furnished room in Boston. There were a lot more driving jobs in the Boston area. He did not pay the support regularly. He would frequently pay me one week and skip two weeks.

Times were very tough. I could not work because the cost of a baby-sitter for three children would approximate my salary, I was getting by on the gifts of food and Jesse's occasional check. I was not on speaking terms with my mother. I resented her lack of support. She treated Sal's wife, Carol, as her daughter.

I rarely saw Robin. My mother still did not want me near her. I still dreamed of having my four children together but would have been content if I could have been able to adequately support my three boys.

Jesse's infrequent support checks eventually stopped coming altogether. My lawyer advised me to get a divorce instead of a separation. At first I refused, but I relented after several months of suffering.

I was surprised when one day the doorbell rang and the visitors were Dorothy and Ted, her husband. I put my hand on the edge of the door, preparing to slam it in their faces. *"Please, Jenny, don't slam the door; we want to talk to you."*

I took my hand off the door. "Okay, Dorothy. Come in."

I did not have much in the way of furniture, so I invited them to sit on a couple of milk cartons that I was using as chairs.

When they were seated, Dorothy spoke first. "Jenny, I'm worried. I have not heard from Jesse for weeks. I went to his place on Charles Street, and he wasn't there. Nobody knew where he was. I don't know what to do."

"Well, Dorothy, now you understand how I felt being married to him."

Ted wanted to change the subject. "Jennifer, I can't believe that you are living like this. What are you going to do?"

I said, "I'm going to file for divorce. I have to put my life together."

Ted was sympathetic to my plight. "Jenny, I know you had things tough. Maybe I could help you. I know that it's tough taking care of three children without any support. Why don't you let me take the boys back to Maine . . . temporarily, until you get back on your feet?"

"I'm sorry, but I want to keep the boys with me. I just don't trust Jesse with the boys. I'm afraid that he will go back to Graysville and hurt them."

Ted persisted, "It would only be temporary custody. I know that you love your boys and before you see them suffer you will let me help."

"I'm sorry; I won't change my mind." They left shortly thereafter.

The next day, I called both the Home for Italian Children and the Sisters of Charity to see if they could board my sons for a week. Both organizations said the same thing; they were filled up and could not help me. Mother Superior at the home told me to place the children in a state facility. I refused. I had to find a job, anything, and I needed someone to care for the boys while I looked. I tried some other charitable organizations, with the same results.

Again, I was backed up against the wall. I could not take care of three small children and work at the same time. I could not live on "nothing."

I called Ted and asked if his offer was still good. I wanted to send him the two older boys, while I could afford to keep the baby in day care. He agreed, saying that Leona could help care for the boys. I told him that when I went for the divorce I would give him temporary custody of the boys.

My mother escorted me to divorce, court. I was granted the divorce along with custody of the children. I told the judge that I was granting temporary custody of two children to my in-laws until I could get a job and instructed my lawyer to make it clear that I could regain custody of my children at any time. He told me that everything would be taken care of.

My marriage was over. I felt relieved; it was never really a marriage to begin with. But it had produced three children that had become my whole life. It broke my heart to know that I would soon be separated from my sons.

One of the hardest things that I have ever had to do was tell the boys that we would be separated. I sat down and held the two older boys close, while Greg crawled around the house.

"You guys will have to be very brave. I'm going to have to go to work to so that I can make money and take care of us. We are going to have to be apart again, I don't know for how long.

"You'll be going to Maine to live for a while. You should like it there. Greg will stay here because he is still a baby. You are my little men; I'll miss you so much."

Giving up my children for an indeterminate amount of time was one of the hardest things that I ever had to do. I had no idea how I would pull this off. I didn't know if I could make enough money to support my family. I only knew that I would do anything to bring my family back together.

Ted called and said that he would be by later that week to get the boys. Several days later, he arrived in a pickup truck. My mother and Aunt Theresa showed up shortly thereafter. I felt numb as I brought the boys out to the truck. The ladies were talking to Ted as I brought the kids downstairs.

I had just put the boys in the front seat when my mother approached me. I could not hold back the anger and resentment that I felt for her. "What the hell do you want? *Are you happy now?* Well, if you are hear to gloat, this is the perfect opportunity. Because of you, my family is split up. *It's only temporary.* This won't be forever. You'll see. I'll show you!"

I couldn't say good-bye to the boys. I had my back to the truck, crying, as Ted drove off with the boys. If I saw my boys leaving, I would collapse and beg for someone to have pity and help me hold my family together. There was no help available, only my mother.

I went back to the apartment, picked up Greg, and ran through the apartment like a madwoman, kicking and throwing things around. I was angry, angry at my mother, and frustrated by my helplessness.

My Aunt Theresa followed me upstairs. My mother followed close behind her. My aunt saw the mess that I was making and tried to settle me down. "Jennifer, things might not be as bad as they seem. If you could reconcile with your mother, she might help you."

"You just don't understand. I have no mother! I have no family. My boys are my only family. My mother took my daughter. They are the only ones that I have left.

"I was an outcast in my family. My brother just became a father. Was I invited to the christening? *No!* Because his multidivorced sister is a disgrace to the family. Things haven't changed. They never will."

The anguish was increasing. I screamed at both of them. "*Get out of my house! I have no family! Get out!*" They left without saying a word.

I did not sleep that night. How could I? I had given away my children. I spent the next few days trying to find boarding for Greg. I finally found a woman who boarded children. The house was clean, and the woman seemed kind. She charged thirty dollars a week to care for one child. Greg would stay there Monday morning to Friday evening.

I was preparing to work double shifts or two jobs and could probably not give him much care during the day. I made arrangements to start boarding Greg the next day.

The following morning, I brought my son to to Mrs. Maloney. I gave her my number and told her that I should be called if even the slightest thing went wrong. I kissed Greg and started to choke up. I left before I started to cry.

I started my job search. I had no car, so I either walked or took public transportation. I filled out what seemed like hundreds of applications, for office jobs, salesgirls jobs, factory jobs. I finally found employment at Palmer Electronics in Revere. The hours were seven in the morning to three-thirty in the afternoon. I had either to walk or take two buses. I walked most days.

I was assembling boards that were used in military applications. I liked the work and got along well with everyone. I felt especially lonely when the other women would talk about their families. I hurt when they spoke, so I usually remained by myself.

I was only semiunskilled, so I could not command a good wage. Even so, my first paycheck threw me for a loop. I netted forty-five dollars for forty hours. After I paid the baby-sitter, I would have about fifteen dollars to live on.

I worked very hard. I had to stay glued to my workbench, with only a short lunch break. I would come home and collapse across my mattress, as I did not have a bed. I had very little to show for my labor. Most of my fifteen dollars went to phone calls to Maine. I wanted to speak to the boys as much as I could. I skipped many meals to be able to hear their voices.

I was able to get a temporary part-time job at another electronics plant. At best I was able to take home fifteen dollars a week. Between both jobs, I was able to maintain a minimal subsistence.

I lived like this for about six months. I would have Greg on weekends, but I could only keep in touch with Jesse Jr. and Todd by phone. I was suffering, but I was not getting anywhere. I could not save anything. I wanted to get a car so that I could visit my sons, but I could barely buy food. I had to do something.

My only choice would be to give up Greg. If I had the thirty dollars that I was paying to Mrs. Maloney, I should be able to save enough to buy a car and put something away so that my family could have a better life.

I called Ted and explained the situation to him. He agreed to take Greg, and arrangements were made for him to pick up Greg that weekend. I blamed Jesse for all this. Ted told me that Jesse had moved back to Massachusetts. I told Ted, "I no longer care where Jesse is or what he is doing." Ted came by Saturday and picked up my baby.

CHAPTER NINETEEN

When the baby was gone, my life seemed really empty. I felt that I had nothing, no family; I just existed. When I did not come home straight from work, I frequently visited Aunt Theresa.

Most of her children were grown and had left home. She had one son, Jimmy, living with her. He was going to college, studying to be an engineer. He looked like Mario Lanza and had a great sense of humor. When my aunt had to go to a doctor's appointment, I sat in the living room and told my problems to Jimmy. He was very sympathetic. I felt better after I talked to him.

With Greg in Maine, I was able to save some money. I went shopping and bought clothes and toys for the boys. I planned to rent a car and go to Graysville to bring the boys all the goodies.

Cousin Jimmy called me that evening to find out how I was doing. I told him how happy I was that I would be seeing my sons in a couple of days. I confided to him that I would be seeing my boys for the first time in months. When I told him that I was planning to rent a car, he volunteered to drive me to Maine. "That way you can spend the car rental money on extra gifts," he told me.

That weekend he picked me up to take me to Maine. I was ashamed to show him my apartment. It had no furniture, but he did not comment. He just helped me load the boys' stuff into the car, and off we went.

I was thankful that someone was with me, because my nerves were shot and I felt nauseous. It was about a three-hour drive but seemed to take forever.

When we reached the house, the boys were playing outside. They did not realize that I was in the car until we pulled in the driveway and I got out. The three of them ran toward me as I ran toward them. I grabbed them in my arms and started crying. It felt so good, I never wanted to let them go. Jimmy turned around; he did not want to see us cry.

Ted came outside and Jimmy introduced himself. Dorothy and Jesse came out of the house moments later. I had thought that Jesse was still in Boston. He walked up to me, his face red as a beet. Jimmy went up to him and introduced himself. Jesse ignored him and kept staring at me, without saying a word.

I did not want to be near Jesse, so I asked the boys if they would like to go out for ice cream. They loved the idea, so they piled into the car and we drove off. We found a drugstore, and the boys had big dishes of ice cream. We then took them to the lake, where they spent the remainder of the day telling me about their lives. They kept asking when they could go home with me. "Soon," I said. "Soon."

The time flew by. I did not want to leave my sons. They did not want to leave me, either. After we drove back to the house, Ted had to drag them out of the car. I waved good-bye as he brought them back into the house. I turned my head away as Jimmy was backing out of the driveway. I couldn't look at them.

The trip back to Boston was terrible. I cried and did not talk to Jimmy. He tried to be sympathetic, but there was nothing that anyone could say that would help. I only wanted my children.

I went to visit my sons most weekends. I would usually rent a car, but sometimes Jimmy would drive me there. I would always bring the boys something. It was difficult to leave. I would lock myself in the apartment after returning from Maine. I could not face anyone.

I had a one-week vacation coming, and I planned to have the boys for that week. I had arranged it with Dorothy. It was the best vacation that I could ask for. I was able to slowly furnish the apartment. I bought a secondhand triple bunk for the boys and stocked the refrigerator with things that little boys like to eat.

Jimmy and I left early Saturday morning to pick the boys up. Dorothy greeted me as I pulled up into the driveway.

"Hi, Dorothy. Are the boys ready? I can't wait to get them home."

"What do you mean, get them home? They *are* home. I have custody, and I'm not going to turn them over to you."

I turned red with anger. "What are you talking about? They are my kids, and I am going to take them. We had an agreement!" I charged after Dorothy. She ran into the house and locked the door. I was crying as I banged on the front door. I heard the boys yelling inside.

I banged on the door until my hands got sore. Jimmy finally was able to drag me to the car, and we drove back to Massachusetts. I cried all the way home.

I made Jimmy promise to take me there the following weekend. I did not tell anyone else that I was going. We went next Saturday, and this time someone opened the door for us, a stranger to us. She introduced herself as Arlene, Jesse's cousin. She looked about four or five months pregnant. She invited us to sit down while she got Dorothy.

Dorothy was not glad to see me this time either. "Jennifer, what are you doing here? I thought we got rid of you last week."

Just then, my sons found out that I was there and came running downstairs. They threw their arms around me, and we hugged.

Jesse heard the commotion and came into the living room. "Well, Jenny, I see that you met my cousin Arlene and our future family."

"What?" I said. "What the hell are you talking about?"

"Arlene and I are getting married. We are starting our family a little early, just like you and me, Jenny, remember? Arlene and I are also taking the boys permanently. We'll raise them so that they grow up to be men."

"Jesse, you asshole! You can't do that. They're my kids. You can't take them; you just can't!" I was crying and screaming at the same time. "There is a court order. You can't do this; you can't. Your parents have *temporary* custody!"

Again Jimmy grabbed me and dragged me to the car. I was fighting him every step of the way. I was afraid for my kids, and I was in shock. He finally got me in the car and drove off. On the ride home I put my head on his shoulder and cried my heart out.

I consulted with several attorneys. They told me the same thing: unless I had a home ready for the children, I could not regain custody, as they had a home in Maine. But it wasn't much of a home. The boys were being cared for by a bunch of degenerates.

If I could not have the boys, I could at least visit them. When I went to see them, Dorothy would not let me take them out of the yard. She was afraid that I would kidnap them. She told me, "They're my children now."

The boys would confide in me about their life in Graysville. Jesse and Dorothy were drinking as much as ever; only now they had to clean up their own mess. Jesse and his fiancée (cousin) had no shame when they practiced their lovemaking, which was not confined to their bedroom. After several beers, they would fornicate in front of my sons. The boys wanted to know more about what they were doing. I changed the subject.

I was finally able to buy a car. It was a used 1964 Chevrolet. This gave me the opportunity to see my children every weekend. I transferred to the graveyard shift at the factory. The 10 percent salary differential was a big help.

Dina and her husband bought a three-family house and needed a tenant for their attic apartment. It was smaller than the dump that I was living in, but a hell of a lot nicer, and the rent was about the same.

I had been able to accumulate some furniture and build up a nice wardrobe.

It was nice living in the same house with Dina. I always had a friend nearby. I was very disconsolate not knowing when or if I would ever be reunited with my sons. I did not have very many friends. I kept to myself at the factory.

I enjoyed the single life. I had four male bosses at the factory who liked me. They were always asking me to go out with them, and I was always refusing. When I returned home, I would tell Dina all about it and we would laugh together.

Like in the old days, Dina and I would go out together, dance, have a few drinks, and return home together. I was always running into someone that I knew, frequently a relative.

My mother's family was close, and if one of them saw me with a drink in my hand, this information would travel back to my mother. Instead of my mother hearing that someone had seen me at a club, she heard that I was drunk and acting like a slut.

Some of my relatives were especially cruel. While at my mother's house, I overheard my mother's sister Carmen talking about me: "Well! That's why she had so many husbands. After all, a man wouldn't beat his wife unless she had it coming to her. If she is always seen with a drink, you can well imagine what her poor husbands had to put up with."

I was in Robin's room when I overheard Aunt Carmen's comments. I came stomping out. "Shut your damn mouth, and the rest of the family should do the same. When I had no food for my sons, you never even offered a crumb. In the future, mind your own damn business."

Aunt Carmen turned to my mother and said, "*Angelina,* are you going to let your daughter talk to me like that?" My mother just threw up her hands. Carmen stormed out of the house.

I was the victim of a horrible old-world stereotype. Having multiple divorces, I was forever branded. It made me very angry and frustrated. I built a shell around myself. I did not want to get hurt anymore.

I was alienated from my family, considered an outcast. As a child, I had been very close to my father. He was one family member that showed some compassion. Now it seemed that I always had to go through my mother to see him. He allowed my mother to build this wall between us. I was angry at him because of it.

My life settled into a routine. I would work at the factory during the week, and I would drive to Maine every Saturday to see the boys. Once or twice a week I would go out with Dina. We would usually go out to dinner, but sometimes we would just go out and have a few drinks.

In order to avoid any familiar faces, we went to one of the clubs

216

along the waterfront. The place was too dark, and the band was too loud. The women in the place looked like they just got out of bed, and the men were very tough looking. Most were longshoreman; some were sailors. I felt very out of place.

Dina and I sat at a booth and ordered a couple of daiquiris. Dina got up to call her family while I sipped my drink.

A large drunk man staggered over to the booth, shoved me to the inside of the booth, and sat down beside me. "Hi, doll. My name's Paul; I really like you."

I started to think of Jesse. "Well, I don't like you. Why don't you get lost? Get out of here and leave me alone!"

"Whassa matter, honey? You too good for me?"

There was another man who was sitting in the next booth. He was quietly sipping his drink and watching us. He saw the trouble that I was having with the drunk and rose from his seat, walked to our booth, and addressed the drunk, "Hey, Jack! Why don't you get lost? The lady doesn't want you around."

The drunk looked up at the man, looked at me, and said, "Well, see you around, honey." He got up and staggered to the door and out into the night.

"I don't know who you are, but I'd like to thank you."

He looked at me and smiled. "You can thank me by letting me buy you a drink."

"Sure, that's the least I can do."

He sat beside me in the booth and introduced himself, "Boatswain Mate, Second Class, Tom Rickerts, United States Navy, at your service."

"I'm Jennifer Rollins, civilian. How come you are not in uniform?"

"I only wear my uniform when I'm on-duty. I feel more comfortable in civilian clothes."

He was a large man, well over six feet tall and well over two hundred pounds. He was not handsome; he had a tough, ruddy complexion. He had a very mean look, but he was very friendly and very easy to talk to. He was from Albany, Georgia, and had been in the navy for seven years. His family had a hundred-acre farm. He joined the navy at seventeen to get away from the farm.

When Dina came back to the booth, I introduced her to Tom. We spent several hours drinking and talking. Dina and I nursed our daiquiris, while Tom was putting down the beers. I did not know how many he had, but he never acted drunk, so I felt comfortable with him.

I told Tom about my life. I took out my wallet and showed him a picture of Jesse and the boys. I told him about my divorce and about my separation from my sons. He listened intently.

217

It was getting late, about eleven o'clock. Dina and I agreed that it was time to go home. It was Friday night, and I always liked to leave early Saturday morning to see my sons. Tom asked me if I would drive him back to his ship. I did, and when he got out of the car he asked if he could call me.

I said, "Sure," and wrote the number down on a match cover. He stuck his head in the driver's side window and tried to kiss me goodnight. I pushed him away, saying, "I never kiss anyone on the first date." He looked at me dumbfounded, then walked away.

As soon as I got home, the phone was ringing. It was Tom. He wanted to know when he could see me again. We made a date for Saturday night. We went to another place on the waterfront where we ate, drank, and listened to the band.

This was the first of many dates. Tom was different from the men that I had gone out with before. He never wore his uniform. He was always dressed casually in slacks and sports shirt. We never went to fancy places. Our favorite place became Sully's Tap, a barroom near the Charlestown Navy Yard. We usually went to a movie and had a simple dinner in a cafeteria or in one of Tom's favorite waterfront joints.

Tom did not dance. I found out why one night when we went to a dance club. When we danced, his feet spent more time on my toes than on the floor. We never went dancing after that.

I had not told Tom all that much about my life, and he never asked. He did know that I was divorced, with three sons in Maine. He did not know about Robin. I liked him, but I did not think that I could trust any man.

Tom found out about my past one night by accident. We were double-dating with Dina and her husband, Johnny. Johnny asked me something about Robin.

When I said that she was fine, Tom asked, "Who is Robin?"

Well, I told him about Robin and about my three marriages.

Tom looked at me in disbelief and said, "Jenny, why didn't you tell me all this stuff before?"

"Tom, there are many things that I would like to forget."

"I don't care about the reasons; I just thought those were things that you should tell me about."

"Look, Tom; it was none of your business. I don't have to tell you my life story. If you don't like it, take a hike!"

He did. Tom got up and walked out of the place. I liked him, but I had made up my mind to never again be dominated by another man. Any future relationships would have to be on my terms.

My biggest pleasure was still seeing my boys every Saturday. I was

218

disappointed, since I still had to follow Dorothy's rule that I could not take the boys away from the house. After a while I didn't mind. Just seeing my boys was enough.

Jesse had married his cousin when she was nine months pregnant. They had a girl, and my sons told me what it was like to have a little sister around the house.

Tom called me up and apologized, about a week after we had our little spat. I started to develop feelings for him. He was like a big kid with a big heart. Our dates remained very simple. We never did very much. Sometimes we just took a walk and window-shopped. I was beginning to feel very comfortable with him.

After a while Tom would accompany me on my weekend trips to Maine. He met my sons and they got along well. He never met Robin. I did not want to take him over to my mother's house. My relationship with my mother was shaky at best.

Tom's ship was docked in Boston. He was scheduled to go on a six-month cruise. We were sitting in my car two days before he was scheduled to leave when he pulled me into his arms and said, "Jenny, I love you. You need someone to care for you. You need me!"

"Don't worry about me, Tom. I'll be okay."

"It is getting late and I have to return to the ship. You know, Jenny, no matter what you say, I'm worried about you. You're a dippy broad. In my four trips around the world I've never met anyone like you."

We promised to write. I refused Tom's request that I come to the dock to see the ship off. He did not believe me when I told him that. I could not handle any more good-byes. He said that he would look for me on the pier. I never showed up.

With Tom out to sea, I felt lonelier than ever. Dina pestered me constantly about reconciling with my parents. I had only seen Robin once in the last six months. I had visited my sons almost every week, and they were hundreds of miles away. My parents' home was less than a mile away.

I figured that Dina was right, and on Sunday I went over to my parents' home. Robin was nine years old. She looked very pretty and very well taken care of. She was a tall girl, not short like her mother. I kissed her and asked her all about school and all the other stuff that fills the life of a nine-year-old girl. She was very friendly toward me and felt comfortable talking to me. This was a refreshing change from our past meetings.

Later my mother told me to sit down so that we could talk "about things." My mother's scorn had alienated me in the past. I wanted to have a reconciliation. I was separated from my children by forces that

219

were out of my control. I was lonely. I wanted my family. I talked to my mother about my alienation and about my loneliness.

"Jennifer, I understand how you feel. Would you like to come home to live?"

"Yes, Ma. I'd like to. Only I'd like to be treated like a mature woman, not a child." My mother did not answer me. She stood up and walked into the kitchen.

I gave Dina notice that I was moving out and moved into my parents' house. They had a huge empty garage, and I was able to store a lot of my furniture there.

I had an ulterior motive in wanting to move in with my parents'. I still wanted to get my sons back. I was hoping that my mother would soften and allow my sons to live with us. I was happy living with Robin, but I wanted a home with all my children.

Several times after I moved in, I approached my mother about reuniting my family.

"Jennifer, I thought we settled this issue a long time ago. I *do not* want those little animals in my house. They are up in the woods where they belong. Leave them there," was always her answer.

My letters to Tom were getting more romantic as time went on. Our first letters were cold and formal, because our final meeting was not especially warm. I wrote asking him to forgive me for the way that I had behaved. He accepted my apology, and our correspondence warmed up. It got so warm that he proposed marriage. I accepted his proposal.

I was lonely. There was something that was missing from my life. I needed a stabilizing influence, someone to love me. The more that I was separated from Tom, the more I missed him. I had tried to build up a shell around myself. I was hurt too many times and did not want to get hurt again. But I trusted Tom and thought that he could provide the affection that was missing from my life.

We were married two weeks after his ship returned. As with my other marriages, there was no religious ceremony. It was a justice-of-the-peace ceremony.

Tom's ship was docked in Newport, Rhode Island. We rented a small apartment there. I moved some of my furniture there, but I still had things in my room at my parents' house.

Shortly after we were married, Tom received his orders for a nine-month Mediterranean cruise. We celebrated the Christmas and New Year's holidays together before he departed. I loved him and I wanted him to provide the stability that was missing in my life.

This time, I did say good-bye to him at the pier. I stood on the pier with the other wives and girlfriends. I did not cry like the others. I was crying on the inside.

Even though Tom and I rented a place in Newport, I spent most of my time at my parents' house. About a month after Tom left, I became very ill. I was very weak and had a splitting headache. I was losing weight and weighed barely ninety pounds. I went to the clinic at the Chelsea Naval Hospital. After a series of tests, the diagnosis was thyroid cancer.

I went to the hospital weekly for treatments. I was weak for several months, but after several months I responded to medicine and the radiation. I gained weight and got stronger.

Tom and I wrote to each other nearly every day. I did not tell him about the cancer, as I saw no reason to worry him. We were making plans for our new life together. We would buy a house. We would have a home for my kids. I would finally have the family that I wanted.

When I recuperated, I made the decision to get back to work. I did not enjoy hanging around the house and had to start earning some money.

I did not want to go back into factory work. I decided to try to utilize some of the hospitality industry experience that I had gained while I was married to Victor.

A new club opened on the waterfront. It was one of the biggest in the city and was owned by a local sports celebrity. I decided to apply for a hostess position, as I enjoyed dressing up and always got a favorable response when I did. I had my interview in the afternoon and received a call that evening saying that I had the job.

I wrote to Tom telling him about the job. He wrote back saying that he did not want me to work there. He did not think that was a good environment for me to work in. He considered it a big barroom when in reality it was a lavish nightclub with a huge restaurant, bar, and banquet facility. The best part was that the money was excellent, far more than I was making in the factory.

I was saving my money because I wanted to make a fight for my children. I wanted to establish a home, with Tom and my kids. For the first time in ages, I felt that I was making progress toward my goal of reuniting my family. Tom would make an excellent stepfather, and I was saving enough money so that when he returned my dream could come true.

While Tom was away, I spent most of my time in my mother's house, but I kept the apartment in Newport. The nine months went by quickly. I worked evenings at the club, and I spent my weekends in Maine.

My relationship with Jesse and Dorothy became even more

strained. Even though I went to Maine every Saturday, I was not allowed to see my sons every trip. It was a six-hour round-trip that was sometimes for naught. But I felt that just the possibility of seeing the boys was worth the trip.

When I went to Graysville, Jesse and Dorothy were always there. They would sometimes tell me that the boys were at their friend's house or make up some other excuse. Sometimes they would just slam the door in my face.

Jesse Jr. was eight, Todd was seven, and Greg was five. I had missed much of their childhood, I did not want to miss many more years. With Tom, I would be able to establish the home necessary to get my boys back.

I often thought that I married Tom because of love, not for love of him, but for love of my boys. I knew that the only way that I could get my boys back was to present a stable home. I needed a husband for that. Tom was the perfect father figure. He was a huge, friendly, kind teddy bear of a man.

When Tom returned, I went to Newport to meet the ship. I stood on the pier, straining to see him. I finally spotted him standing at the rail. I waved at him wildly. He saw me and waved back. When the ship docked, the wives and girlfriends ran up the gangway to the ship. The women ran up to their men and hugged and kissed them. I was one of the last women on the ship. When I saw Tom he approached me with a dirty, oily cloth in his hand. He greeted me by shaking my hand. There were no passionate kisses. He was just as nervous as I was.

We stayed in Newport for a few days, then drove to Malden to visit my parents. My parents liked Tom. He was very friendly and respectful to them. He told them about our plans.

He was finishing up his second four-year enlistment. He had enough of service life and was planning on getting out. We were planning to rent a place near Boston and get all new furniture. My parents seemed pleased and nodded as he spoke.

While waiting for his discharge, Tom made several trips back and forth between Newport and our new home in Stoneham. We got a three-bedroom apartment. I wanted enough room for everyone.

Tom got a good job at the waterfront loading tankers for an oil company. I continued to work nights at the Boston 1800 Club. I enjoyed the work very much, but Tom did not like me working there. He was jealous because I had a glamorous job. I had to get dressed up every night, and I attracted the attention of many men.

This issue was settled one night when I slipped on some spilled food. I fell hard on my behind and broke my tailbone and strained my back.

I was in the hospital for a month and recuperated at home for several months after that.

My biggest regret was not the pain, suffering, or lost employment time. It was that I could not make my weekly trips to Maine.

After about six months, with the help of a rubber doughnut on my seat, I was able to make the trip. The boys were thrilled to see me and asked why I had not visited them. I explained my little accident. We hugged and talked and had a great reunion.

I walked with Tom and the boys into the house. Dorothy was tense as she said, "Ya know, Jenny, things have been tough here. Jesse Jr. ran away a couple of weeks ago, and they just found him."

"He looks okay to me. Why did he do it? What's going on around here?"

"I've been raising these boys all by myself. Jesse is gone most of the time, and my no-good husband doesn't do a thing. I need a rest from the boys for a while. Do you still want to take them?"

I glanced at Tom. "Sure, Dorothy. We'll take them home right now. We'll pack their things right now." Tom, Dorothy, and I went upstairs and packed their stuff.

I was stunned. I did not believe that it was this easy. It was too good to be true.

CHAPTER TWENTY

On the ride home, my boys were as happy as I was. They kept standing up on the backseat and wrapping their arms around me. This was the first time that they would be home with me in years. They were looking forward to it.

When they arrived at our place, they were full of questions. Their most persistent question was whether they could live with us. We did not have beds for the boys, so we let two of them sleep in our bed and borrowed a roll-away for Greg. Tom and I slept on the convertible sofa.

The boys were shabbily dressed. They each had one pair of shorts that weren't really shorts; they were cutoffs. When I opened the boys' suitcases, I realized what little they had. I had gone upstairs with Tom and Dorothy, but they had packed the boys' clothes while I brought some of their playthings downstairs.

Each boy had a small suitcase filled with dirty clothes. They had underclothes, socks, and a couple of shirts, in addition to a jacket. That evening when I offered to help them bathe, they refused, saying, "We had to do it ourselves in Maine."

The following morning, I cooked a big bacon and egg breakfast. The boys ate as though they hadn't eaten in weeks. They explained that they never had eggs for breakfast, only cold cereal.

That day Tom and I were going to take the boys out to get them new clothes. I told them to "wash up superclean to try on new clothes in the stores." They were so excited about getting a new wardrobe that they lined up while I filled the bathtub.

When they undressed, I became sick to my stomach. Todd had sores all over his body. I questioned him about them. He said, "Well, we had no hot water, and we could only take a bath on weekends." I was so upset that I called Tom in to see the sores and help me bathe the boys.

Greg was in the same shape, but in addition, he had teeth marks on his back and shoulders. He did not want to talk about how they got there. Jesse Jr. had another problem. He had spasms. He would strike himself on the head and would not or could not stop.

I called the doctor and made an appointment for the boys. Tom and I then took them shopping. After we returned, I called Al Petrone, my attorney. I explained the situation to him, from scratch. He was the attorney that had represented me in the negligence suit that I filed against the Boston 1800 Club. I had sued the club for damages when I fell and was hospitalized. The suit was still pending.

He told me that since Dorothy had custody, I had to return my sons to her at her request or I could be charged with kidnapping. I did not want to believe him; I could not send the boys back to Maine to be abused and neglected. Al told me that the law was pretty clear and I did not have any choice.

The boys had told me that it was Jesse, not Dorothy, that was raising them. Dorothy and Jesse had warned the boys not to tell anyone about this arrangement.

Dorothy had decided that one week was enough time for me to be reunited with my boys. I did not want to take them back to Maine. Al advised me to return them to Maine and file for custody. He thought that we had a good case, since I was married and had a home for them. Tom agreed that we should follow our attorney's advice.

When the departure day arrived, the boys were very upset. They were eating well, had a hot bath every day, and had clean clothes. Most important, they were living with people who loved and cared for them.

The boys loved Tom as much as they loved me. He was what they wanted for a father, much kinder to them than their own father. He was the stable father figure that they desperately needed. I could not bear to take them back.

I choked back the tears as I loaded them into the car. I loved my babies and did not want to give them up . . . again. It was a tearful trip to Maine. When we arrived, the boys did not want to get out of the car. Tom had to drag them out.

I walked with the boys up to the front door and kissed them good-bye just as Dorothy was opening the front door. They reluctantly went into the house, as Tom took my hand and led me back to the car.

I cried all the way back to Massachusetts. Tom kept reassuring me that we would win a custody battle. The only thing that could make me feel better would be having my family back.

My lawsuit against the Boston 1800 club was settled out of court. I netted $7,000 and used part of this money to put a down payment on a two-family house in Boston. The house had a huge yard, but it needed a lot of remodeling, so we used the remaining proceeds from the lawsuit along with borrowed funds to fix up the place. My father was especially helpful. We utilized his expertise at fixing up old houses.

Our main reason for buying the house was that we could show the court that we could provide a good home for the boys. We bought twin beds for the boys, as well as bureaus and other furnishings for their rooms. We wanted everything to be perfect when we brought them home for good.

We were allowed to bring the boys home on weekends while the custody litigation was in process. One Saturday afternoon, while the boys were playing in the yard, Jesse Jr. had a convulsion. He stood and shook. Tom and I rushed out to the yard. Jesse collapsed, unconscious, just as we reached him.

I called the police, who sent over an ambulance. I accompanied Jesse to the hospital while Tom stayed home with the other boys. Jesse was revived in the emergency room. They could not give us an immediate diagnosis and recommended that he stay overnight for tests and observation. I stayed with him as long as I could and finally went home about midnight.

I was exhausted when I arrived home and not ready for what I found. Greg was screaming in pain and holding his stomach. For the second time that day, we had an ambulance at our home. Greg had an attack of appendicitis. I now had two sons in the hospital.

The doctor who examined Greg noticed the marks on his body, called me into the examining room, and got very indignant with me. He thought that I was the one who was responsible for the abuse. I wound up telling him the whole story. They decided that Greg did not need surgery. They kept him in the hospital for a week of recuperation.

Jesse was discharged from the hospital but would have to return as an outpatient. He would have to undergo brain-wave and other neurological tests. After two weeks he was diagnosed with epilepsy. Due to his condition, Jesse stayed with us when I brought Todd and Greg back to Maine.

Jesse spent most of the next few weeks in the hospital. He had confided things to the doctors that he never confided to me. He told them about the treatment that he was receiving at the hands of Dorothy and Jesse. He had been beaten and occasionally knocked unconscious by his father. He was knocked over by a truck and never received proper medical attention. Jesse Sr.'s sister, Leona, was a nurse. She was the one treating Jesse Jr., with medicine taken from the clinic where she worked.

Dorothy had the legal custody, but the boys were living with Jesse. He had them living in the cellar and sleeping on the floor next to the furnace. My sons were treated worse than dogs.

I wanted to confirm what the doctor told me. I talked to Todd and Greg separately. They tearfully supported Jesse Jr.'s allegations. They each vividly described their life in the cellar. They were reluctant to discuss Jesse Sr.'s cruelty because they feared retribution.

I called the doctor to make sure that Jesse Jr. would be healthy enough to testify in court. The doctor said that he should be fine, but he must not be returned to Maine. He could not survive the abuse that he was receiving.

When the court date arrived, I was a bundle of nerves. The boys were very frightened. We would have a hearing before a judge in the Suffolk County Probate Court. All the parties would present testimony to the judge, and he would make a decision.

I was very nervous and insecure. I thought Jesse Sr. would say that my multiple marriages made me an unfit mother. Tom reassured me, saying, "Look, Jenny, you have nothing to worry about. You're happily married, I think. You have a home. Getting the boys back should be a snap.

"It's not you that has something to worry about; it's Dorothy and Jesse. They broke the custody agreement. The kids are kept at Jesse's house, not Dorothy's. They were just bringing them to Dorothy's when you visited."

Tom and I went to the courthouse with Jesse Jr. Our attorney meet us there. Jesse Sr. and Dorothy, in addition to bringing Todd and Greg, brought what seemed like half of the state of Maine. Some of them were relatives that I recognized, but there were many more that I didn't know. Most of them looked like Jesse's drinking buddies. They were men with boots, plaid shirts, and about a week's growth of beard.

Greg and Todd were surrounded by this bunch and appeared very nervous. One of the seedier-looking members of this pack walked up to Tom and tried to provoke him. "Hey, Tommy, which one of you is the woman of the house?"

Tom moved closer to him, but I grabbed his arm and whispered, "Tom, stop. This asshole is just trying to provoke you. If you fight in these halls, we'll never get the kids."

Tom saw the wisdom of my words and backed off. He was twice as big as this jerk and could have leveled him, but there was more at stake here.

We sat and waited at least three hours before our case was called. Tom and I kept taking the boys for walks so they would not be so jumpy. Finally, a bailiff appeared and took my sons to talk to the judge. Their faces drained and became white. I hugged them and reminded them to tell the truth and everything would work out fine.

The bailiff took the boys upstairs to speak to the judge. The rest of us followed and waited in the hall outside his chambers. My sons would speak to the judge first. Jesse and Dorothy would then speak to the judge. Tom and I would see him last. Tom and I sat on the bench on one side of the hall. Jesse and Dorothy sat opposite us.

For about a half hour I sat opposite Jesse. I thought about all the beatings. I thought about the baby that I had lost because of him. I thought about how he abused my sons. It was a sickening half hour. I also thought about Dorothy. How could a woman let this happen?

I was deep in thought when the door to Judge Hack's chambers opened and the children came out. Todd and Greg came out of the judge's chambers in a somber mood. Jesse Jr. came out with a smile on his face and a bounce in his step. Whatever he had said to the judge, he was proud of himself.

Jesse and Dorothy were ushered into the judge's chambers, while Tom and I remained outside with the boys. They were in the judge's chambers no more than twenty minutes. The judge spent less time with them than he had spent with the boys. I thought that odd.

It was now my turn. I decided to go in alone while Tom stayed with the boys. I was so nervous that my stomach felt queasy. This was the first time that I ever had any dealings with a judge.

A bailiff led me into the judge's chambers and closed the door behind me, remaining in the chambers with me and the judge. The judge was in his fifties, balding, and extremely heavy. I thought that the bailiff remained in the room to help the judge if he attempted to stand up. After the introductions, Judge Hack instructed me to sit down at the desk across from him.

"Well, Mrs. Rickerts. Let's start from the beginning. Tell me, how was Dorothy Rollins awarded custody of your children?"

I told him the whole story in as much detail as I could. I started with the separation and later the divorce proceedings. I told him about a technical mistake at the divorce proceedings that kept me from regaining custody at my discretion. I ended by relating Jesse Jr.'s condition, caused by his abuse in Graysville.

The judge did not say anything as I spoke. When I finished about fifteen minutes later, he said, "Thank you, Mrs. Rickerts. Please wait outside."

The bailiff opened the door for me. I went back into the hall, where Tom was waiting with the boys. "Jenny, how did it go?"

"I haven't the slightest idea. I told him my story; he said, 'Thank you; wait in the hall'; that was it."

I was only waiting about ten minutes when I was called back into Judge Hack's chambers. "Mrs. Rickerts, I wish I were God, or at least a Solomon, but unfortunately I am not. I spend a lot of time in Maine, in

Miller's Falls, a town near Graysville. In fact, I was born in Augusta. I know Graysville well. It is a wonderful little town with some of the prettiest birds in the country. It is a great place to bring up children. I am going to send the boys back to live in what I consider to be a better environment. There have been some allegations of mistreatment, so I will send an investigator to look into the matter."

I broke down and cried. Through the tears, I tried to explain, "Please, Judge Hack, you can't do this. Please reconsider. Jesse is a drunk who does not even want the boys. The boys are abused. They are not fed properly or taken care of. Please, anything but that. Put them in a foster home. Don't send them back to live in that place. PLEASE!"

"I'm sorry, Mrs. Rickerts. That is the way that it has to be. Bailiff, please escort Mrs. Rickerts out of my chambers."

The bailiff almost had to carry me outside. Both Tom and Mr. Petrone tried to reassure me that everything would be all right. I just sat there and cried. I could not be consoled.

Jesse Jr. came over to me and asked what was wrong. I held him tight and said, "I'm sorry, but you boys are going to have to return to Maine, but just for a short time."

He started screaming and crying, "I can't go back there! Daddy will beat me because of what I told that judge. You promised that if I told the truth, I could stay with you. *You promised!*"

"I'm sorry; I did the best that I could do. We'll be together again."

He broke free and ran down the stairs, screaming that he was going to kill himself. Tom and I ran after him, while Jesse, Dorothy, and their attorney were restraining the other boys.

When we got to the first-floor landing, we saw that a police officer had grabbed Jesse Jr. and was holding him. The officer carried him upstairs. After a short discussion with the bailiff, the officer handed Jesse over to his father, who threw him over his shoulder. Jesse Jr. continued to kick and scream, but it was of no use. Mr. Petrone had me by the arm and would not let me go.

I watched as Jesse Jr. was carried out by his father. Dorothy and their attorney dragged the other boys out of the courthouse. All three boys were crying and screaming that they did not want to go back to their private hell. But they had no choice. Lady Justice had put their lives in the hands of an incompetent Massachusetts judge.

I was horrified as I watched this scene. Tom and Mr. Petrone tried to comfort me. When that did not work, they tried to drag me away. They finally got me into the car, and Tom drove us home.

I was in a state of shock for days. I did not speak and felt ill. I could not believe that a judge could send my children back to Graysville, where they would face more abuse. I gave evidence, we presented medical evidence, the boys testified, and that ignorant judge was influenced by the pastoral setting of Graysville. Why were my boys being punished? Why was this nitwit on the bench?

Even though I could not get custody, I still wanted to visit my sons. I telephoned Dorothy several weeks later informing her that I would like to see the boys.

"Jennifer, I'm so glad to hear from you. I didn't think that you would want to talk to me since we whupped you in court," she told me.

"I just want to see my children. I'll be up there this weekend and—"

"What do you mean, you'll be up this weekend? You have no visitation rights. You lost everything. The boys are mine, and I'll do as I please with them. Anyway, the boys don't want to see you, not after the way that you lied to them."

"Look, Dorothy; just let me speak to my sons—that's all I want."

"I'm sorry, they are out playing. *Good-bye!*"

As soon as I hung up, I called Mr. Petrone and told him about my conversation with Dorothy. "Look, Jennifer. Wait until the investigator comes to interview you. Please stay away from Graysville until the investigator comes, because your case depends on his findings. You have to play a waiting game. I wish that I could be more helpful."

I played a waiting game. I waited and waited. After a month, I still did not hear from the investigator. I called my attorney. He said that he would take me into court to seek visitation rights.

Mr. Petrone and I went to see Judge Hack, who asked me if I would like to "take the boys for a weekend."

"Of course," I replied.

He issued an order allowing me to see take my sons home for the weekend.

Mr. Petrone said that Tom and I should go to the local police in Graysville and present the court order in case we had any trouble with Jesse or Dorothy. We promised to take his advice.

The next morning we rose early and headed for Maine. The trip seemed longer than I remembered. When we reached Graysville, we stopped at the police station. We went inside and Tom told the officer on duty why we were there and asked him if he would assign someone to go to Dorothy's house with us.

When Tom finished speaking, he handed the court order to the officer, who read it, looked up at us, and said, "Well now, you're from Boston, huh? Yup, this looks like a real court order. Then again, it might not be. Well, we do things different up here than they do in the city. I can't be going around stepping on people's feet. By the way, miss, why don't you have your kids?"

"Look, Officer; it's a long story."

"Well, just because you're from Boston, that doesn't matter. We don't have to obey this court order."

I hung my head. All I wanted to do was see my sons. I could not understand what was going on. I turned to walk out when the officer said, "Look, missy; I can't accompany you to the Rollins place, but maybe the county sheriff can help you. I'll notify him. Why don't you two wait outside?"

We sat outside in the car for a half hour and waited for the sheriff to appear. When he arrived, he got out of his car and approached us. He took the court order and stared at it.

"Y'know that I cannot enforce this, but I can take you to Dorothy's place and see what happens. You is goin' to have to go with me."

Tom waited in our car, while I got into the sheriff's car. The sheriff knocked on the door, and Dorothy answered. She did not say a word as she answered the door. She did not have to say anything. The look she gave me said it all.

After she opened the door, the sheriff said, "Sorry to bother you, Dorothy, but I got this court order. It seems like the little lady has a complaint."

While he was talking, I spotted Jesse Jr. in the living room. I ran up to him and hugged him. He looked terrible and was very frightened. He was weeping as he told me how much he loved me and missed me.

I asked him where Todd and Greg were. He whispered, "They are living with Daddy. I'm staying with Grandma, so people can think that she is caring for us. I shouldn't tell you this; I could get a beating for it."

I walked back to where the sheriff and Dorothy were standing. Dorothy excused herself and made a phone call. Within fifteen minutes Jesse and Arlene arrived with four goons. Jesse walked over to the sheriff, who said, "Hi, Jesse. I'm glad that you showed up. I have this court order."

"I don't give a shit about no court order. I am not going to obey it, and you can't enforce it."

The sheriff turned to me and said, "He's right, missy. There is not much that I can do."

"Well," I said, "at least document what went on here so I can have something to take to court. Record that two of my sons were not living here. Look at my other son. Write down the way he looks."

The sheriff did as I asked, scribbling something on a piece of paper. This whole scene was a farce. When he was finished writing, I requested a transcript. We then walked out to his car and drove back to the station. When Tom saw the expression on my face, he surmised what had happened.

I ran to my car and only said, "Let's get out of here." On the ride back to Boston, I explained my adventure to Tom. He was not surprised.

As soon as we got home, I telephoned my lawyer.

"You know, Jennifer, this case is becoming a pain in the ass. I won't stand for this. We are going to have to go back to court."

Several weeks later we were back to see the judge. I was there with Mr. Petrone. Jesse's lawyer, Mr. Block, represented the Rollins family. We went into Judge Hack's chambers to tell our stories.

Judge Hack was planted behind his desk as he addressed Mr. Block and asked why the order was not enforced.

"Your Honor, my clients could not obey the order because they were not informed. Two of the boys were not present. Mrs. Rollins has every intent to obey the court's ruling, but adequate notice is required."

"Okay, okay, Mr. Block. That sounds reasonable to me. I don't see any problem here. I am still waiting for the results of the investigation in order to make my determination."

"Your Honor, I'm sure that the investigation will support Mrs. Rollins's contention that she is the rightful guardian."

I could not take this shit anymore. I turned to Mr. Block and said, "How could you know what the report will say? I've never even talked to the investigator."

He looked at me and smiled. "Maybe I phrased it wrong, okay."

Well, that was it. More indecision. More wasted time. Tom was waiting for me outside. He could sense my frustration. I told him what had happened in the judge's chambers.

More weeks passed before we finally saw the investigator. He was a very young man, with a slight build. He interviewed Tom and me for about an hour. I told him all about myself and my history with my children and gave him a list of people who would support my answers. He was very polite, wrote down everything that I said, and asked Tom and me several follow-up questions.

In the months that passed, I called Maine each week to speak to the boys. Each week Dorothy refused to let me talk to them.

Finally, I heard from my lawyer. The investigation was finished. He told me, "I'm sorry, but we lost. The case has been dismissed. Dorothy gets to keep the kids."

"How can we lose? Didn't they see the boys? Couldn't they recognize abuse? Don't they know that I'm their mother and can give them a loving home? What idiot is making the decisions?"

"I know how you feel. I did not believe it myself, but there is nothing that I can do."

"I want to see the investigator's report. I want to read the lies. I want to know what I am fighting."

"I'm sorry, but you are not allowed to read it. It can only be read by the attorneys and the judge."

"If I can't have it, I want my file. I'm going to get another lawyer. I want all the documentation of my case. Someone has got to be able to help me."

Mr. Petrone was angry, but he agreed to give me whatever records he could get. Tom went to his office the next day to pick up the file. He brought the file home, and we went through it. It was filled with legalese and we could not understand it. We had to get another attorney.

I went to see Mr. Donnelly, the attorney that had represented me in my divorce from Jesse. He stated that he would review the case, but an up-front payment of $1,000 would be required. He would have to read all the documentation associated with the case. We told him to "go ahead," even though we had to borrow the money to make the payment.

It took him a week to become acquainted with the case. He called us to his office, told us to sit down, and said, "I have read everything, and I have to tell you that I don't think that you have a chance of winning. If you want, I will still take the case, but it would be futile."

I was upset and asked, "Why are you so sure that we will not win?"

"It doesn't negatively reflect on you. It's just a weak case. The court decided that your sons are better off in Maine. It's up to you; do you want me to proceed on your behalf?"

"I don't want you taking the case if you think that it is a lost cause."

We paid him the money and walked out of the office with nothing. Tom put his arms around me and tried to console me as we walked to the car. I was depressed, very depressed. I had started to feel that everything was hopeless. I deserved to have my children. They should not be given to those derelicts in Maine.

Tom was working on barges and tugboats and was frequently away from home for three or four days at a time. During one of these trips, I felt lonelier than I had ever felt before.

The first night that Tom was gone, I went to the bathroom and took a bottle of Valium from the medicine chest. I poured a handful into my palm and swallowed them, one or two at a time. I went to bed and awaited the end of my problems.

As I settled into a stupor, I started to regret what I had done and called the emergency phone number. That was the last thing that I remembered until I awoke in the hospital. Tom was standing over me.

He explained that they had had to pump my stomach, but I would be okay.

I had been looking for a quick solution. I was depressed and felt like a huge failure. I just wanted it to be over.

When I started to lose consciousness, I had received a shock. All of a sudden, I came to my senses. I did not want to leave my children forever. I wanted to keep fighting for them. I thought about Tom. I loved him and did not want to leave him. I could not leave yet. I reached for the phone.

I had been working in a beauty salon. Soon after I recovered from my accident at the Boston 1800 Club, I went to school, became licensed as a hairdresser, and started work. I liked the job because it was more pleasant than factory work and it provided me with a flexible schedule. I worked my way up from shampoo girl to salon manager, supervising twenty-five employees.

This salon was part of a regional chain. While employed there, I met an attorney who represented the chain. We became close friends, and when I told him about my sons he sympathized with me. He sympathized so much that he obtained a copy of the investigator's report and gave it to me.

It was a thick volume, and it took me three hours to read it. I cried as I read it. It was packed with lies. Perhaps the biggest lie was that I was related to a famous criminal. It lied about my life-style; it said that because I had three previous marriages I was promiscuous. It did not document the boys' abuse at Jesse's hands. It said that they were living with Dorothy and how happy the boys were living in the country. It read like it was written by Jesse.

This lawyer reiterated the opinion of Mr. Donnelly: It was a lost cause. The evidence supported Jesse and Dorothy. But in my heart, I could never give up my children. I could pray to God for a miracle.

CHAPTER TWENTY-ONE

I tried to pull my life together, no matter how painful it was. I immersed myself in my work, twelve hours a day, six days a week. I enjoyed what I was doing, and my employer was satisfied with my work.

My boss, Irving Cohen, owned a chain of fifteen salons in the northeast. In addition to being my boss, he became my friend. I talked to him about my custody battles, and he was very supportive.

I was a novice at business management, but Irving was very patient and taught me how to run a salon. It had been about ten years since I had learned the restaurant business from Eric Lomax. Some of the administrative and financial details of the restaurant business were applicable to the beauty salon business, but for all practical purposes I was starting from scratch.

In addition to Irving, I also became close to Max Levine, the attorney for the chain who had obtained the investigator's report for me.

Without my sons I felt empty. My support system became Tom, Irving, and my father. My father was always very supportive of me. Unfortunately, my mother kept him from being more expressive. I don't recall him ever really criticizing me, even though I made my share of mistakes.

Even though I could not have my sons, there was still Robin. She had just turned thirteen and had spent her childhood with her grandmother and grandfather. Robin had become very spoiled because of the way that my mother indulged her. She was raised as an only child, who was never deprived of anything but her real mother. My mother had never allowed Robin to call me "Mother"; instead she had to call me "Jennifer" or "Jenny."

Even though I did not raise Robin as my daughter, I knew that she was provided for properly. I could not say the same for my sons. I stayed up many nights thinking of how they were being mistreated. They were forced to live with a couple of sadistic alcoholics. I thought about the beatings and the starvation. I was haunted by this nightmare.

I did not give up the custody battle. I spent lots of time and lots of money trying to get my boys back. Although I did not get custody, I was able to regain visitation rights, and I kept battling to get full custody. I would not believe the people who told me that it was futile. Through Mr. Levine, I retained an attorney, who was constantly petitioning the court for custody.

This turned out to be a very expensive proposition. I was fortunate that I had Tom's support. He knew how much my sons meant to me and never questioned the legal expenses.

I became totally disgusted with the Massachusetts judicial system. It was a great big farce. My father had told me that a little authority in the wrong hands was the most dangerous weapon of all. I now knew how right he was. I thought that probably half of the judges sitting on Massachusetts courts should be impeached. They had no right being there, deciding the fates of mothers and children. I fervently wished that there were more women judges in their place. A woman has a natural instinct to protect children. Woman had that maternal instinct, whereas men had to learn compassion.

I was bounced around from one court to another. I was completely frustrated by the manner in which my children and I had been treated by the judicial system. No one had time to listen, and no one cared. The lives of my children were reduced to an enormous, growing legal file that was tossed around among a bunch of apathetic bureaucrats.

My sons were not my only concern. My father was past sixty, with a severe coronary condition. He was barely able to maintain his job in the shipyard. He curtailed most of his outside activities. He no longer bought houses and fixed them up. He spent his spare time in more sedentary pursuits, like playing the stock market.

I felt that my father and I had much in common. My family was split, and so was his. I had always felt closer to my father, while my brother, Sal, gravitated toward my mother. My father helped to raise Robin, but she bore my mother's imprint. She had become a spoiled little brat.

My mother had also spoiled Sal. He got a car as soon as he turned sixteen. When he married, he received a house as a wedding present. He was always self-employed. He had an auto parts store, a tire store, and even an auto dealership purchased for him.

Sal was a chronic gambler, who lost houses and businesses at the Las Vegas crap tables and elsewhere. He was a pathetic character, but my mother would never recognize this. He never changed, and neither did she. He married a woman in his own image. They were like a pair of matching bookends, both greedy and self-centered. The only love that they had was a love for money.

My father's condition slowly deteriorated. He had to retire from the shipyard and was under the constant care of a cardiologist. Dad, along with the rest of his family, was told by the doctor that he required constant care. He could suffer a heart attack anytime.

Tom and I were the only ones who took the doctor's warning seriously. We would run errands for Dad and help around the house. I wanted to do anything to make his life easier. The other members of his family seemed oblivious to his needs. Since they did not have hearts, they probably could not conceive of heart disease.

Religion was always very important to me. I had grown up in a convent and felt close to the church ever since. The Catholic church was a very good and a very strong presence in my life.

Unfortunately, the church had a dark side. Its name was Fr. Nino DeMarco. He was a priest that I had known my entire life. He had been a close friend of my mother's for as long as I could remember. He would come over to my parents' home and make himself at home. He was like no other priest that I had ever known. He would come over, remove his collar, put his feet up, and make himself at home, usually when my father was not there.

Over the years, my father and I had many secret discussions about the priest. Neither of us liked him, but we tolerated him. My father said, "I don't like Father Nino personally. I respect the cloth, not the man."

My father was a very religious man who only missed mass when he became too ill to attend. He went to church every morning before work. I admired his piety and wished that I could match his devotion. It was due to my enormous respect for the church that I had contempt for Father Nino.

He was too bold and too familiar for a priest. My memories of him went back many years. I was about seven years old and home for the weekend from the convent. Father Nino was at our house visiting my mother. Sal was only three at the time and confined to his playpen. My father was remodeling one of his houses.

I was upstairs in my room in my nightgown. Father Nino came upstairs and said that he wanted to talk to me. He walked over to me, and instead of talking, he lifted my nightgown. I ran downstairs screaming. My mother grabbed me and asked what was wrong. When I told her what Father Nino did, she grabbed me, threw me to the ground, and beat me, while calling me a "lying little bitch."

I never forgot that incident. I later told my father, but all he did was shake his head. In the ensuing years, I did my best to stay away from Father Nino.

Whenever Father Nino would visit my mother's house, he acted very familiar toward her, making off-color un-priestlike remarks, like, "Angelina, you look good enough to eat."

My mother would welcome his advances and encourage them, saying, "Well, what's stopping you?"

A priest is supposed to repress his carnal feelings. Father Nino was the exception. He was very bold, even in front of my father. The man would frequently hold my mother's hand or touch other parts of her body. Ever since I was seven years old, I knew that this guy was a pervert. My mother told me that my suspicions "are all in your mind."

I grew to realize that my mother desired Father Nino as a woman wants a man and the feeling was mutual. I am sure that my father realized this before I did, but he did nothing to prevent this relationship from developing. I never understood why. He never wanted to discuss this matter with me.

My father had made quite a lot of money, but not from his job as a shipfitter. It was earned from real estate development and his stock market investments. He was a simple man, not requiring a lot of material goods. He rarely bought new clothes for himself, and he usually drove his car until it fell apart.

On the other hand, he was generous with his family. My mother had a new car almost every year. She also had a lavish wardrobe, packed with furs. My brother always had new cars. He was always conning my father out of money to support his gambling activities. My father knew his son was a creep, but my mother treated her little boy as if he were a deity.

Marriage had not changed my brother. He was given a house and a business as a wedding present. After repeated trips to Las Vegas, the house and the business were heavily mortgaged. I always thought that our irresponsible family contributed to my father's illness.

Since my father's physical condition deteriorated, I was spending more time at my parents' house. It was almost as though I did not trust my mother to care for my father. The more time that I spent there, the more I saw of Father Nino. I tried to stay out of his way, but sometimes I could not control myself, especially when he became familiar with my mother in my father's presence. After I told him, "Get your damn hands off of my mother," both Father Nino and my mother would attack me.

I felt sorry because my father was not respected. Through his labors, my family was very secure financially. My mother never had to work outside the house. Robin never had to want for anything. My brother and his wife had a very comfortable life-style. Whatever my brother lost was replaced. They were not thankful for their good fortune.

Tom or I had to go to the drugstore for my father's medicine. Tom would have to shovel the snow or mow the lawn of my parents' home.

My mother and brother would do nothing for my father. They would let him die with a shovel in his hand.

I felt very frustrated and sought an outlet. I was frustrated by the courts. I was frustrated by my family. I was becoming a hateful person. I needed a release.

One day after I left work, I went straight to see my father. I was excited and wanted his opinion. He saw my enthusiasm and asked, "What are you so excited about?"

"Dad, I want to write a book. You know all that stuff about the pen being mightier than the sword? Well, it seems to make sense to me. I have a lot to tell. I think that it would be a thrilling experience," I bubbled over.

"Jennifer, do you remember the book you wrote when you were twelve years old, *The Little White House on the Hill?*"

I chuckled, "I sure do. It never amounted to anything, did it? This book will be different. It will be an autobiography. If I can't get justice in the real world, I can get it in the literary world."

"No, it didn't amount to anything, but that was the start of becoming a writer. A hairdresser's license is not the proper credential for a writer, but you have the heart of a writer and should do well. Anyway, what the hell do you have to lose?"

My father gave me the confidence and inspiration that I needed. When I left him, I ran out and bought a typewriter. Now I had a typewriter, some paper, and an idea. What more does a writer need?

I did not find writing easy at first. I struggled, but the more I banged on the keys, the easier it became. I barely had enough time to tell my story. I had to sneak a few hours whenever I could. I was working long hours at the salon, helping my father, and spending the weekends in Maine.

Visiting my sons was still a hassle. I would frequently make the trip for naught. Jesse and Dorothy were playing the same old game of not having the boys available when I went to visit. They frequently had to be threatened with *more* court actions before I could visit my sons. The years were slipping by with my boys seeing me sporadically.

I was suffering from stress and anxiety, caused by my not being able to see my sons and by the financial burdens of the litigation. Tom and I were working and bringing home healthy paychecks, but the continuing litigation costs were a burden. We eventually had to go into debt to pay for the continuing legal fees associated with the custody battle.

Finally, I completed my book and was totally thrilled with it. This book was my life story. I told about my experiences as an abused wife. I told about losing my children. I told about my family.

239

The book was a catharsis. It was a vehicle that allowed me to release my frustrations. I spent many evenings talking to my typewriter not knowing what to expect. I felt as though the manuscript was my child.

I decided to call it *A Woman's Heart*. I brought it to my father, as I respected his opinion. He knew that I was writing it and was so excited when I finally brought it to him. He told me that he would read it that day and give me his opinion tomorrow.

My father knew my life and wanted me to finally achieve success. He knew how much I had strived, with little success. I desperately wanted him to like the book. I wanted and needed his approval.

When he telephoned, I held my breath while I waited for his opinion. I felt as though I were being critiqued by the *New York Times*.

My father loved it. He thought that it was honest, down-to-earth, and written with emotion. He was surprised that I could write such a book and advised me to submit it to a publisher.

After a pause, I asked, "Well, Dad, how do you submit a manuscript?"

He laughed and said, "Jennifer, why don't you go to the library and take out some writers' books to find out?"

I was ecstatic and could not wait for Tom to come home that evening. When he arrived, we sat down at the kitchen table and I told him what my father had said.

Tom was not a true believer. Although he supported me, he never believed that my writings would amount to anything. But although he was not as excited as my father, he wanted me to follow through and get the book published.

I was very proud of this accomplishment. A woman with little formal education and no literary training, I wanted this book published for several reasons. I needed the money: my legal fees had put Tom and me deeply into debt. I also wanted to tell my story.

It was an autobiography filled with abuse: wife abuse, child abuse, and abuse at the hands of the legal system. This book might be the only justice that I would ever receive.

I took my father's advice and got several "how to" books for writers. I submitted the manuscript to two different publishers, a royalty house and a subsidy house.

When I arrived home from work three weeks later, Tom handed me two envelopes. I scanned the return envelopes and smiled. I was sure that they were rejection letters, but they weren't. The manuscript had been accepted by both publishers.

The letters contained a lot of technical stuff in addition to reviews of the manuscript. The royalty house offered 10 percent, versus 40 percent for the subsidy house. But in return for the 40 percent of sales, I would have to subsidize the book.

Thaler Books was a vanity press, which means that the writer has to pay for the cost of publishing the book. In this case, the additional 30 percent royalty would cost $6,000.

I did not have $6,000, but I wanted the 40 percent deal because I was very optimistic that the book would be a huge success.

I went to my father to discuss my options with him. He warned me that the only way that I could come up with the money would be if I sold my house.

I went home and explained the options to Tom. I told him that I wanted to sell the house so that we could get the better royalty deal. He sat and shook his head and said, "Now look; if this is the only way you can get your children back, then go ahead and sell the house. We'll publish the book."

I had a primary objective in my life. That objective became an obsession. I wanted my boys home with me. As the years passed, my love for them and my desire to be with them did not diminish. It was 1975 and two of my sons were teenagers. I had missed most of their childhood and did not want to miss any more.

The legal system is structured for the benefit of those with money. The rich can afford the high-priced lawyers and private investigators. I was convinced that if I had had the funds to pay for an adequate custody battle, I would have had my family with me. I knew that Dorothy and Jesse were not providing anything close to an adequate home for my sons. I just did not have the money to prove it.

I called Thaler Books and spoke to one of their representatives. I wanted some personal assurance from the publisher that it was a good manuscript. He quickly reassured me that he saw great things in store for it. He started to talk about screenplays, foreign rights, and other things that I did not understand. He was talking as though it were already a best-seller.

He seemed to be too optimistic. I did not completely believe him, so I decided to call the other publisher, the Chaneysville Press, whose offer I had refused. I talked to David Bradley, one of their representatives. He was very friendly, and we hit it off quickly. He was also optimistic over the manuscript and wanted me to change my mind. He said, "I don't think that you should go ahead with that other publisher. You're more or less committed to me."

I liked David personally, but money was the issue. I wanted to make a cold-blooded business decision. I needed to make money so that I could

241

get my boys back. I resisted David's congenial pitch and stuck to my decision.

I sold my house, sent the publisher the $6,000 and waited for a response. I had kept this book a secret from everyone but my family. I received encouragement from everyone but my mother.

Thaler Books was based in New York City. My publisher was John Nolan. We were on the phone constantly, discussing editing, cover layout, jacket blurbs, etc. I did not realize all of the things that had to be done with a book after it was written. Mr. Nolan was very cordial and businesslike. The more I spoke to him, the more optimistic I became.

In one of our conversations, he recommended that before the galley proofs came out I take a trip to Manhattan so that we could meet. I was ashamed to tell him that it would be difficult because of financial problems. I said that I would get back to him.

I had sold my house and barely got enough out of it to pay the publisher. Tom and I were renting an apartment and still subsidizing the legal profession through my custody fight.

I discussed the situation with Tom. I would have liked to go but was hesitant. In addition to the cost of the trip, I did not want to go the big city alone. Tom could not go with me because he could not take the time off from work. He told me that I should go alone. I decided to ask my father's advice.

I went to see him that evening. My parents were home watching television. I sat next to my father and asked his advice. He said, "Jennifer, I agree with Tom. You should go, even if you have to go alone."

"Well, Dad, I'd like to go, except I feel uncomfortable going alone. I've never been to New York City before. I'd rather not go by myself. But . . . Dad, how about you? How would you like to go with me?"

"I don't know. I . . . I don't see why not."

My mother was sitting quietly listening to my father and me discuss the trip. When she heard that my father might accompany me to New York, she exploded off the chair and said, *"Dominic,* what the hell is the matter with you? You're a sick man. With your heart, you can't go on wild goose chases. You're staying home. Let your daughter go alone."

My father threw up his hands and said, "Okay, okay. I won't go."

Later that evening my father took me aside and told me that if I was afraid of going alone, I could take Sal's wife, Carol. He said that he would be willing to pay the expenses for the trip.

I disliked her and said, "Dad, I don't want to take that bitch along."

"Well, Jennifer, you have two choices. It's either take Carol or go alone."

I called Carol and gave her the good news. She was thrilled. It gave her an excuse to get out of her house. I then called John Nolan, and we set the date for our meeting.

Tom drove us to the airport so that we could catch the seven o'clock shuttle. I was very nervous. This was a completely unique experience. When we landed at La Guardia, I felt as though there were a million butterflies in my stomach. We arrived in New York a little after eight and took a cab to Thaler Books.

Thaler Books was located in lower Manhattan, near Greenwich Village. Their offices were located on the seventh floor of an office tower. Their offices were not what I expected. I was expecting ultramodern offices, packed with overdressed sophisticates. These were average-looking offices with normal-looking people sitting at their desks.

Mr. Nolan's secretary let us into his office. We introduced ourselves and shook hands. He had to go to another office to get a chair for Carol. He was not pleased that I had brought along a traveling companion and said, "I had planned to work with you on your manuscript. Your friend is going to be very bored. What are we going to do with her?"

I sat there, unable to say anything. Mr. Nolan broke the ice, "Well, why don't I take you on a tour of the company?"

He gave Carol and me a fifteen-minute tour of Thaler Books. They rented the entire seventh floor. Their suite of offices was like a rat's maze. We stuck close to Mr. Nolan because we would surely get lost if we didn't. I would have liked to see how books were produced, but the tour only included administrative functions.

Carol was thrilled by the whole scene. She had married right out of high school and never held a job. This might have been the only office that she had ever seen. After taking us back to his office, Mr. Nolan left us alone for a few minutes.

When he finally returned he announced, "Jennifer, I've decided to take you and your sister-in-law sight-seeing in Greenwich Village." I was getting tired of these tours; I wanted to get down to business. Carol did not have a clue as to what was happening; she just wanted to be entertained.

"Mr. Nolan! I would rather get to work and put off the sight-seeing."

"Jennifer, call me John. It makes for a warmer relationship between us. There will be plenty of time for work. I think that we should get to know each other first."

We took the elevator to the first floor and started walking toward Greenwich Village. We walked a few blocks with him pointing out the sights. He then said, "Jennifer, I'm going to take you to a restaurant where Ernest Hemingway did some of his writing."

I was expecting to go to a big fancy restaurant, with expensive food and well-dressed waiters. It was another shattered image. He led us downstairs to a dirty, dumpy, dimly lit café. There was a band playing, but I could barely see it through the cigarette smoke. There was a bar in the center of the room, with small tables all around it.

John picked out a table and seated us. The waiter came by and handed us menus. He stood there as we looked at them. "What would you like to eat?" John asked.

I was very nervous and did not feel like eating, so I told him, "I'm not hungry; we ate on the plane."

Carol gave me a quizzical expression and blurted out, "No, we didn't, and I'm starved!" I realized that I had made a big mistake taking her along. I wished that my father had come instead.

Carol ordered a club sandwich; I just had a cup of coffee. John was asking many questions about the manuscript. He did not believe that it was a true story. He wanted to know all about the characters, especially Jesse and my mother.

The waiter came back, and John ordered drinks for all. It was barely lunchtime, a little early for me to drink, but I went along with him and ordered a daiquiri. Before I was half through with my drink, John was ordering his fourth martini. Our conversation, which had started as very formal, became very friendly.

"Jenny, I want you to know that I read between the lines."

I stared blankly at him and said, "I have no idea what you're talking about; what do you mean by that?"

"I mean that I read between the lines. Your meaning transcends your words."

"But there is nothing to read between the lines. It is an autobiography. Everything is written as it happened."

I thought that the alcohol had affected his thinking, so I let the remark pass without further comment. I was still on my first drink while John and Carol were getting drunk. While John was talking to me about the manuscript, Carol was sitting and babbling to herself. John was slurring his words and weaving in his chair, but he still managed to maintain his conversation about the manuscript.

Suddenly, he turned to me and asked, "Would you do me a favor if I asked you?"

I replied, "Sure, if I can."

"Would you say 'fuck'?"

I stared at him, astounded. I felt as though my eyes were about to pop out of my head. Carol began to laugh. John turned to her and said, "Carol, why don't you say the word for me?"

Carol looked at him with a dazed expression and with slurred speech asked, "Just ask Jennifer when she loses her temper. Then everything could come out of that mouth." I closed my eyes and said a silent prayer. I was expecting a dignified business meeting; I got something quite different.

Just as I thought that this scene could not deteriorate any more, it did. I had my hands under the table, on my lap. I felt John take my left wrist and move it toward him. He placed my palm on his erect penis and held it there.

I was in shock. I did not know what to do; I could not move my hand. I sat there and *held it,* while I stared at Carol, who was as drunk as John. Within seconds, I came to my senses and started flexing my wrist, trying to get free. With one big tug, I was able to free my hand from his grasp. I moved my chair away from him, as I tried to regain my composure.

Needless to say, John was no longer the conservative businessman. He pulled a huge wad of bills from his jacket pocket, threw it on the table, and said, "Jennifer, call your husband and tell him that you won't be in Boston tonight. You've got to spend a night in the city. We are going to have a party in your honor."

"I'm sorry, but I can't. I told Tom that I'd be home. Besides, you didn't tell me about any party."

"Well, it's sort of a surprise."

"Who's going to be there?"

He smiled. "You and me."

Carol was in a drunken stupor by now, and John had trouble zipping his pants over his hard-on. When everything was back in place, he stood up and opened the top buttons of her blouse, while staring at her ample cleavage. She seemed flattered; I was totally amazed.

"Would you like to stay in the city, Carol? I have a friend whom you would really love. His name is Sal."

Carol convulsed in hysterical laughter.

"Why are you so amused?"

"That's my husband's name."

John led her to a dark corner of the café, where he pinned her to the wall while fondling and kissing her. Carol was obviously enjoying it, because she returned his affection.

After they were all fondled out, they came back to the table and sat down. I turned to John and said, "I'd like to leave the restaurant."

Carol had her eyes on the wad of bills on the table as John said, "I'm all for that!" He picked up the money, leaving some on the table, and pressed two 100-dollar bills into my hand and said, "Here, come on. We're getting the hell out of here."

245

He clung to Carol as they staggered out of the restaurant. Once outside, he hailed a cab and instructed the driver to take us to the Commodore Hotel, after the cab dropped him off at his office. He told me to get a suite with the $200. He would go to his office and make some excuse to take the rest of the day off. Then he would round up his friend Sal and meet us at the hotel.

He continued to babble in the taxi about what a great time we would have. Carol would be entertained by Sal, and he would entertain me. He even promised Carol and me a midnight cruise on his yacht.

When the taxi stopped in front of John's office, he kissed me on the cheek, jumped out of the cab, and ordered the driver to take us to the Commodore. Carol jumped up and down on her seat as she waved good-bye to him. Then as the taxi sped off, she sat back, turned to me, and, still laughing, said, "Isn't this exciting, Jennifer?"

I lashed out at her, "You make me sick!"

"What do you mean?"

"I mean we're not going to any hotel. We're going back to Boston."

Carol was enraged. "But why? I don't have to tell Sal. I'll keep your secret."

"Humph! You'll keep my secret? You'd be the first one to hang me if you could."

I turned to the driver and said, "Forget about the Commodore. Take us to La Guardia, the Eastern shuttle."

I had my hands full trying to get Carol on the plane. She was acting like a complete ass and was furious because I did not want to stay in New York City. On the flight, she passed out drunk.

When we got to Boston, I put her in a cab and sent her home alone. Taking Carol along was the worst piece of advice that my father ever gave me.

CHAPTER TWENTY-TWO

I was emotionally drained when I arrived home. Tom was waiting for me as I sat down, poured a glass of wine, and proceeded to tell him the whole story.

Tom stood up and had rage in his voice as he said, "Well, you'll probably get screwed out of that book. I don't know how, but somehow you're going to get screwed again." I did not tell him what I was holding under the table at the café. I'd wait until he settled down.

At that moment, the phone rang. It was my father, anxiously calling Tom to see if he had heard from me. He was surprised when I answered the phone. Again I repeated the story of my adventure in Manhattan.

When I finished, my father groaned and said, "My poor daughter. Your book will never make it. This man is going to cheat you out of everything. If you didn't go to bed with him, he will take advantage of you in another way. I don't know how, Jennifer, but I know that you are going to be hurt."

I felt a familiar surge of terror inside me. I said, "Oh, God, please don't let me be hurt again." All our money was tied up in the book. We had sold our home because of it and were living in a four-room apartment. But as God would have it, what my father had told me proved to be true.

My father told me to call John Nolan and tell him that I would be returning the money. When I called, I got right through to him.

"Hello, John. It's Jennifer."

"Yes, I know. You're in Boston?"

"Yes, I'm in Boston. John, I still have your $200. I'm going to send it right back to you."

"Forget it, Jennifer. Don't worry about the money. Look; I'll be sending you some things through the mail. Just watch for them."

I received correspondence, keeping me aware of the book's progress. Before it was to be published, I received the galley proofs. I did everything necessary, and the book was finally published. I was eagerly expecting my first royalty payment when I found out that my father was right. I had been screwed.

I did not check out this subsidy house. I had no legal representation when I signed the contract. I basically believed this publisher, which was a bad mistake. I wound up getting 0 percent rather than 40 percent. This was not a reliable subsidy house, so I could not trust them to honor their contract. I knew that the book had some success in the Boston area, but I never received an accounting.

I was in a familiar situation. I needed help and did not know where to turn. I knew nothing about the literary world and was looking for someone to represent me. No attorney in Boston would represent an unknown author with no money. Most of the literary attorneys were in New York City, and I did not have the money to go hunting for one.

The only positive to come out of this whole mess was David Bradley. We kept in contact through the publishing process, and he was the only one that I could turn to. He knew that I was treated unethically, and after many "I told you so's," he said that the best that he could do was get one of the attorneys for his firm to break my contract with Thaler and retain my copyright. I would not get any money out of this, but I would get my book back. David kept his word, and I was able to retain my copyright.

I felt as though I had hit bottom. I was counting on *A Woman's Heart* to provide the funds that I so desperately needed. Instead it broke my heart. I brought a simplistic attitude into the business world, and I got screwed.

I gave up any ideas of writing anything else. My first attempt was thoroughly discouraging. I decided to concentrate on my other pursuits, which were my job and my continuing fight to get my children back.

Just as the shock of my publishing experience was wearing off, I received another surprise. While at the beauty salon, I received a call from my son Jesse Jr. I was amazed that he could find me. It had been several months since I had seen him, and I was surprised when he asked if he could come and visit me. He was seventeen and he could make some decisions on his own. He said that he would see me this weekend.

I was walking on air. The people who worked with me were very excited for me. They were hugging and kissing me when I told them that I was seeing my son after all this time. I went home early and couldn't wait for Tom to come home so that I could tell him. I telephoned my parents as soon as I got home. I was so excited, I did not know what to do.

I had given Jesse Jr. my home number so that he could call me that evening. There was so much to catch up on. I did plenty of food shopping and cooking. I wanted this reunion to be something special.

Jesse Jr. was coming to Boston by bus. I was at the Greyhound station several hours before his bus was scheduled to arrive. Tom and

Robin were with me. About ten of the employees from the salon met us at the terminal. Some had drawn a picture of a bus and a mother waving to her son. Another had a sign that said: WELCOME HOME, JESSE.

As the bus drove into view, my stomach was filled with butterflies and my mind filled with anxiety. What if Jesse resented me for not going to see him? What if he didn't recognize me? What if he didn't show up?

We walked up to the gate and watched the passengers get off. I did not recognize anyone when suddenly I felt a tap on the shoulder. I turned and faced my son.

Jesse was not what I visualized. I had imagined that he would be taller, but the boy who stood before me was a poorly dressed, baby-faced young man with a laundry bag thrown over his shoulder and a baseball mitt in one hand. He was barely five feet tall. "Hey, look at me," he said. "It's me, Ma. What's the matter? Don't you recognize me? It's me, Ma. It's Jesse."

I threw my arms around him and sobbed. I did not want to let go of him. My actions embarrassed him. He pleaded, "Please, Mother. We're in public."

He then ran to his sister. I was amazed that he remembered her. He said, "Hi, Robin. Look what I brought you," as he handed her a baseball mitt. "I have another one in my laundry bag."

Robin took it without saying anything. Her face had no expression. I sensed Jesse's disappointment and wanted to change the subject. "Come on, everyone; the car is parked around the corner. Let's go home."

On the way to our apartment, I barraged him with questions. "How are your brothers?"

"Oh, they're fine."

"Do they ever want to visit?"

"Sure, Ma."

"What were you doing?"

"Not much, Ma." He was obviously uncomfortable, so I left him alone.

I wanted him to feel comfortable and at home. "Jesse, I borrowed a roll-away cot for you, because our apartment is so small, but if you'll be patient, Mother will work hard and we'll get another house where you'll have your own room."

As I emptied Jesse's laundry bag and sorted his belongings, I noticed bottle after bottle of medications. He looked like a very frail child. These medications confirmed it. He was still having epileptic seizures. As he explained it, "Mommy, I have to tell you something. I do many funny things, and you may not want me. After I do these things, I don't remember them."

As I went through Jesse's stuff, I said a little prayer. "Oh, God. For the first time you have given me my wish. I have one child back. It's not all that I want, but it's better than nothing."

I was thrilled that he called me "Mommy" or "Ma." Robin, at my mother's insistence, still referred to me as "Jennifer" or "Jenny."

Later, when we got Jesse settled, he told us some horrendous stories of abuse. We knew about him having to live in the cellar and about the beatings at the hands of his father. Jesse told us about his brother Todd, who had turned completely wild due to the abuse.

As he related these and other stories, my hatred of Jesse Sr. and Dorothy was rekindled. My hatred grew so strong that I wanted to grab a gun and race to Maine and shoot those assholes.

In addition to epilepsy, Jesse had multiple hernias and had been brain-damaged during one of the beatings that fractured his skull. The doctors wanted to know how he got so beaten up. I told them all about his father.

I had little money and no medical insurance, but I took Jesse to specialists and tried to provide as much care as I could. I had taken time off from work to be with him, but as much as I wanted to stay home, I couldn't, as we were sliding deeper into debt.

I tried to get some kind of public funding to help with Jesse. Again, the system was cold toward me. I was refused welfare. I thought that he would qualify under a Social Security disability, but I was wrong again.

While I was at work, I arranged for one of my cousins who was a nurse to look in on Jesse during the day. Some days I took him with me to the salon. The hairdressers fell in love with him. Each one volunteered to play hooky from work to watch over him. They would take him for long walks around town and buy him stuff. He was a lovable boy, a joy to have around, very innocent, and very immature.

Jesse was always looking for his sister. He wanted to get acquainted with the family that he never knew. Unfortunately, his family was not as anxious to be with him. He used to telephone Robin, but she would never speak to him. He tried to contact Sal and Carol, but they wanted no part of my family. They were very selfish and greedy people.

My father, on the other hand, was great to Jesse. He tried to bring him into the family. He would take Jesse to mass. Jesse was baptized a Catholic but raised a Protestant. He decided that he would like to be a Catholic like his grandfather. I took Jesse to a priest who began to give him instructions in the Catholic faith.

Jesse was a great kid. He had a wonderful attitude and did not have to be ordered to do anything. He would run errands and clean the apartment. He ate whatever he was fed. I wished that I had him with me much sooner. He was a happy child, who was ecstatic to be home with his mother again.

Just as I was starting to enjoy my son, there was a problem with my daughter. I had not seen Robin for a while and was becoming suspicious. I questioned my father, who would not give me a straight answer. Even Jesse knew something was wrong. He said, "Mom, I tried to call Robin again today, but she wasn't there, and I haven't seen her at Gramp's house. Doesn't she like me? Doesn't she want to see me?"

I knew something was wrong. I called my brother and asked if our parents or Robin was at his home. He avoided giving me an answer; I only got a wisecrack about my losing my family again. I hung up on the asshole.

I drove over to my parents' house. My father was there alone. "Dad, what's wrong? Where is Robin? What are you hiding from me?"

He sat me down at the kitchen table and proceeded to explain, "Okay, Jennifer. This is what happened. One night when your mother and I were out, Robin had packed her clothes and left. It happened about a week ago. Your mother and I did not want to worry you. We have been taking turns looking for her. Your mother is out right now, looking for her."

I got up and screamed, *"How could she run away!"*

Although Robin was raised by my parents, she was still my daughter. I had trusted them to take care of her. I was heartbroken when my father told me what had happened. Just as I found one child, I lost another!

Suddenly a thought appeared to me, that if anyone knew about Robin's disappearance, it would be my sister-in-law, Carol. Since Robin had turned nineteen, she had been very friendly with Sal's no-good wife.

I went over to their house. My brother was working, but Carol was there, and I confronted her. "Where is Robin?"

"How the fuck should I know!"

Suddenly I grabbed her and pinned her to the wall and shook her. "Where is my daughter? You tell me now, or I'll beat the shit out of you. I don't give a flying fuck for any of you!"

Carol was turning white, as I had my hands at her throat. "Yes, I know where your daughter is, but I have no intention of telling any of you. I don't give two shits for your family."

I grabbed her blouse and pushed her to the floor, then sat on her, while I pounded on her with closed fists. Sal came through the door, just as I was about to turn his wife into hamburger.

Sal saw what was happening when he opened the door. He ran over to us and started yelling, "*Are you crazy?* You can't come into my house and beat my wife. What the fuck is wrong with you?"

I stood up and turned on him. "Why, you arrogant little shit! Mom and Dad have been out every night looking for Robin. I've been going crazy worrying. Even my son is concerned about Robin's disappearance. You two assholes don't give a fuck. I should kill the both of you."

Sal, in a somber voice, said, "Carol, tell my sister where Robin is before there's more trouble."

"Sal, you fuckin' asshole, I'll tell your sister *shit!*"

I ran from the house and slammed the door behind me. I went home mad and stayed mad. I remained awake all that night thinking about Robin.

Several days later, one of the hairdressers told me that he had seen Robin and had followed her home. He gave me her address. She was living in an old apartment building on Main Street in Malden.

I went to visit her after work. She was living in a run-down apartment with two older women, two sleazy-looking women who appeared to be in their thirties. She did not have her own bed; she was sleeping on the floor. The place looked as though it had not been cleaned in months, if not years. There were empty beer cans all over the place, and the aroma of marijuana was in the air.

One of her roommates opened the door for me. She was high on something. "Yeah, what do you want?" she greeted me.

"I'm Robin's mother. I've come to see her."

"*Hey, Robin!* Your mamma's here."

I walked into the apartment and felt nauseous. Robin was sitting on the couch. "MA! What are you doing here?"

"What am I doing here? I'm here to see you. What the hell is the matter with you? Why did you run away from your home to come to a dump like this? Don't you have any consideration for other people? Don't you know that your grandparents and I are worried sick over you?

"Your grandfather is seriously ill, and you are making his condition worse. This is the man who raised you, the man who worked like a dog to give you everything, and this is how you repay him?"

"Look, Ma; I don't give a *fuck* about anyone. I'm going to do my own thing. The only one that helped me was Carol. She is my only friend. She is the one who helped me get this place. The rest of you can *go to hell!*"

My daughter and I did not speak the same language. I lowered my voice and tried to reason with her. "Robin, you are ruining your life. You have a home. You have people that care about you. You can correct your mistake. Please come home."

"I'm happy here, Ma. Why don't you leave me *alone*?"

"Good-bye, Robin!"

I made repeated unsuccessful visits to Robin's apartment to try to change her mind.

My children were in opposite situations. My daughter had a family that cared for her and wanted her back. Nobody but Tom and I wanted my son. Jesse's brain injuries left him a perennial child. He had a childish desire to be loved and accepted.

Jesse would continually call my brother in a vain attempt to win his love and acceptance. Sal constantly brushed off his nephew. He did not even want to speak to him.

Jesse had to be admitted for neurosurgery to relieve the pressure on his brain caused by too many beatings at the hands of his father. He was afraid of the surgery. He called Sal, his grandparents, and Robin, in a vain attempt to get them to visit him in the hospital.

Tom and I were his only visitors. Jesse's grandfather was too ill to visit but sent flowers.

The surgery on Jesse was successful, and he was home within a few weeks. Robin was still sharing an apartment with the two degenerates.

My father had raised Robin as his daughter, so her new life-style exacerbated his heart condition. He was deeply worried and broken-hearted, and rather than fighting, he was slowly giving up. This incident with Robin might have been the last straw. He had worked his whole life to be a good husband and father, without a whole lot to show for it. He had been married to a woman for close to forty years, a woman who did not respect him. His son was a chronic gambler. His granddaughter, whom he had raised as a daughter, shunned him to live the life of a streetwalker. Then there was me!

I frequently lost my temper when I called Robin. "Robin, if anything happens to my father because of you, I'm going to come over and beat the shit out of you!" She just laughed and hung up the phone.

The next night, the doorbell rang and Jesse, who was home from the hospital, answered it. Two policemen were at the door. They asked for me. "Mrs. Rickerts, we have a harassment complaint against you filed by a Robin Vicci."

I was enraged and lost my temper. "WHAT! Harassment! That's my daughter. She can't do that." I related our recent mother and daughter history to the officers. They looked bored.

"Look, Mrs. Rickerts; she has rights."

"*Rights!* Robin has rights!" I turned to Tom and said, "Isn't it a joke? Everybody has fucking rights but me." The officers gave me a copy of the complaint and left.

253

I was in the process of buying another house with a $4,000 down payment loaned to me by my father. I was determined that Jesse would have his own bedroom. The house was in Medford, very near where my parents lived. It was a "handyman's special" that needed a complete overhaul, from wiring to plumbing.

It was a two-family house. We occupied the first floor and advertised the second floor for rent. We rented the second floor to a couple of newlyweds, Patricia and Ed Mastrangelo. Very quickly, they became like a sister and brother to me, instead of tenants. Coming home after work, before going upstairs, Ed would often stop by our apartment to see what was for supper, as I cooked Italian food, a skill that Ed's Irish wife had not yet learned. In the evening they would come downstairs to watch television with us.

One day Jesse did not return home from school. I became frantic. I was afraid that he had had an epileptic fit. I went to the police, who because of his condition put out an all-points bulletin for him.

They found him back in Maine. His father had contacted him and told him that he had to rush back to Graysville. I was completely shocked and did not know what was going on. I spoke to Jesse Jr. on the phone. He would not tell me why he had to leave so suddenly. He just said that he would have to stay there "for a while."

My father would frequently come over to our house and spend the evenings with Tom and me. Dad became more and more alienated at his home. My mother spent more time with Father Nino than with my father, even though he was weakened by his heart condition. My mother and Father Nino would spend the evenings with Sal and Carol. My father did not want to spend the evenings alone, so he came over to our place.

He confessed to me how lonely he was and how alienated he felt. He missed Robin and would not accept the fact that she had left. He was destroyed by my mother abandoning him for Father Nino.

Father Nino had been close to the family for as long as I could remember. Since my father's illness, he had gotten closer. Father Nino, even though he was a priest, was not a kind man. He was rude and crude.

Even though Robin's leaving had hurt my father, he never wanted to punish her. He just wanted her to come back. He did not want her to get hurt.

One evening when I was at my parents' house, I witnessed the conflict between a pious man and an impious one. My father and Father Nino were discussing Robin. My father said, "I know that Robin is making a big mistake. I just hope she sees the light before she gets hurt."

Father Nino had a different opinion. "Dominic, what are you worrying for? Leave her out on the street. It is a fit punishment for the girl."

My father stood up and screamed, *"Nino, get out of my house!"*

My mother joined the fray. "Dominic, don't you *ever* talk to any of my friends like that. Never open your mouth to Father Nino again. If you don't treat him with the proper respect, I'll leave you. I'll leave you here to die!"

I felt that my mother and Father Nino were abusing my father. He was a man who had earned respect, not indignities. I could not stand by and say nothing, "Don't you ever talk to my father like that again. Who the hell do you think that you are? You know, you've done nothing but neglect my father, and abuse me. No one fits your image but Sal, Carol, and Father Nino. There is something wrong with you people. The world does not revolve around you."

My mother struck back. "You, you little tramp, shut your mouth. You think you're a hairdresser. You think you're a writer. You think you're a mother. Let me tell you what you are. You're a whore! You were a whore, and you will always be a whore."

My father struggled to stand up. He had to lean with one hand against the couch. "Angelina, you can't talk to our daughter like that . . . " My father could no longer stand up and collapsed back onto the couch.

My mother ran out of the house and jumped into her car. Father Nino followed close behind her. I stayed with my father and tried to console him. At that moment I hated my family and was ashamed of them.

Several weeks later, I was sleeping soundly when I was awakened by the persistent ringing of the doorbell. There was also a loud banging on the door, and Tom was shouting, "Jennifer, answer the door!"

I was accustomed to medicating myself with Valium, so I was very weary as I staggered to the door and fumbled with the lock. I opened the door to find my brother standing there. "Sal, what the hell are you doing here?" I mumbled.

He did not look at me as he said, "Jennifer, Daddy's dead. He died in his sleep."

The shock woke me in a hurry. I was incredulous. My father would not die. My father would not leave me. God could not be this cruel.

I went berserk, screaming and punching Sal across the face. *"He's not dead! He's not dead! You're a fuckin' liar. Where's my father?"*

I woke the house. Ed and Patricia came running downstairs, and Tom raced to the front door. They saw me pounding on Sal and screaming, *"You dirty, rotten liar!"*

Everyone was trying to calm me down, without success. It was a wild scene. Tom was yelling, "Jennifer, go to your mother! Let's go to your mother's house! C'mon, Jennifer!"

I wildly replied, "I want my father! Where's my father? I have to see my father!"

Sal told me, "Jennifer, he was taken to Malden Hospital."

Without a word, I ran to get the car keys, grabbed my coat, and hurried out the door. Tom, Ed, and Patricia rode with me to the hospital.

I raced into the emergency room of the hospital and demanded to know where my father was. *"Where is my father! Dominic Vicci! Dominic Vicci! Where is he?"*

I was surrounded by Tom, Ed, and Pat. They were trying to control me. I was out of control in the emergency room. Doctors and nurses were starting to gather around us, trying to calm me.

"I just want to see my father. All of you get away from me."

Finally one of the doctors said that if I settled down, he would take me to the morgue to see my father.

I was not prepared for what I was about to see. The memory is just as vivid now as it was then.

I was led to the basement, with Tom and Ed holding me up on each side. *Oh, God,* I thought. *It looks like a room full of operating tables on wheels.* There were about ten gurneys with bodies covered by green sheets.

We started walking through the morgue when I identified my father on one of the tables, by the ticket attached to his big toe.

I broke free of Tom and Ed and threw myself across my father's body, sobbing wildly. "Please don't leave me, Daddy. Don't leave me. Please don't do this to me. Please don't leave me, Daddy."

I was not the only one crying. Even the nurses who accompanied us wept. I was lifted off my father's body and dragged to a wheelchair. They injected me with a sedative. Although I was sedated, I sat in the wheelchair for only a few minutes. I got up, ran from the hospital, and drove straight to my mother's house.

A crowd of mourners had gathered at her house. I went inside, and one of the first people that I recognized was Robin. I said to myself, *Of all times for Robin to come home.* My resentment toward Robin surfaced.

I grabbed her and pinned her to the wall and screamed, *"You killed my father!* He was the only member of the family that I ever loved. It had to be my own child who took my father's life. You took my father. I'll never ever forgive you for that." At that moment I felt nothing but contempt for my family, contempt for Robin, Sal, and especially my mother.

I was striking Robin while I was yelling. People gathered around us and tried to restrain me. The sedation kicked in and I passed out.

The wake was held at the funeral parlor. He was in an open coffin in a large room filled with mourners. Tom held my arm as he escorted me into the room. When I saw my father's body, I broke free from Tom, ran to the coffin, and threw myself over it and sobbed uncontrollably. Tom and others were able to pull me from the coffin and seat me in a corner.

With the help of Valium, I was able to settle down. But I was not prepared for what was to come next. Father Nino appeared and stood before the coffin, with my mother, and began to say the Rosary.

I saw it as such an insult to my father. Here were my mother, and the priest who was fucking her, praying over my father. I could not control myself. *"Nino, get the hell out of here!* You will not say my father's eulogy. You are not going to walk in my father's shoes."

People tried to restrain me, but I just kept screaming, "You're not taking over my father's life or walking in his shoes!"

I sat and watched as the line of mourners passed in front of my father's coffin. I wondered, *How many of them cared for him? How many are here as an obligation?*

My mother's family, the DeVitos, were together as they approached the coffin, saying, "Doesn't he look wonderful?"

I exploded again. "You fuckin' hypocrites, kneeling at my father's coffin, saying he looks wonderful! You never gave a shit about him."

Their words burned in my head. My father had helped so many of them, but not one of them had come near him during his illness.

I turned to my mother and said, "I'm going to take a vow that no one will shut my mouth again. My father had to be quiet every minute of his life so that you and your son would not be upset. Well, I will never shut up. I will say everything that my father wanted to say and couldn't. I swear before my father's coffin that you will pay."

I meant every word of it. As the procession of mourners approached our family to offer condolences, I just stood there, with an angry expression, muttering, "What a fuckin' farce," and staring at the coffin.

As they approached me, I called many of the mourners "fuckin' hypocrites." The wise among the mourners avoided me, offering their respects to my mother, Robin, Sal, and Carol.

The wake lasted three days.

CHAPTER TWENTY-THREE

Following my father's wake, I suffered a breakdown and eventually ended up in the hospital with heart problems of my own. My prolonged grief included visits with psychiatrists. They were not able to help me. I could not deal rationally with the loss. I felt I was the only one truly mourning. I was the only one that missed Dad.

I would run to the cemetery, where my father's grave was covered with flowers. I would take some of the flowers home and staple them to the wall of my room.

I was angry because my family did not miss my father as much as I did. Soon after the funeral, I went to my mother's house and found her sitting amidst a crowd who were all eating and drinking.

To the Italians, a death was just another excuse for a party. If someone died, you ate. If someone was born, you ate. If someone got married, you ate.

While they ate, I rummaged through my father's room with a trash bag in my hand, collecting all of my father's personal belongings. I took his clothes, his spiritual bouquets, his sympathy cards, his jewelry, everything that could remind me of him. I could not accept his death.

My family avoided me. I was doing crazy things. I continued to dress in black months after he was laid to rest. I had his clothing sent to the dry cleaner's and then hung it in my closet.

I adopted a ritual of leaving the house early in the morning and spending much of the day at my father's grave site. It had become so bad that when Tom arrived home from work and I wasn't at home, he knew where to find me. He would drive to the cemetery and pull me from the grave.

I could not accept the fact that my mother did not mourn. I was the only family member that cried at the wake. People who did not know mistook me for my father's wife. I broke down, while my mother was emotionless. She acted as if the dog had died.

Father Nino's presence intensified after my father's death. He would spend more time at my mother's house, eating most of his meals there. He would wear my father's clothes, the ones that I had not removed. It was as though he were my mother's new husband. She did not believe in a mourning period. She went from one husband to another.

Tom came home one night and saw me clutching my chest. He rushed me to the hospital, where they at first thought I had suffered a heart attack. But the tests did not reveal a heart attack.

They thought that it might be psychosomatic. I was despondent and refused to speak to the doctors. Instead, they questioned Tom about my childhood and my relationship with my parents, especially my mother. He gave them what background he had, but they needed the details that only I could provide.

I did not want to reveal the details of my personal life. I had been taught from childhood to suppress my feelings and not disclose them to anyone outside my family.

I was admitted to the psychiatric ward of the hospital. Every day I saw a new psychiatrist. I would not talk to them. When they asked me a question, I just turned my head. One day I was visited by a psychiatrist who was more persistent than the rest. He arrived with Dr. Madden, our family doctor.

When I turned away from this psychiatrist he yelled, "How long are you going to continue this? Do you realize how young you are? You have your whole life ahead of you! You're emotionally crippled! Let us help you!"

I turned to stare at the psychiatrist, a young man in his midthirties with a pad of paper in his hand. I thought that he and the others thought that I could tell my life's story in thirty seconds. That was impossible.

Dr. Madden stood over me and said, "I'm just an internist. You require two doctors. One for your body and one for your mind. You have to accept the death. You need a psychiatrist to help you."

I turned to him, suddenly hating all men. My words dripped with sarcasm. "What the fuck can you do to help me? Do you think that the man over there sitting down with a pencil and a piece of paper is going to cure what I have? *In ten minutes* he's going to help me?"

Dr. Madden had been patient with me; he wanted to soothe me. "Jennifer, please!"

"Don't 'please' me, Dr. Madden. Do you truthfully think that the psychiatrist can help me?"

"Yes, Jennifer. I do! Give him a chance."

"You really think that he is a good psychiatrist?"

"Yes, I do, Jennifer."

"Then have him bring my father back, and then I'll tell you if he's a good psychiatrist."

I turned to the psychiatrist and said quietly, "Get out of my room. I don't believe in psychiatry. I have no use for you. You can't cure my mind, because you could never understand my problems. Get out!"

I looked at Dr. Madden and asked, "Are you going to commit me to a mental institution?"

"Why, no, Jennifer."

"Then I want to be released!"

"Jennifer, at least stay in the hospital for a rest."

"Am I going to be committed?"

"No, you're not!"

"Then I want out! I can do better by myself. I know how to heal my own wounds. I've learned from a very young age how to heal my own wounds."

Dr. Madden had me discharged on the condition that I see a psychiatrist of my own choice, as an outpatient. He called Tom and told him that I was being discharged immediately. I got dressed and waited for Dr. Madden to sign the papers.

When he came back into my room he was infuriated. I was dressed in black from head to toe. "Jennifer, they don't do that anymore. That was done in the Dark Ages. You can't go through life like this, totally in black. It's not going to bring your father back," he told me.

I did not want a lecture. I snarled, "Mind your own fucking business!" He started to back away from me, just as Tom came into the room. He heard my last remark and hurried me out of the room. He took me home where I could brood in peace.

Several days after I left the hospital, I was in the backyard of our house. I thought that I was hallucinating. I saw my son Jesse approach. I thought, *Oh, God, I'm seeing things. It can't be my son.*

I raced to him and hugged and kissed him. He was dirty and tired. He had hitchhiked from Maine. He said that his father no longer wanted him. Jesse Jr. was running away to join the circus. He had stopped by to say good-bye to me before he joined the Big Top.

I was stunned as I sat in a chair and listened. I pulled him close to me and questioned him about his health. He said that he was "okay, and I'm not taking any medicine."

Jesse had just been released from a detention center where his father had him committed. He had been unable to contact me. I did not want to believe what he was telling me. He then gave me a big surprise. Dorothy was dead. Alcoholism finally killed her. Jesse did not want me to know because he feared that I would heat up the custody battle.

My life was as confused as ever. I was sure of at least one thing: I did not want my son to run away. I wanted him to remain with me. He had changed. He was not the same compliant, malleable boy who was with me before. He refused to change his plans.

Jesse told me that he had stopped by my mother's house to visit Robin, but my mother would not let him. It seem that she was entertaining Father Nino and did not want to be disturbed. My mother did not gently turn him away. She had to be cruel about it. She told him that she did not want him near Robin because he had "bad blood."

I asked him why he went to his grandmother's house before he came here. He explained that he had gone to see his grandfather, not knowing that he was dead.

I was about to go the cemetery and asked Jesse to accompany me to see his grandfather's grave. He refused, saying, "Mom, I don't want to see it. Please don't show it to me."

"Don't be silly, Jesse."

"Please, Mom, I don't want to go to the grave."

I did not force him to go. I left him at home while I went alone.

Aunt Theresa came by and told me that my mother was "ill from stress" and could use a vacation. My aunt asked me to take my mother away for a week or so.

I laughed scornfully. "What do you expect me to do with my son Jesse? He's epileptic. Besides, he just came home. How can I accompany my mother anywhere?"

I felt my first obligation was to my child. I did not feel right about leaving him, since he just came home. Sal or Carol or one of the other family members could go with her. She didn't need me.

My mother began to call, pleading with me to take a vacation with her. I had an uneasy feeling. My mother had stabbed me so many times before this. I did not know what she was up to. I explained that I did not want to leave Jesse alone while Tom was working.

My mother informed me that she was planning to take a Caribbean cruise with Robin and wanted me to make it a threesome. My mother was persistent, but I was resentful. I was angry at both my mother and Robin.

"Look, Ma; I have no further use for Robin. If Robin is accompanying you on the cruise, she should be sufficient company. You shouldn't need me."

"Well, if that's the way you feel about it, good-bye."

Jesse was still insisting that he wanted to run away and join the circus. I did all that I could to talk him out of it. I called an attorney and the police. I wanted Jesse put under protective custody. I was informed that he was of legal age and he could do as he pleased. I explained about his epilepsy, but it made no difference.

261

Tom, Ed, and Patricia also tried to persuade Jesse to change his plans. They explained that he finally had a home that wanted him and he should not give it up.

My mother had a different approach. She did not think that children should be coddled. She told me to "play hard. Throw him in the street. Throw him out, like I did you. Show him what it feels like to be thrown in the street. Then he'll want you." I knew what my mother meant. The more I thought about it, the more bitter I became.

Jesse told me that he was going to New Jersey to meet up with the circus. I did all that I could to stop him. I sobbed; I pleaded; I begged. I even telephoned his father, who told me, "I think that it's a great idea. It'll be a thrilling experience for the kid to join the circus. It'll be something that he will always remember."

I was very distraught and did not know what to do. Tom saw how upset I was and tried to talk me into taking the cruise with my mother and Robin. He thought that it would do me some good to get away from things for a while. He said that with the help of Ed and Patricia, he could easily take care of Jesse for the week that I would be gone. He also hoped that I would be able to reconcile with my daughter and mother. Against my better judgment, I decided to go on the cruise.

I regretted the decision immediately. What was supposed to be a trio became much more. Two aunts and two cousins joined us. My mother did not need or want my companionship. She had wanted to separate me from Jesse.

By the time that I realized this, Tom had already paid for the ticket. I wanted to back out, even after the travel agent informed me that I would have to forfeit the money. Tom, my mother, Ed, and Patricia spent the next three days trying to talk me into taking the cruise. I relented and decided to go.

Even though I decided to go, I was not very enthusiastic about the trip. As Tom helped me pack, I told him how bitter and resentful I was about the whole thing.

My mother arranged for her, Robin, and me to share a cabin. I could not stand the sight of those two during the cruise. The cabin became very crowded. I smoked heavily, and my mother screamed that she could not tolerate cigarette smoke. I responded, "Then how come you don't holler when Sal smokes?"

"Sal smokes a better quality cigarette that doesn't bother me as much," she said.

I spent as much of the cruise as possible isolated from my mother and daughter. I did not have a good time. My aunts and cousins were having a ball. I was worried about my son and still mourning my father. The journey was uneventful, and I could not wait to return home.

The night before the ship was to dock in New York, I had a crazy dream. I dreamed that everyone was looking for a little boy who was lost in the ocean, but no one could find him. I awoke very frightened.

When we arrived in New York, there was a Greyhound bus waiting to take us to Boston. When the bus made a rest stop, I made a call to Tom. I had a premonition that something was wrong, and I had to speak to him right away.

I could not reach him, so I called Ed and Patricia. I reached Ed and began to question him. "Have you seen Jesse? Where is he? Where is Tom?" Ed reassured me that everything was fine and I shouldn't worry.

The trip to Boston seemed to last forever. Ed's reassurances did not help. My mind was not at ease, and the nearer that we came to Boston, the more unsettling were my feelings. I sensed an impending disaster.

When the bus pulled into the Boston Greyhound terminal, Tom, Sal, and Carol were there to meet us. My mother and Robin left with Sal and Carol, without even saying good-bye to me. Tom drove me home.

As I was unpacking my luggage, Tom had something to say to me. "I don't want you to get excited . . . but Jesse ran away. Probably to New Jersey like he was talking about. He must have hitched a ride while the three of us were out. We tried to always have someone watch him, but there was nothing that we could do."

I did not say a word. I took three Valiums and collapsed on the bed.

It must have been five or six hours later when I heard the telephone ring. I heard Tom talking but could not make out his words. All of a sudden his tone changed and he began to yell. *What is he screaming at?* I wondered.

I went into the living room where ribbons from my father's flowers were still stapled to the walls. I said to myself, *Death is still in the house.*

Tom looked at me, his face completely white. He did not say a word. He only stared at me while he held the telephone. I felt a sudden panic and knew that something was wrong. I screamed, "Tom, what's wrong?"

He dropped the phone, ran to me and pushed me into a chair. He blurted out, "Jesse Jr. is dead."

Everything went still. I said to myself, *This is a dream. It can't be true. God could not do this to me . . . again.*

I did not believe Tom but wailed, "Please, God, not this. I could not just bury my father, take a cruise, come home, and have my son be dead."

Ed and Pat joined us. They were also shocked, as they tried to console me. An hour later, Jesse Sr. called me. "Jennifer, we have the

263

body here. You have four hours to view his body. He's being buried in the morning."

I sat in the chair and cried. I was still wearing black. It was only eight weeks since my father had died. I knew that the room was filling with people. "Another procession," I murmured, "another death."

I remember taking Valium. I remember voices in the background. They were asking could they make the trip to Maine with me.

I screamed, "No one, no one! I brought my son into the world alone. I stood by him alone. I will put him to sleep alone."

Aunt Theresa was Jesse's godmother. She insisted on making the trip with me. I vehemently told her, "No!"

She solemnly stated, "Either I go with you or I follow your car up. You have no choice. He's my godchild."

I lost interest in the argument. There was too much agony and too much pain.

Someone in the room notified my mother of her grandson's death. She called back shortly and asked to speak to me. I took the phone as she offered her condolences. "Jennifer, I'm sorry that Jesse is dead. I would go to the funeral with you, but it's Sal's birthday and we ordered a special cake to celebrate."

I went crazy and screamed into the phone, "Your grandson is dead, and you're having a cake? You're crazy! You killed my father and now you've killed my son by forcing me to go on that fucking cruise!"

My mother replied bluntly, "The cake is paid for, and there is no sense in wasting it."

As soon as I could compose myself, Tom and I got in the car for the trip to Maine. Tom sped the whole way in an attempt to reach Maine in time for me to view the body. Aunt Theresa sat in the backseat trying to talk to me. I don't think that I said one word the entire trip. I was still dressed in black, as I had been since my father's death. I felt as though I was on a perpetual death voyage.

We arrived in Graysville within three hours, but it was early morning and the funeral home was deserted, with no cars in sight. I stared at my black dress. It was as worn, tattered, and tired as I was.

Tom and Aunt Theresa assisted me from the car, propping me up on each side. The funeral director appeared and asked who we were. Tom did all the talking. We were the only ones there.

We were ushered into a small, dimly lit room where I noticed an enormous wooden casket in one corner. My legs were like jelly as I approached the coffin, which from a distance appeared empty. I was not prepared for what I was to see. Inside was my son. I bellowed in pain. *"Jesse-e-e!"*

He was so tiny that his body could hardly be seen inside the large casket. He was lying there without a pillow, in the same clothes that he was wearing when he left for New Jersey. No one had bothered to dress him in a suit. He held a large piece of paper in his hand, a note from his father to me.

Aunt Theresa had a shocked expression as I ripped the paper out of Jesse's hand and read it. Jesse Sr. had written that he would miss his son and that he had tried to be a good father.

I lifted Jesse Jr.'s shirt to inspect his body. I ran my fingers through his hair and kissed his face. I brought a scapular of the Blessed Mother and placed it around his neck. I did not have time to get flowers.

His body was badly bruised and battered, and he had an autopsy scar down the length of his torso. I stood there motionless and sobbed, "My poor baby."

I reread the note and it made me sick. I went berserk, racing through the funeral parlor, screaming, "MURDERER!" I could not be controlled as I ran to the register and scribbled "Murderer" all over the pages. The undertaker, Tom, and Aunt Theresa ran to calm me.

It was the last time that I saw my son. I never made it to the funeral. I was taken to the car and taken back to Boston and brought to the hospital.

Jesse Jr. had been found dead in a ditch outside Hagerstown, Maryland. He had been beaten to death. His murderer was never caught.

The psychiatrists were astounded and did not know what to do for me. The events of my life resembled an outlandish soap opera. Again I refused to speak to them.

I overheard the psychiatrist explain to Tom that never in the years that he had practiced had he run into a case similar to mine and he was uncertain how to handle me.

I turned to him in a rage. "That's a fucking joke. You don't know what to do with me? I don't want to live. What purpose do I serve? Nothing in my life has ever gone right. I was even screwed out of my book!"

My train of thought was broken. My mind was swamped with memories of how my mother's family had ridiculed my manuscript as well as my life. "Well," they would say, "you will wind up in the trash can. Anyone can write a book."

Whenever they would see me pass by, they would say, "There goes Liz Taylor." They were not referring to my looks, but to my multiple marriages.

I lay there and thought of how often I had been persecuted by my mother and her family. My mother had never once supported me. I felt like an empty shell, a zombie. I felt empty. I had no substance, no body. I was alienated from my family. My mother, my brother, Carol, Robin, and Father Nino were the family. It was especially painful to me to know that the priest was walking in my father's shoes.

I was obsessed with feeling that my life had no purpose and no accomplishments. Tom would listen to me for hours while I ranted endlessly about my worthlessness and how I hated my family, my mother, Sal, Carol, and even Robin. I hated them all. I especially hated Father Nino, who was trying to play husband and father to my family, a family that did not give a damn that my son had died. "Nothing matters anymore," I told Tom. "It's useless!"

While I was working as a hairdresser, one of my part-time jobs was working for funeral homes, doing the hair of the deceased. There was one undertaker whom I became friendly with. After Jesse's death, I talked to him frequently. I wanted Jesse's body brought back from Maine. I did not have the money to pay for the transfer, but my friend was compassionate. He promised that if I arranged for a burial plot, he would move the body, without charge.

I was thrilled by his promise. My family owned nine grave sites, and I was sure that I could get one for my son. I phoned my brother and said, "Sal, I want to talk to Ma."

"For what?" he replied.

"I need one of the graves. I want one of them for Jesse."

"Well, then, you can't talk to Ma," Sal stated. "You have to talk to me. The deeds to the plots are in my name."

"Okay, Sal. I want one of the graves."

"Sorry, Jenny. I can't help you."

"Why not?"

"Because we don't want your son buried with us."

I became hysterical and screamed, "I want one of those graves! If I don't get it, I'll come over and *kill you!*"

"I don't care, Jennifer. The answer is *no!*"

My mother had turned some of the family business over to Sal, and I was stunned that I was refused. My mother treated him as though he were the Christ Child, and I wanted to be the one that crucified him.

I never got over the shock. They would not even give a burial site to my son. They were the lowest of the low and the cruelest of the cruel.

I talked to Sal a number of times, but the answer was always the same. "*No!*" He told me, "Neither Carol nor I want to be bothered. Dead is dead! We ain't interested in Jesse's death. Carol and I are busy with

Father Nino. We are his only family. Anyway, he has been very busy consoling our mother."

"Sal, you're a sick fucking boy."

Sal was upset by my remark. He did not like me swearing. It was a new experience for the family to deal with a tougher Jennifer.

I hung up the phone and dwelled on my hatred for my family. I had been refused a grave site because they did not want my son buried near them. My hatred was not limited to my immediate family. I hated the judges, the investigators, and the aunts who in the past would ignore me. I felt like a time bomb ready to explode.

Tom and I had decided to sell the house. We had bought the house anticipating the return of my sons. A shortage of funds and grief over Jesse made the decision for us.

Before we decided to sell the house, Ed and Patricia told us that they would be returning to Ohio, as they could no longer view the tragedies that occurred within this house. Ed came to me one night and confessed that they could not stand to watch my agony much longer.

He also wanted to tell me of an experience that he and Pat had in the house. He explained that one night he and Pat were looking out of the window when they saw my father walking along the side of the house. He said that it was the morning that I had gone to Maine to view Jesse's body. Pat confirmed the story. I realized that the couple were frightened and wanted to leave the house. I wished them luck and said that I would miss them.

I went hunting for a one-family house by myself and purchased one, without Tom's input. Even though I bought the house, I had trouble describing it. I was unable to relate to Tom, and he was unable to talk to me.

I lashed out at him, "I don't give a shit. I don't care if I'm an author or a toilet cleaner. I don't care if I'm a hairdresser or salon manager. I don't care if I'm dead or alive." I just wanted to be left alone.

I did not allow my employees or close friends to be near me. They were all crushed by my rejection, but I had decided that no one would ever be close to me again.

Tom was stunned that I had bought a house without even confiding in him. When he saw it, he was disgusted and did not want the place.

I had wanted that house, although at the time I did not know why. Tom knew better than to argue with me, so he agreed to buy it.

We did the paperwork and moved in. The house was a mess, with no working bathrooms and no kitchen. It needed the same thing as always . . . money, money, money. It was something that I never had and which my mother had sworn I never would have.

267

It finally dawned on me why I had chosen this particular house. The front was similar to that of my mother's home. I realized that I was still searching for my father. I was unhappy with the house from the day that we moved in.

My mother frequently telephoned me to remind me that God was punishing me. I was beginning to see God as cruel. The more my mother told me I was being punished by God, the more I hated him.

I was very unhappy. I quit my job at the beauty salon and spent more time in the cemetery in my black outfit. Besides my father's belongings, I now clung to Jesse Jr.'s clothes and toys and would sit in the midst of his baseball gear night after night.

CHAPTER TWENTY-FOUR

A year had passed since the deaths of my father and son. Things were no better. I continued to spend much of my time in the cemetery. Money was still a problem, and Tom was experiencing layoffs. My hatred for my family did not abate.

Father Nino's presence in my mother's house was as strong as ever. I was repulsed that he was still running around in my father's clothing, hiding his priesthood. He had destroyed my image of "men of God."

I needed a release, as I was still obsessed with the deaths and my family's attitude toward my grief. I had all sorts of crazy thoughts racing through my mind, which I did not tell to anyone.

I thought about killing my ex-husband Jesse. Night after night, I would try to develop different plans to kill him. But whatever plan I thought up required money, and I did not have any. It just added to the frustration.

I was filled with anger, but I started to realize that my anger at the church was unwarranted. I knew that Christ had been crucified for mankind and rose again. It was not his intention to crucify men. I realized that I had to find a purpose to live.

One day, I drove to Reading and discovered a little statuary shop where I found the most gorgeous little statue of the Blessed Mother in a grotto, along with many figurines of little children. I purchased the Madonna and all the children. Two men loaded everything into my car, and I drove home.

When I got home, I told Tom about my purchase. He no longer argued with me; he ignored me. I wanted the Blessed Mother in the grotto and the children placed in the backyard. The statues of the children represented my own children.

Tom chuckled and rubbed my head. "Now look, Jennifer; you're torturing yourself. Don't build up your hopes. Your son is gone, your father's gone, and all you have left is me."

"I won't accept it. I still believe in miracles, and with my life, I need a miracle every day. You just watch and see. God will find a miracle for me."

Tom just shook his head and smiled.

I was a night owl. I was up each night with Percodans for the pain. Tom was up late with me one night when the phone rang.

When I answered it I heard a young boy's voice. "Hi," he said.

"Who is this?" I asked.

"I'm Todd."

I hesitated. "Todd who?"

"I'm your son."

My mind raced as I answered, "If you think that this is some kind of a joke you're playing, you have a sick sense of humor." I hung up the phone, feeling that someone was attempting to harass me.

I did not trust the voice on the other end of the phone but thought it may have been my ex-husband Jesse, with his warped sense of humor.

The phone rang again. This time I questioned the boy, "If you are my son, where do you come from?"

"Maine," he replied.

I questioned him further about the family, and he replied, "I had a brother who died." He then proceeded to tell me how Jesse had died.

Since my number was unlisted, I asked, "How did you get my phone number?"

He said, "It's too long a story to go into right now, but I'm at the local Dunkin' Donuts right down the street from you. If you come down here, I'll be waiting for you." He hung up.

I was astounded because I had just put the Blessed Mother outside and miracles, I thought, did not happen that fast.

Tom had been calmly watching television, totally oblivious to what was going on and unaware that his life was about to change. I sat down completely stunned. "Jennifer, what are you sitting there like a zombie for?"

I jumped up like a maniac and proceeded to dress. "It's my son Todd. He's come home."

Tom stood up and demanded, "What? Are you crazy? Oh, come on, Jennifer. How the fuck can your son come home?"

"I don't know how, but I'm going to Dunkin' Donuts to find him." I looked at Tom, who wasn't moving fast enough to suit me, and said, "I'm going with or without you."

Tom threw his clothes on. He was not about to let me go by myself.

Quickly we drove to the doughnut shop, and while we were searching for my son my mind raced. What did he look like? Would he recognize me? The doughnut shop was jammed with teenagers, and I scanned every face looking for an image of Jesse Jr., but I did not find a familiar face among them.

Once more, there was a tap on my shoulder. I turned to face Todd. I was speechless. I threw myself over his shoulder and sobbed.

Everyone in the store was staring at us. I didn't care, although Todd was embarrassed. When I looked into his face, it was as if I were looking into a mirror. He had my facial features. He was very thin. He was several inches taller than I was, but he probably didn't weigh a hundred pounds. He was shabbily dressed and had long hair with a headband across his forehead.

I held him close, not letting him go. Although I realized that I was meeting a young man that I did not know, I wanted to love him. I felt that God had answered my prayers.

I hurried Todd into the car and drove home, where again I heard mind-boggling stories of how he had suffered. At the age of thirteen he had been placed in the state's custody and shuffled from foster home to foster home. His first foster mother had been a young woman of twenty-two who had initiated him sexually.

He had later endured starvation and beatings. His life was more horrifying than Jesse Jr.'s. I asked why I had not been informed of what had gone on and why he had never tried to call me.

He said, "My father and grandmother always covered up everything. When you visited and were told that I was out playing, I was in foster homes."

I ran around the house preparing things for my son. He was not at all like Jesse Jr. He had a bitterness that his brother did not have. Physically, he resembled me.

My family was not kind to Todd. Robin came to meet him the night that she notified me that she was getting married. Todd was not Robin's image of a brother, but she recognized that he was not as naive as Jesse Jr. Todd was streetwise.

I was aware of the love that my sons had for their half sister. Robin had no time for them. My mother, Sal, and Carol had taught her well. She was as cold as they were.

Soon after I brought Todd home, I called both my mother and Sal and asked if they would welcome him home. I brought him to my mother's house to meet everyone. He was treated more like a criminal than a long lost child. My mother, Sal, Carol, and Father Nino sat like a jury ready to render a verdict. Their verdict was not in doubt.

Todd was sadly disappointed with his grandmother and hated her instantly. He also hated Sal and Carol but tolerated Robin. "After all, she is my sister," he said.

I argued with Robin about her impending marriage but could not change her mind. I felt that she was too immature and selfish to become

271

a wife. At first I fought with her. Later I tried to reason with her. It was all in vain. Robin was determined to get married.

Carol announced that she would help plan Robin's wedding and would split the wedding costs with me. That was appropriate, since Sal was doing so well.

Since my father's death, Sal had grown wealthy. He did not earn his wealth, it was given to him. My mother turned over many of the assets that she inherited from my father to my brother. I received nothing.

I was never given an accounting of what my father had left, but there was enough for my brother to purchase an auto dealership soon after my father died. Sal and Carol reaped the benefits from my father's lifetime of work. They never visited my father's grave. On holidays, birthdays, and anniversaries, I was the one who placed flowers on his grave. No one else remembered.

I finally got a chance to meet my future son-in-law. He was about my age, nearly twenty years older than Robin. He was Italian, of Sicilian ancestry, with a dark complexion. He was nearly bald and was missing most of his teeth.

He was about five feet, seven inches tall and had the wildest eyes that I had ever seen. I could not believe that Robin had chosen this man for her husband. He did not know his place and only opened his mouth to change feet. The only thing that he had going for him was a flashy car.

I questioned Robin closely about him, but I felt she was lying, even about how she had met him. I asked the typical questions. I asked about his employment, his financial status, and how he would be able to support her.

As I was talking to Robin about her future, my mother joined the conversation, saying to me, "Mind your own business; this is none of your concern. You're nothing but a whore, and I don't want Robin near you. I don't want your son at the wedding. He just brings bad blood."

There was no way that I would allow my family to hurt Todd. He had been through too much. He had even slept on park benches for eight weeks while he searched for me. Tom and I had passed him many nights while walking the dog, never realizing that he was my son.

He had found me by accident. Todd explained how he had walked into the Dunkin' Donuts and, while talking to one of the counter girls, mentioned that he was from Maine and had a brother who had died. The girl knew me but did not have my address or phone number. Fortunately, she also knew my cousin, who did have my number.

My mother and Carol were causing a lot of commotion while

planning a large, elaborate wedding for my daughter, who was about to become Mrs. Rocco DiCarlo. The invitations were mailed, and I had no input regarding the guests. Father Nino had become the head of the household. My mother, Robin, Carol, and Sal all turned to him for advice on the guest list. It made me sick.

Whenever I saw Father Nino, I totally ignored him, pretending that he was not even there. I was disgusted by his sneakiness and found out that when he left the rectory at night he told the other priests that he had to officiate at a wedding. He would laugh and boast to our family about his lies.

On those evenings that he would sneak out of the rectory, he would meet my mother at Sal's house, which had become their favorite rendezvous. If Robin was not home, they would meet at my mother's house. He was careful not to spend the night so as not to arouse suspicion at the rectory.

I was in constant conflict with my mother over Robin's wedding. Whenever I called to inquire about the wedding, my mother would tell me, "It is none of your business." I pleaded with my mother to cancel the wedding. Robin was not ready for marriage.

Even though I was violently opposed to the wedding, everyone else was delighted, my mother in particular. Robin's fiancé had a flashy car and a nice wardrobe. That was enough for my mother.

I was concerned about Robin's sense of responsibility. She had never worked a day in her life. My father had spoiled her. She never had the opportunity to grow up.

My mother did not understand this. She was only concerned with material possessions. If you looked like you had something, you were something. One of my mother's favorite sayings was "nothing from nothing is nothing." If you had nothing, you did not fit in with her.

My future son-in-law was an idiot, but he had a nice car and dressed nicely. Therefore, he was acceptable to my family.

This attitude was completely opposite from my father's. I felt that they were not part of his family. Father Nino advised them not to visit the cemetery. As he phrased it, "There's nothing there."

My mother frequently complained to Father Nino about how difficult life had been with my father. I thought, *My poor father must be turning over in his grave.*

I told my mother that I would not attend Robin's shower or the wedding, since I was shut out of the planning. I did not have enough money to pay for my one-half of the wedding expenses, as I had promised Carol.

I noticed that since my father's death, my clashes with my mother were increasing. After my father's death, I felt that I had no reason to be quiet. In the past, I had tried to avoid conflicts with my mother out of respect for my father. My mother still visited me on occasion, but always in the company of Father Nino.

My family often gossiped about Todd's abuse of drugs, including alcohol. They acted as judges, with no compassion in their hearts. I knew that Todd had developed dependencies while growing up in Maine.

I wanted to do something to help him, but I was financially restrained. Tom's health insurance policy did not cover Todd, and I was unable to obtain any other coverage for him. Fortunately, I was able to get some medical assistance through public clinics.

Todd was very sick. He was a bad substance abuser, and he had undergone several operations in Maine as the result of abuse at Jesse's hand. Todd was very bitter. He stated, "I'm going to live my life as well as I can. I don't give a shit for anyone. I only want women and booze."

I tried to talk to him but couldn't. He had deep emotional problems, and when I tried to reason with him, he said, "Well, what the fuck? I'm going to be in a funeral basket like my brother anyway."

I was experienced in dealing with Jesse Sr.'s alcoholism, but I had no knowledge of other drugs. Todd would come home every night stoned on something. I never realized which substance he was abusing.

Often when Todd arrived home at night he would tell me that he had the "munchies." I would run to the kitchen to prepare a meal, no matter what the hour. Sometimes I would be cooking at two or three in the morning, but it never bothered me as long as he was eating.

Tom became disgusted. He had changed and became somewhat bitter and selfish. I sensed that he was starting to resent my family, especially my children.

My mother did all that she could to ruin my relationship with Tom. Whenever she got the opportunity, she would take Tom aside and tell him that I was a "bitch" and he should leave me. My mother's world revolved around Sal and Father Nino. To her, Father Nino was God and Sal was the Christ Child. But their actions did not fit her ideas. Father Nino's relationship with my mother was anything but holy. My brother was hopping from bed to bed, while his righteous wife was doing the same. Sal had even caught Carol one afternoon screwing a vacuum cleaner salesman in the living room.

My mother was aware of their activities but condoned their behavior and helped to conceal it. I was shocked by the attitude that my mother had developed since my father's death. My mother had condemned me for my multiple marriages and had crucified me for them.

Now Sal and Carol were committing flagrant adultery, while my mother was cavorting with a priest.

As the days passed, my hatred grew. It got to the point where I no longer considered my mother to be my mother. I thought my family was a mockery to the memory of my father.

My father worked hard his whole life, investing his money wisely and living simply. After his death, much of his ample savings was wasted by Sal. He had gone crazy, buying fancy cars and taking trips to Las Vegas and Florida and many trips to the local horse and dog tracks. Whatever he lost my mother would replenish.

I thought, *Here I stand with a dead son and another about to die. I'm struggling to make ends meet, and my family doesn't even offer a crumb.*

Tom's frequent layoffs added to the financial burden. We needed the income, but I did not want to go back to hairdressing. I decided to return to electronics and was hired by a temporary agency that provided contract support to electronics companies. I chose the midnight to eight shift but ended up working seventy to eighty hours per week for the overtime. I was proud and determined not to ask for anything from my family.

I worked hard until I became very ill. My heart condition worsened. I had to take time off from work to be fitted with a portable heart monitor. I was in constant pain, facing possible surgery.

Todd's larceny was out of control. He helped himself to my belongings, stealing jewelry and clothing. He took anything that he could hock. He had even written 1,000 dollars' worth of bad checks against my account. I had to come up with the money in order to keep the bank from prosecuting him.

I tried everything possible to win Todd's love, even sneaking into his room at night to hug and kiss him. He would push me away. I realized that he had been raised as a child in an atmosphere without love. He was breaking my heart.

I was willing to take all the blame for how his life had turned out. I begged his forgiveness for not being the mother that I should have been.

I did not talk to him about my life with Jesse during Todd's very early years. I could not explain things to someone who was as hurt and bitter as he was. He was seventeen and had received little education. He could barely read and write. I offered to hire a tutor, since he refused to return to school. He wanted no part of education. He thought that he knew everything.

I sought advice from Dr. Madden, but he was thoroughly disgusted with Todd. "Jennifer, you're the worst person possible to deal with this boy. He's an alcoholic, drug addict, and punk. You have to throw him out of your house, or he will kill you some night."

I realized the truth in his words, but I knew that he didn't care for Todd as much as I did. Todd was not his son. No matter what anyone said to me about Todd, I would not listen. I had this need to be accepted as a mother. I loved my children and had already buried one. I could not bear the thought of burying another.

Robin's wedding day drew near, and Todd realized the extent of his family's rejection when he was not invited. We were both crushed. I decided not to go, since I did not give a damn for any of them.

My invitation was waiting at home when I arrived home from work. It was handwritten by Carol, listing the date, time, and place of the ceremony. It listed my mother as the mother of the bride, making no mention of me. I was totally left out and was heartbroken and angry.

I had already fought with Robin over my refusal to attend her bridal shower. Her attitude was, "I don't give a shit if you don't go. How do you like that?" Robin behaved like a little snot with me.

My mother pleaded with me to attend the wedding. She whimpered and whined, but I knew why she wanted me there, so that she could save face in front of her family and friends. I had no intention of going to the wedding.

I was crushed that the wedding invitation did not recognize me as Robin's mother. But I tried to suppress my feelings and camouflage my emotions. Nobody knew what I felt.

Todd was also offended by my family's attitude. He had known one brutal family. He was being introduced to another. My family was a cruel, insensitive bunch. They were a group of small-time characters who thought they were the Kennedys. It was unbelievable to see them with their Cadillacs, accompanied by the priest wearing my father's clothing.

I tried to talk to Todd, to console him, but I could not reach him. He simply said, "Life's really a fucking bummer, isn't it, Mom?" I couldn't answer him.

As Robin's wedding day drew closer, my son's behavior became more and more reckless. He called me one night to ask permission to stay overnight at a friend's house. I said that I preferred that he return home. But he was quite a con artist and I was an easy target, so I consented to his request.

The following day, I waited for my son to return, but he never did. I became frantic, visualizing him dead on the street. I ran to the police to have him reported missing.

My imagination was vivid and ran wild as I imagined Todd winding up like his brother. I was miserable and desperate to find him. It seemed like I had just found him and now he was gone again.

Robin's wedding day was fast approaching, and I had still not located my son. My mother had arranged for a gown to be delivered to me. It was a perfect fit. She was still insistent that I attend Robin's wedding.

I discussed the situation with Tom, who advised me, "Jennifer, your mother did not show up for your first wedding. Don't do the same thing to Robin." I thought it over and decided to attend the ceremony but would not sit at the head table.

I was ignorant of the wedding details, as I had no part in the arrangements. I realized that my family wanted me there solely as an image. They wanted to present the proper facade for the DeVito tribe. At the last moment, I received a phone call informing me that Sal would walk Robin down the aisle.

I was sick from the problems with Todd and Robin and on the verge of a nervous breakdown. I felt like a bitch who had delivered a litter of pups from which everyone had taken their pick. Later, when the pups had become diseased, they had returned them to her.

The wedding day arrived. Dr. Madden had read the wedding announcement in the paper, arrived uninvited, and sat next to me. Robin was a beautiful bride. My mother had outdone herself, dressing Robin in a Victorian gown, with a wide picture hat and carrying a parasol. The groom was a pathetic picture standing next to her.

The ceremony was not held in a Catholic church, but in a college chapel. I questioned it but received no answers. As Robin walked down the aisle on Sal's arm, I visualized how my father ought to have been there to give his granddaughter away. As the photographers flashed their cameras, capturing Robin's moment, I had the strangest feeling that my father was sitting with me.

As I was sitting at my table, I could no longer stand it. I put my head down and sobbed. Dr. Madden pushed me back in the chair and said, "Jennifer, this should be your day." He picked up a napkin and wiped the tears from my eyes, saying, "This is such a shame, Jennifer."

I felt mixed emotions. I turned to him and said, "Let them have the glory. Let them have everything. I think that I can hold up through this."

But I could not. I could overhear biting remarks from the DeVito family about my marriages. I was disturbed by their remarks, by Todd's disappearance, by everything.

The wedding reminded me of a circus. My brother, the car dealer, used it to hustle customers for his business. My mother was acting like his sales manager, extolling the virtues of his new Chevy dealership. While my mother was continually rebuilding my brother's life, she was destroying mine. She had made my crown of thorns.

My new son-in-law was an ass. Every time he opened his big Italian mouth, I wanted to slap him. After the wedding, Robin started to treat me as competition, afraid that I wanted to steal her husband. Tom sat and observed without saying anything.

I was amazed by how much Tom had changed. We were beginning to argue constantly. He was out of work, and I sensed that he enjoyed staying at home while I worked. He was not looking for another job, and his attitude was putting a strain on our relationship.

My relationship with Robin was also strained. I loved my daughter and longed for a mother-daughter relationship, something that I never had with my mother. Whenever I attempted to become close to Robin, she would ask for money. I gave her what I could, because she and her husband quickly squandered the money that they had received as shower and wedding gifts. Once she had received what she wanted from me, Robin would no longer have the time to see me and I would be totally ignored.

My mother and Father Nino were still going around together, without shame. I decided to speak to Sal about the situation. Although it would be difficult, I felt that it would be necessary for my mother's sake as well as for the memory of my father.

When I approached Sal, he said, "I don't think that there is anything wrong with the relationship. On the contrary, it is a good thing. Nothing will ever come of it."

I screamed, "What? Are you crazy? He's walking over Daddy's grave. Don't you care?"

Sal stared at me and said, "Well, I never was too close to Dad. That was your problem. I've always been Mommy's boy, and it's going to be that way till the day Ma dies."

I was furious and retorted, "You all think that you're going to walk over my father's grave. You're going to get paid back in spades for everything that you've done. You will pay. I'll make sure that you pay."

My coworkers never knew about my life because I built a facade and camouflaged my true feelings. At work I joked and clowned, but at home I brooded.

My thoughts of killing Jesse had become stronger as the years passed. I thought, *That bastard, hiding up there behind the law. They're letting him get away with it.*

The more that I thought of the judges in Boston, the more I despised them. *Idiots,* I thought. I wanted to reopen the case, but there was one thing that I wanted to do first. I wanted to see a cardinal in the church about Father Nino.

I knew that my action would have repercussions, but I could not let things go any further. I decided not to do anything behind Father Nino's back. I would see him alone, and we would discuss the situation.

I phoned him and made an appointment to meet him at the local church. At the meeting I told him, "Father Nino, I'm shocked by your relationship with my mother. You are alienating my family, and not living up to the image of a priest. I truly love my mother; I am crushed that we never had a normal mother-daughter relationship. As a priest you should have noticed how the family disintegrated and how you contributed to the turmoil."

His response shocked me: "Jennifer, your mother's life is none of your business. None of this concerns you."

"This *does* concern me. She is my mother. If she wants to date, she should go out with an available man, not a priest."

"Look, young lady; I'll tell you one more time: mind your own business."

I left without saying another word.

I made an appointment with Bishop Lacey. He sat and listened attentively as I told him the whole story. When I finished, he told me that he would take care of the whole situation. I left comforted, knowing that things would change.

I then proceeded to contact the Maine state police in a frantic attempt to locate Todd. I telephoned Max, who mumbled, "I should go to the *Boston Globe* with this. No one would believe this story." He continued, "If it wasn't for your bad luck, Jennifer, you'd have no luck at all."

I received a call from the police notifying me that Todd was locked up in the Graysville jail. When Max heard the news, he immediately went to court with me to try to regain custody of Greg, the youngest. Maybe he could be saved.

Max obtained a warrant that gave me custody of both Todd and Greg. If I went to Maine with the court order, and presented it to the authorities, I could procure Todd's release from jail. They both could then return with me to Massachusetts.

Even though Tom was driving, the ride to Maine was difficult. The long winding roads and the endless highways gave me a feeling of complete isolation. When we arrived in Graysville, it appeared that it was still full of the illiterates and alcoholics that I remembered. If history were to repeat itself, I would run into some sort of opposition. I decided to proceed first to the school to pick up Greg.

When I entered the school building, I went to the rest room to freshen up from the long drive. I heard someone banging on the door and shouting for me to come out. I opened the door and faced a plainclothes policeman who brandished his badge. He held a large pistol that looked like a small shotgun.

Someone had spotted the Massachusetts license plates and called Jesse, who in turn had called notified his cousins on the police force.

I produced my warrant and demanded to see my son. The policeman read me my rights and drove Tom and me to the local jail. They informed us that we would be detained for a couple of hours while the police tried to "reach someone with authority."

I demanded my right to make a phone call, but I failed in my attempt to reach Max. Tom and I were detained for several hours with guns pointed at our faces.

Jesse had told the police that I had made threats on his life. They rushed over to the school to apprehend me.

The police questioned me, asking if I had threatened Jesse. I replied, "No." I did want to reveal what was in my heart. I would have liked to kill him, especially after what Todd and Jesse Jr. had told me about the beatings. Todd had added to Jesse Jr.'s tales of terror by telling me how his stepmother used to beat the boys with boards and knock them down the stairs.

I had demanded to see Todd but was refused. Again I produced my court order but was informed that it was worthless in Maine. I was told: "What goes on in Massachusetts doesn't change anything in Maine."

I had enough with the courts, the police, and the people in Maine who had destroyed my life. I was fed up with all of them. I thought to myself, *You're all assholes. You can all go fuck yourselves.*

It was all a big farce. Once again, my court order was being ignored. Everyone preached about child abuse, but when they were aware of an actual case, they closed their eyes.

After three hours, Tom and I were informed that we could go back to Boston, alone. We had another fruitless drive home.

Soon after we got home, the phone was ringing. It was the chief of police in Graysville. He told me, "After due consideration, I have decided that you can take your son Todd back to Boston with you. The other boy, Greg, will have to remain here.

"Y'see, Todd is a nuisance. He does nothing but get into trouble. We here talked it over and decided that if you're willing to take on the problem, he's yours."

Tom and I got back in the car and returned to Graysville. Todd was released in our custody. I was still worried about Greg, but at least I was able to salvage one of my sons.

The police warned me to stay away from Greg. They also wanted to escort us to the New Hampshire–Maine state line.

I became angry and told the policeman, "You'd better be prepared to lock me up, because I am going to leave when I am good and ready. I have a son buried here."

I turned and asked Todd, "Do you know where Jesse's grave is located?"

"Sure, Ma. I know where it is. I'll take you there."

I was not prepared to visit my son's burial site, but I felt that it was something that I had to do. I had not attended his funeral and did not know if I would be in Maine again. I had to see his grave before I left.

The cemetery was located in a small, isolated area at the end of a ravine. I was unsure how to cope with the ordeal. Todd and Tom led me to a lonely little spot. There were no gravestones, just small markers. I felt a terrible sensation but knew that I had to see the grave before I left.

Todd turned to me. "Do you think you should do this, Ma? Maybe we should just go back to Boston."

I gave him a quick, flashing look. "No! We're going to see your brother's grave. I want to see where my son was laid to rest. I never made it to the funeral."

Todd was becoming increasingly upset with me. "Look, Mom; I hate this fucking state. Let's get out of here. I don't want to see the grave. I just want to get out of here."

I refused to listen to him, so the three of us struggled to search up and down the rows for Jesse's grave site. We finally discovered his grave, isolated, under a big tree. There was no stone or tribute, just a tiny marker, and when I saw it, all the tears that I had been suppressing flowed. I fell to my knees and sobbed. It was such a lonely spot beneath which my son lay. I put my head to the ground as if I could touch him.

Todd grew impatient and ran to the car, slammed the door, and sat in the backseat, not making a move. I sat on the ground and screamed, "Oh, my God; my son, my son!" Tom picked me up and carried me to the car.

As Tom started up the car, Todd began to scream, "This fucking state. My fucking father, my brother!" On the ride home, Tom had a terrible time trying to control both mother and son.

I made a vow that I would never return to Maine, not even for Greg. Since both Todd and Jesse had made the effort to find me, in time Greg would also.

CHAPTER TWENTY-FIVE

I despaired that it probably was too late anyway. Greg had most likely been ruined by his father. If I ever did find him, the situation would be similar to that of Jesse and Todd. Greg would be rejected by my family. I decided to wait and see.

Todd was raised as an atheist. I tried to teach him basic religious values, but it was futile. He continued his binges with drugs, including alcohol. My problems were like a three-ring circus, with Father Nino, Robin, and Todd.

One night there was a knock on the door. I opened it to discover Father Nino standing there. I had been waiting for this visit. I invited him into my home.

"Well, Jennifer, you're looking well. What have you been up to lately?"

"I haven't been doing much of anything. What have you been doing?"

There was a slight pause before he said, "I would like to speak to you privately."

"Certainly, Father."

I ushered him upstairs into the bedroom so that Tom and Todd could not hear the conversation. "What can I do for you?"

"Jennifer, have you discussed your conversation with the bishop with anyone?"

"Are you asking me to relate something I've discussed with a priest?"

"Yes, yes, I am asking you this."

"Well, I'm sorry, Father Nino, but I was instructed that whatever transpired between the bishop and myself was strictly confidential."

He persisted, "What did you tell the bishop?"

"I came to you first, but you were not interested in what I had to say. So whatever my conversation was with any other priest is like a confession. I don't have to tell you."

He hesitated, then asked, "Do you know that I'm being transferred?"

I was surprised. "No, I didn't know that, but I think that it's for the best."

"You are not going to admit anything, are you, Jennifer? You are not going to admit that you were the one that squealed on me."

"I have nothing to say to you, Father Nino. You have divided my family. You are no help to us. I think that it is better that you are out of our family."

At this point, my mother strolled into the room. Something told me that I had been set up. My mother started to scream, not caring who heard her, "Confess, you fucking little slut! You know what you've done. You're my child. What a disgrace! How could you disgrace your mother *and* a priest?"

I lashed out at my mother, "How dare you talk to me like that?"

She answered, "You've incriminated me. You accused me of having an affair with a priest."

I turned. "How do you know what I said? I didn't accuse anybody of anything. I never said that you had an affair."

I realized that my mother was probing to find out about the conversation that had taken place between me and the bishop. I looked at her and said, "I did tell him that I felt that Father Nino has divided our family."

My mother was boiling with hatred as she said, "Well, you fucking little bitch, you'll be sorry. You'll see changes now that you've never seen in your life. Your brother, Sal, will have everything. He'll have an empire, and I'll make sure that you're in the gutter."

I looked her straight in the eye. "I don't want your blood money. I don't even want you. All I want is my father. You've already taken Robin away from me. You've made my sister-in-law my enemy. You've never accepted my children. How much more do you think that you can hurt me?"

Father Nino turned to my mother. "Why don't you just stay here with her? I'm leaving." He left the room, slamming the door on his way out.

My mother stood and gave me a vicious stare. "I wouldn't stay with you if you said that you were dying." With that, she ran out of the room and down the stairway, yelling after the priest, "Nino, Nino, wait for me!"

Tom appeared at the door and said, "What the fuck? It's a good thing that I'm not a Catholic. Who could become a Catholic after a scene like this? Your father would turn over in his grave if he could see what was happening to his family since his death. There are no loyalties, no prayers, no remorse, no family."

I looked at him and said, "Well, what do you expect? My father *was* the family."

My mother, although she was in her sixties, did not consider herself to be a senior citizen. She preferred to socialize with younger women and one in particular, named Francesca. I remembered her when in her teens she was dating my brother, who had dumped her for Carol. Francesca was a small, chubby girl with large brown eyes. She had gotten lucky when she married Roberto Turelli, who was tall, dark, handsome, and wealthy.

I had heard rumors of my mother and Francesca making the rounds of the Boston nightclubs. I thought that she would be a better companion for my mother than Carol.

One day while shopping, I bumped into Francesca. I had not seen her since my father's wake. We decided to have lunch and picked a small restaurant in downtown Boston. She was very friendly and especially inquisitive about my family.

Francesca was subtly pumping me for information about my family. I was vague and did not get very specific. She continued to ramble on to different subjects, trying to find some common ground, until she mentioned real estate.

She had been an unsuccessful real estate broker, while I had friends in the business. It seemed like a logical topic. With one breath Francesca would make a comment about property, and with the next she would direct a question to me about Sal and Carol.

I finally explained to her that I was alienated from my family, had not spoken to them, and had no intentions of doing so. My bluntness stunned her. I was getting tired of playing games and asked her, "What is it that you want to know?"

She acted embarrassed. "Nothing, Jennifer. I just want to become friends. I feel so bad about your father and your son."

Francesca had such a sweet little voice and big cow eyes. I was suspicious and knew that she was up to something. "Did you know, Jennifer, that your brother and I have remained close through all these years? We've never lost touch with each other."

"No, I didn't," I replied.

"I've always wanted to have a closer relationship with you, Jennifer, more like a sister. Although I have a sister, we're not close."

I smiled. Secretly, I had always longed for a sister, but I knew that this was not the one that I wanted. She was still carrying a torch for Sal. That came across loud and clear.

"Well, Francesca, how's your marriage?"

"Wonderful! I have two little boys."

"How is your husband?"

"Fantastic!" Whenever Francesca spoke, she jiggled, reminding me

284

of Carol. "I have a twenty-room house, income property, and all the money in the world. Everything that I want."

"Then why would you be interested in a little asshole like my brother?"

Her face drained and became white. "You know, Jennifer, that I always loved him."

"Well, I suppose that's something that you just can't help, but I've got to admit that you've got very poor taste."

Francesca giggled nervously and timidly asked, "Can I tell you something like a sister?"

"Sure, Francesca. Go ahead."

The chubby little girl spoke. "Since the day that your brother married Carol, I've been seeing him."

"What you're saying is that he's been cheating on his wife since the day that he got married."

"Well, I always thought that he was going to leave Carol and marry me."

I was amazed by what I was hearing, although I realized that I shouldn't have been shocked. My family was thoroughly screwed up, and I was the only one chastised. I was the victim of their double standards. My sins were spotlighted, but theirs were kept in the dark.

I did not think that Francesca was lying, but I sensed that she had an ulterior motive in telling me this story. Whatever the motive, it did not keep us from becoming close friends, almost like sisters.

Francesca often called in the middle of the night and asked me to take a ride with her. She thought a nocturnal drive would be good for me. "Oh, come on, Jennifer. We'll just go for coffee."

I usually refused, but one night, because I was unable to sleep, I took Francesca up on her offer and was amazed where she took me. She drove high up on a hill, directly behind Sal's house. She stopped the car, got out, took out a pair of binoculars, and aimed them at his house.

I stared at her and said, "I hope you don't think that this is going to be an everynight occurrence. If this is your idea of an evening out, I want you to take me home."

She became very nervous as I continued, "Francesca, I have no intention of spying on Sal. I am not interested in his business or his life. Now bring me home."

She was extremely anxious, but without hesitating she obeyed my order. On the way home she wanted to stop at my mother's house and spy on her. I got angry and just told her to "take me home."

On the ride home, Francesca gave me the details of her affair with Sal. She was also aware of my mother's affair with Father Nino. She divulged how she was using her friendship with my mother to get closer to Sal. As she put it, "I want to be the daughter that your mother never had."

I just stared at her and thought to myself sardonically, *Another one trying to replace me as the daughter.* She did not realize that she was lighting a fuse that could lead to a nasty explosion.

Francesca continued to babble on about how Sal had told her that I disgraced the family. He was unable to hold his head up to people who knew that I was his sister.

My thoughts raced. Who the hell was he talking about? He was out pretending that he was a hot water bottle, warming every bed in sight. He had a right to look down on me? And his wife—she was no different.

When I got home, I discussed things with Tom. I was still enraged when I said, "I think that I'll lay my cards on the table with my family. If they're so worried over images and that I don't fit in, just wait until I finish with them."

He agreed with me and said, "Your father was the only decent member of that family. It's a wonder that you can function after what they did to you."

I stood up and said, "Tom, I have some unfinished business with my family." I ran down the stairs and drove off. I had decided to visit Carol, knowing that my mother would be there.

When I arrived at her house, I knocked on the door and heard her squeaky voice ask, "Who is it?"

"It's Jennifer."

Carol opened the door a crack, and I could hear Sal holler from the kitchen, "Who is it?"

Carol yelled back, "It's your sister, Jennifer!"

"Well, let her in!" he shouted.

I was brought into the kitchen, where my mother and brother sat over cups of coffee. Sal greeted me, "Well, what's new? What have you been doing?"

I thought to myself what a bunch of bastards and hypocrites they were. I looked at them. Their mouths were hanging open, and I could sense that they were uncomfortable by my presence. They knew that I had changed since my father's death and they could no longer relate to me. I also could not relate to them.

"Well, seeing that you think I'm nuts," I said, "I've decided to have group therapy right here among all of us." I pulled up a chair and sat down.

Sal's mouth dropped wide open, as he was stunned by my announcement. I turned to Carol and said, "Do you know that your husband goes out and cheats every night?" She became hysterical.

Sal stood up and demanded, "Who the hell are you to tell my wife that?"

"Didn't you tell my daughter that I was a slut?" I responded.

He didn't answer, so I turned to Carol. "Do you know about Sal screwing around? I'm sure you do. I know that he knows about you screwing around." Her face turned white, but I proceeded with the group therapy, turning to my mother.

"And seeing that you are the head of this group, you're the one who don't give a shit for your grandchildren or for the memory of my dead father, how about you, running around with a priest? How dare you tell my daughter to stay away from me? You, pretending to be her mother. You have some nerve!"

I felt wonderful. They were hysterical, as they were standing and screaming. I thanked them for the coffee and walked out of the house.

When I got home, I told Tom what I had done. He stood with his mouth wide open in astonishment. "Jennifer, I don't believe that you could do something like that. You're so filled with hate."

"Why shouldn't I be?" I replied. "Do you think I can keep going on like this? Nobody cares. I don't even care anymore."

Everyone had come along and taken a piece of my heart, used it, and thrown it away when they were finished. My life was in continual disarray. Tom was out of work. Bills were piling up. My health was failing, and Todd was always in and out of trouble. How much could one woman take?

Tom and I were in serious financial trouble. Whenever I spoke to our attorney, Max Levine, he would advise us to file for bankruptcy. Things had been bad for some time, but I wanted to avoid bankruptcy. I was very proud and did not want to admit to a financial failure.

My father had had his his assets in joint tenancy with my mother. When he died, my mother set up the joint tenancy with my brother. My brother used "his share" to purchase a house and a business. He also managed to gamble away much of what he was given.

I was given nothing. Since there was no will to probate, I could not even get an accounting of what my father had left unless I sued my mother. That was something that I was unwilling to do.

Tom and I were on our own. Unfortunate circumstances brought us to the financial brink. Legal fees, Tom's frequent layoffs, my health problems, all made bankruptcy the only option. We took Max's advice and filed for bankruptcy.

My brother could not wait to gloat over my misfortune. He began to telephone me and harass me. The phone would ring in the middle of the night, and as I answered it, I would hear his voice: "Guilty? You killed Daddy. How does it feel to kill Daddy?" Then he would hang up on me.

Sometimes his taunts would change and he would mock my misfortune: "If I had a loaf of bread, I wouldn't give you or your children a slice."

I would respond, "Go fuck yourself," and hang up. He did not have the courage to come to my house, but the calls continued.

One day, I decided that I had had enough. I drove to his auto dealership. I walked through the lot until I came to the showroom. I asked to be directed to his office. I found him sitting by his desk and laughing as he was talking on the phone.

I walked over to him and grabbed a handful of his hair and twisted him around in the swivel chair. "You fucking little weasel, if you have something to say to me, say it to my face. I should kill you, you worthless little coward."

I assaulted him in full view of his customers and employees. I was screaming so loudly that everyone within earshot heard me. Finally, three men rushed in and pulled me off of Sal.

As I straightened my skirt and blouse, I turned to Sal and smiled, saying, "Let that be a lesson to you." I turned and walked out as if nothing had happened.

Sal was still acting crazy as the three men tried to placate him. I heard him screaming as I walked through the lot and toward my car.

As I drove home I thought, *Hm-m, well, Sal, I guess I'm my father's boy and you're still Mommy's little girl.*

Later I heard that Sal and Carol had separated. I felt nothing for them. I thought, *Well, I had divorces and couldn't even get welfare for my children. I suffered and no one cared. Now they will know what it feels like. Now they will wear the scarlet letter D for Divorce.*

Todd was becoming a huge problem. He had run away to Maine, where he was thrown in jail for burglary. I had done everything that I could to help him. The social workers told me about abused children. They felt that Todd was drastically abused. Abused children always return to the abuser. That explained why he always ran back to Maine, but it did not stop me from feeling like a failure.

I had given Todd everything that I could, a home, clothing, and all the material comforts that I could afford. I loved my son, but he could never return that love. He stole and pawned our possessions. He was always high. When he was bored with things here, he ran away to Maine, to get into trouble there.

The professionals that I spoke to thought that Todd was a lost cause.

I was advised to let him go. He was a punk and I was not qualified to handle him.

After Tom and I went through bankruptcy, we were still able to keep our house. Tom was still unemployed, and I was working for the agency. Francesca was still hanging around, looking for information about my family. I thought Sal and Carol's separation would be enough to keep her busy.

After work, I would frequently come home depressed. I would take out the manuscript to *A Woman's Heart* and update it. I find that writing is a catharsis. I was also hoping to publish an updated version of the book.

Sometimes I would rummage through my father's clothes or Jesse Jr.'s belongings. I would try to bring back things that I had lost. I just tried to escape.

I was struggling with the manuscript when Francesca offered her help. The only catch was that she wanted her name to be included on the book as the coauthor. When she told me that, I just laughed. I knew that she could not achieve a single thing on her own. She had money and real estate, but it was not earned by her; she wanted my book as her trophy.

I told her, "Look, Francesca; I may never finish my manuscript. If I do, your name will never appear on the cover. It wasn't your life; it wasn't your heartbreak. If it ever sold, it would never be your achievement."

My book was my life story, through my marriage to Jesse. I was cheated by the publisher and received no money, even though I knew the book sold. Since I was able to retain the copyright, I wanted to update the book to reflect my recent history, plus revise some of the earlier parts. I was struggling with it at the same time that I was struggling to survive working as an electronics assembler.

I enjoyed my job. Working for an agency, I was able to work for many electronics companies. I made many friends working for these companies. At one of these, Sentinal Corporation, I met someone with whom I established a special relationship.

Mark Griffith was an engineer from Liverpool, UK. Tom and I became friendly with him and with his English wife, Beth, who was also a writer. She had not written any books but had a number of articles published.

As they read *A Woman's Heart* and talked to me about my life, they became sympathetic to my plight. I had a tendency to withdraw into my shell. When I did, Mark and Beth would drag me out of the house and out to dinner.

I had not had any close friends since Ed and Patricia moved to the Midwest. I enjoyed spending time with Mark and Beth. They were sincere, generous, and loving people. They both had poise and compassion. They were so different from my family.

One day, Mark approached me at work and said that he thought that Beth should help me with my manuscript. I was thrilled by the offer. I felt that this was a legitimate offer of help. It was not like the offer that I had received from Francesca.

Mark and Beth took me in hand. Beth edited the manuscript while Mark typed it. They were a happy-go-lucky team who would come into my house at night, frequently uninvited, with a bottle of wine. They would talk in their English accents and Tom in his Georgia accent. It was a wonder that we could communicate.

I was happy that my manuscript was progressing. I wished that I could be optimistic over Todd. He was traveling between my home and Maine. Whenever he went back to Maine, he would do something to wind up in jail. He would get into fights, or he would burglarize homes. He was controlled by his addiction.

My daughter also was not doing well. Robin and Rocky had been evicted from their apartment for not paying the rent. Rocky worked as a bus driver for the Massachusetts Bay Transportation Authority, so he was making more than a living wage. My daughter was working for American Airlines. They had no kids. He was supporting a child from a previous marriage. Even so, I couldn't see how they could not pay rent. I had to put them up in my house until they could find something on their own.

The icing on the cake was the reappearance of Robin's father after twenty-one years. The guy took off and all of a sudden decided that he wanted to get reacquainted with his daughter.

Somehow Bill was able to get in touch with Sal, who told him where to find me. I felt that he wanted to get in touch with his daughter because she was old enough that he did not have to pay child support. She did not need someone to play father at this stage of the game.

When Bill called me it was the first time that we had spoken in over twenty years. He proceeded to tell me how he had changed and how much he loved his daughter. I lashed out at him, "If you loved your daughter so much, why didn't you support her? Why did you turn that responsibility over to my father?"

Bill replied, "I don't want to talk about that. I'm remarried and have a daughter of my own."

"Well, isn't that wonderful?" I answered in a calm voice.

He added, "I'm a Catholic now. I'm married to an ex-nun; I've really changed. I'm also a police officer."

When I heard that, I pulled up a kitchen chair, sat down, and laughed out loud. "Well, aren't you a pile of bullshit?"

Bill was furious and asked, "What are you laughing at?"

"You're a police officer. Isn't that a pisser? Another person hiding within the law."

Bill started to get cocky. "I don't owe you a thing, and in case you're not aware of it, there's a statute of limitations. I made sure I waited over twenty-one years before I called."

I paused for a moment, then said, "Oh, you did, did you? Well, we'll see about that." I never gave him a chance to reply. I hung up.

I then called my attorney, told him the story, and asked his advice. Max told me that he would get back to me in a few days.

I told Robin about her father and about how he had deserted her many years ago. I told her not to encourage him to visit. If he cared about her, he would have come back to Boston many years ago.

Max told me that I would be able to go after Bill for retroactive child support, if he did not agree to pay it voluntarily. Max would have to get his associated law firm in Illinois, where Bill was now living, to handle the case. The law firm in Illinois agreed to handle the case on a contingent fee basis.

Bill did not agree to a voluntary settlement, and legal action was begun. This was not only a dispute between Bill and me. Robin was very upset, and I continually fought with her.

My mother and brother advised Robin to be very "sweet" to her father. After all, they reasoned, he might have money, which he might share with her.

I laughed at their logic. "How could they tell you something like that? It's so asinine, Robin."

She responded indignantly, "Well, what do you know? Just because he did not give you anything, that doesn't mean that I won't get anything. He owes me."

"He does owe you, but he does not owe you money. He owes you twenty-one years of fatherhood. You can't look at everything in terms of dollars and cents."

She just stared at me and said, "Rocco also told me to get close to my father."

"Look, Robin; your husband is a jerk with no common sense. If he had any, he wouldn't have been kicked out of his home. You married a man as old as your mother. You actually married your father."

"Look, Ma; I can handle him. Sal told me to take you to court."

"Take me to court? For what?"

"Over my father," Robin answered. "You're interfering in my life."

"Tell that idiot uncle of yours to mind his own business. All he and my mother have ever done is ridicule me and give me grief. I don't need any shit from you."

Robin tossed her head around, looked at me, and said, "I think you're jealous."

"Robin, get the hell out of my house!" I realized that anything I said to her would be fruitless.

With the help of Mark and Beth, I struggled with the manuscript. I was waiting for the time when I could stand up and shout, "Look, I've achieved! I'm successful!" I was waiting for the time when I could say to my mother, "Do you love me now? I'm someone!"

I wanted the success that a best-selling book would bring. My life was a series of defeats. I needed a victory.

I finally finished the manuscript and had it copyrighted. With the help of Mark and Beth, I made fifteen copies and submitted it to publishing houses for consideration. After about six weeks I received a response. It was accepted. I was Jennifer Vicci, author. I was somebody at last.

CHAPTER TWENTY-SIX

Suddenly a pounding on the door brought me back to reality. Half-asleep and in a daze, I walked to the mirror and gazed at my reflection. The pounding continued. "Miss Vicci, Miss Vicci." Still in a daze, I tried to collect my thoughts. I walked to the door and opened it. It was Stacy.

"Miss Vicci, I've been trying to telephone you, and when I did not get an answer, I came right over."

"Oh, I'm sorry, Stacy. I must have dozed off. All the excitement surrounding the book and the trip from Boston must have worn me out."

"Well, Mr. Ross would like you to be ready in an hour. He has a wonderful evening planned for you. Hans will pick you up."

I thanked Stacy and promised to get dressed immediately. I chose a simple mint chiana cocktail dress with a matching jacket.

As I gazed at my image in the mirror, I heaved a sigh of relief that my troubles were over. I had reached a point where I could see the end to my troubles.

The phone rang. It was the front desk, who told me that the chauffeur was waiting. When I arrived in the lobby, Hans approached me. He was a handsome figure, tall and blond.

"Hello, Hans."

He tipped his cap and said, "Miss Vicci."

"Where's Mr. Ross?" I asked.

"He's waiting," the chauffeur replied.

"Oh?"

Hans opened the door to the newly polished black limousine, and I slid into the backseat. Hans was not talkative, and I felt ill at ease.

"Where are we going?" I asked.

"To Mr. Ross's penthouse."

"Oh?" I commented but thought to myself, *This ought to be something.* I again spoke to Hans. "I thought that we were going to dinner."

"You are," he answered but offered no other comment.

I decided that Jason Ross must have instructed his chauffeur not to be talkative, so I did not pursue the conversation. Instead I looked out the window at the New York skyline.

An hour passed before the limousine pulled up in front of the publisher's penthouse. The lobby was majestic. The huge chandelier, which hovered above my head, sparkled like a thousand stars. The elevator doors slid open. Hans ushered me inside and pushed the button to the top floor. It seemed but a second until the doors slid back to expose an exquisite sight.

My legs felt weak from excitement. I glanced around at a room packed with lavishly dressed people. There were waiters running around with trays of hors d'oeuvres and cocktails. In one corner of the room, a young man sat at a piano, surrounded by a small group of guests.

As Hans led me into the room, everyone became still. Jason Ross appeared and walked toward me. I noticed that he cut quite a dashing figure in his black tuxedo with his wide smile and flashing teeth. He was quite a handsome man.

"Jennifer, dear, you look radiant."

"Why, thank you, Jason," I responded with a smile.

"Come, I've been dying to introduce you to this gathering of friends and associates. Don't be nervous, Jennifer. This party is in your honor, and I must say that it's long overdue."

He took my hand and led me to the microphone, announcing that he would like everyone to be quiet.

"Everyone, please, may I have your attention? Please. This is the moment I've been waiting for. I would like to introduce Miss Jennifer Vicci. Stacy, please?"

Jason motioned for Stacy to come forward. I saw as she approached that she was carrying a plaque. "I had this made especially for you, Jennifer," Jason said.

I took it and was shocked when I read it. It was a copy of my book mounted on a plaque and inscribed: "Jennifer Vicci, Woman of the Year." I could feel tears sting my eyes but the crowd applauded and voices echoed, "Speech!"

"Come on, Jennifer," Jason coaxed. "A few words."

My speech was brief but eloquent. "Thank you, and thank God for giving me the strength to endure."

I was beginning to realize how much my life had changed. Jason was still smiling when he said, "Come with me. Let's go out on the balcony to get away from these peasants." He laughed as he led the way, explaining, "We can go out here to talk, and we won't even be missed. You'll discover that as you attend more and more of these functions."

As he guided me by the arm, he called out to a waiter, "Bring us two champagne cocktails.

"Now, Jennifer, I insist that you have a drink. This is a very special occasion. Come with me.

294

"Ah, that's better, my dear. Life has certainly thrust some blows at you, but that's over now. Come look at this view. I often feel at peace with myself when I come out here, and I wanted to share it with you."

Jason had not exaggerated at all. The view from his balcony was breathtaking. I felt that I was at heaven's door.

The singer was crooning, "I'm Laughing on the Outside and Crying on the Inside." The song suited me well.

Jason interrupted my thoughts, "Well, here's our drinks. Shall we sit down and talk for a while? But before we do, I propose a toast, Jennifer. May your life be smooth and blessed from this day on."

Our glasses clinked, and I smiled and thanked him. As I sipped my cocktail, Jason spoke. "I want to be your friend, Jennifer."

"I know, Jason," I replied. "I think that for the first time in my life I have stability, and I think that God has relieved me of all my problems. After all, what could happen now? I've achieved. I've survived. I can see nothing but good happening in my life from this point on. This is a wonderful night for me, and I want to thank you for making it happen, Jason."

He laughed and leaned over to brush his lips across my cheek. "Oh, Jennifer, I'm happy, too."

We looked at each other and laughed. I was happily sipping my drink and chatting with Jason, thinking to myself, *What could ever go wrong?*, when suddenly the waiter appeared and interrupted our conversation.

"Excuse me, sir. Miss Vicci has a long-distance call. Would you like me to bring the phone out here?"

"No," Jason answered. "Miss Vicci can take the call in the study. Inform the operator that she will be there immediately."

He saw me flinch and become tense. "Come, come, Jennifer. It's nothing. It's probably someone calling to congratulate you on this marvelous occasion."

I attempted a weak, crooked smile, knowing that he was trying to reassure me. I followed the waiter into the study. It was a beautiful room. Books clung to the walls, encased in gorgeous mahogany bookcases. The green Victorian couch looked like no one had ever sat on it. It was flanked by two huge wing chairs. Jason's large mahogany desk looked as if it belonged in a conference room instead of the study.

I approached the telephone with apprehension but picked up the receiver and said, "Hello?"

"Miss Vicci?" a voice inquired.

"Yes, this is Jennifer Vicci."

"Go ahead, sir," the operator prompted.

295

"Jenny?"

"Tom? Is it you?"

"Yes, honey."

"Tom, is anything wrong?" My heart raced as I waited for a response. "What's wrong, Tom?"

"Look, honey; I don't think that we should discuss it over the phone. But I do think that you should fly back to Boston right away."

Fear gripped me as I wondered what could have possibly happened. "Tom, what is it? Please."

His voice was filled with sorrow. "Jennifer, please, just answer me; are you coming back to Boston? I have to know."

"Of course, Tom. I'll take a plane right away. I'll have Jason drive me to the airport right now."

"That will be fine, Jenny." Tom's voice sounded too quiet. "I'll meet you there." He hung up without a good-bye.

I felt cold, and my head was spinning as I wondered what might be wrong. I knew that I had to find Jason, but as I turned to find him, I discovered that he had been standing next to me.

"Jenny, I wasn't eavesdropping. I was concerned. I heard everything, and I've already instructed Hans to take you to the airport. Don't worry about your personal belongings. Stacy will pick them up and bring them there."

Jason put his arm around me as he cautioned me, "Don't let your imagination run away. It may not be anything bad."

"Oh, Jason. Given my personal history, I don't think that it is anything minor." My voice shook, and the words barely came out.

Hans appeared. "Sir, Miss Vicci? Is she ready?"

"Yes," Jason replied. "One moment, Hans." Jason turned to me. "Jennifer, I want you to know that we will always be close friends. If there is anything that I can do to help, don't hesitate to ask." He clutched my hand.

"Yes, Jason, thank you."

I smiled, then kissed him on the cheek before rushing out the door with Hans.

The ride to the airport seemed endless. I jumped out of the limousine, ran into the terminal, and purchased a ticket. Fortunately, the plane was already boarding.

I only spent about an hour in the plane, but it seemed like days. When I left the plane, I scanned the waiting area for Tom. There was no sight of him. There was a cluster of reporters off in a corner, but no Tom.

Suddenly, I heard someone yell, "Hey, there she is!" And another: "Hey, guys, there she is!"

I turned around to see who they were yelling at. As I did, the reporters came running toward me. I finally noticed Tom, who was also running towards me. He put his arms around me as the reporters gathered. I knew that I was in the middle of a crisis, but what crisis?

They circled me and flashbulbs blinded me. *How wonderful,* I thought. *All this attention must be because of my book. Tom wanted to surprise me.*

One of the reporters shouted, "Miss Vicci, do you have any comments?"

I shook my head no, still amazed at all this attention.

Suddenly a man yelled out, "Miss Vicci, did your son appear to be upset?"

I thought, *My son, which one?* I turned to the reporter, "What are you talking about?" I panicked as I grabbed Tom's hand and dug my nails into it, demanding, "What are they talking about?" Tom did not have time to explain.

"Your son Todd, Miss Vicci. Did he give you any indication that he was going to kill your ex-husband?

"Miss Vicci . . . Miss Vicci."

Voices shouted and cameras clicked. My son? Todd? Killing Jesse! *Oh, God,* I said to myself. *I've wished him dead, but not by Todd's hand.*

I stood with Tom's arms around me as the photographers took pictures. This day that should have been the greatest day of my life became my biggest nightmare.

Made in the USA